Creative Beading

VOL. 12

The best projects from a year of *Bead&Button* magazine

KB KALMBACH BOOKS

Waukesha, Wisconsin

Kalmbach Books
21027 Crossroads Circle
Waukesha, Wisconsin 53186
www.JewelryAndBeadingStore.com

Published in 2017
21 20 19 18 17 1 2 3 4 5

Manufactured in China

ISBN: 978-1-62700-405-3
EISBN: 978-1-62700-406-0

The material in this book has appeared previously in *Bead&Button* magazine. Bead&Button is registered as a trademark.

Editor: Erica Swanson
Book Design: Lisa Schroeder
Illustrator: Kellie Jaeger
Photographer: William Zuback

Publisher's Cataloging-In-Publication Data

Creative beading : the best projects from a year of Bead&Button magazine.

v. : ill.

Annual
Vol. [1] (2006)-
Description based on: vol. 7 (2012).
Latest issue consulted: vol. 7 (2012).
Material in each volume appeared in the previous year's issues of Bead&Button magazine.
Includes index.

1. Beadwork—Periodicals. 2. Beads—Periodicals. 3. Jewelry making—Periodicals. I. Kalmbach Publishing Company. II. Title: Bead&Button magazine.

TT860 .C743
745.594/2

Contents

22

32

40

49

99

102

108

118

152

156

166

176

Introduction

Welcome to *Creative Beading, Volume 12*, our newest annual collection of projects from a year of *Bead&Button* magazine. Over the past year, our contributors have designed wonderfully creative pieces with new beads and techniques. You'll find necklaces, bracelets, earrings, pendants, and more.

Like always, *Creative Beading* includes all the various stitches you love and appeals to many different design sensibilities. Whether you're looking for a traditional style with seed beads, crystals, and pearls, or a project that includes a new twist with shaped beads, you'll find it within these pages. Each project is illustrated with complete step-by-step instructions that are fully tested by *Bead&Button*'s talented editors.

As in previous volumes, projects are organized into three categories: single-stitch projects, multi-stitch projects, and other techniques. There are more than 75 great designs, many with color options and helpful tips. If you need a refresher, you can flip to the Basics section for specific stitching techniques. Whether you are new to beading or have lots of experience, you'll find projects to suit your style and skill level.

I hope you enjoy all that *Creative Beading Vol. 12* has to offer.

Happy beading!

Julia Gerlach

Julia Gerlach
Editor, *Bead&Button*

Tools & Materials

Excellent tools and materials for making jewelry are available in bead and craft stores, through catalogs, and on the Internet. Here are the essential supplies you'll need for the projects in this book.

TOOLS

Chainnose pliers have smooth, flat inner jaws, and the tips taper to a point. Use them for gripping, bending wire, and for opening and closing loops and jump rings.

Roundnose pliers have smooth, tapered, conical jaws used to make loops. The closer to the tip you work, the smaller the loop will be.

Use the front of a **wire cutters'** blades to make a pointed cut and the back of the blades to make a flat cut. Do not use your jewelry-grade wire cutters on memory wire, which is extremely hard; use heavy-duty wire cutters, or bend the memory wire back and forth until it breaks.

Crimping pliers have two grooves in their jaws that are used to fold and roll a crimp tube into a compact shape.

Make it easier to open split rings by inserting the curved jaw of **split-ring pliers** between the wires.

Beading needles are coded by size. The higher the number, the finer the beading needle. Unlike sewing needles, the eye of a beading needle is almost as narrow as its shaft. In addition to the size of the bead, the number of times you will pass through the bead also affects the needle size that you will use; if you will pass through a bead multiple times, you need to use a thinner needle.

A **hammer** is used to harden wire or texture metal. Any hammer with a flat face will work, as long as the face is free of nicks that could mar your metal. The light ball-peen hammer shown here is one of the most commonly used hammers for jewelry making.

A **bench block** provides a hard, smooth surface on which to hammer wire and metal pieces. An anvil is similarly hard but has different surfaces, such as a tapered horn, to help form different shapes.

bench block

chainnose pliers

roundnose pliers

wire cutters

crimping pliers

split-ring pliers

hammer

beading needles

Tools & Materials

head pin

eye pin

jump rings

split ring

crimp beads and tubes

clasps

earring findings

FINDINGS

A **head pin** looks like a long, blunt, thick sewing pin. It has a flat or decorative head on one end to keep beads on. Head pins come in different diameters (gauges) and lengths.

Eye pins are just like head pins except they have a round loop on one end instead of a head. You can make your own eye pins from wire.

A **jump ring** is used to connect components. It is a small wire circle or oval that is either soldered closed or comes with a cut so it can be opened and closed.

Split rings are used like jump rings but are much more secure. They look like tiny key rings and are made of springy wire.

Crimp beads and tubes are small, large-holed, thin-walled metal beads designed to be flattened or crimped into a tight roll. Use them when stringing jewelry on flexible beading wire.

Clasps come in many sizes and shapes. Some of the most common (clockwise from the top left) are the toggle, consisting of a ring and a bar; slide, consisting of one tube that slides inside another; lobster claw, which opens when you pull on a tiny lever; S-hook, which links two soldered jump rings or split rings; and box, with a tab and a slot.

Earring findings come in a huge variety of metals and styles, including (from left to right) lever back, post, hoop, and French hook. You will almost always want a loop (or loops) on earring findings so you can attach beads.

WIRE

Wire is available in a number of materials and finishes, including brass, gold, gold-filled, gold-plated, fine silver, sterling silver, anodized niobium (chemically colored wire), and copper. Brass, copper, and craft wire are packaged in 10- to 40-yd. (9.1–37 m) spools, while gold, silver, and niobium are sold by the foot or ounce. Wire thickness is measured by gauge—the higher the gauge number, the thinner the wire. It is available in varying hardnesses (dead-soft, half-hard, and hard) and shapes (round, half-round, square, and others).

STITCHING & STRINGING MATERIALS

Selecting beading thread and cord is one of the most important decisions you'll make when planning a project. Review the descriptions below to evaluate which material is best for your design.

Threads come in many sizes and strengths. Size (diameter or thickness) is designated by a letter or number. OO and A/O are the thinnest; B, D, E, F, and FF are subsequently thicker. **Cord** is measured on a number scale; 0 corresponds in thickness to D-size thread, 1 equals E, 2 equals F, and 3 equals FF.

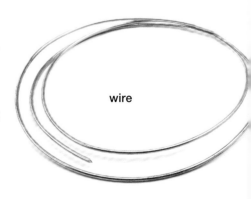

wire

Parallel filament nylon, such as Nymo or C-Lon, is made from many thin nylon fibers that are extruded and heat-set to form a single-ply thread. Parallel filament nylon is durable and easy to thread, but it can be prone to fraying and stretching. It is best used in beadweaving and bead embroidery.

Plied nylon thread, such as Silamide, is made from two or more nylon threads that are extruded, twisted together, and coated or bonded for further strength, making them strong and durable. It is more resistant to fraying than parallel filament nylon, and some brands do not stretch. It's a good material to use for twisted fringe, bead crochet, and beadwork that needs a lot of body.

Plied gel-spun polyethylene (GSP), such as Power Pro or DandyLine, is made from polyethylene fibers that have been spun into two or more threads that are braided together. It is almost unbreakable, it doesn't stretch, and it resists fraying. The thickness can make it difficult to make multiple passes through a bead. It is ideal for stitching with larger beads, such as pressed glass and crystals.

Parallel filament GSP, such as Fireline, is a single-ply thread made from spun and bonded polyethylene fibers. It's extremely strong, it doesn't stretch, and it resists fraying. However, crystals may cut through parallel filament GSP, and smoke-colored varieties can leave a black residue on hands and beads. It's most appropriate for bead stitching.

Polyester thread, such as Gutermann, is made from polyester fibers that are spun into single yarns and then twisted into plied thread. It doesn't stretch and comes in many colors, but it can become fuzzy with use. It is best for bead crochet or bead embroidery when the thread must match the fabric.

Flexible beading wire is composed of wires twisted together and covered with nylon. This wire is stronger than thread and does not stretch. The higher the number of inner strands (between 3 and 49), the more flexible and kink-resistant the wire. It is available in a variety of sizes. Use .014 and .015 for stringing most gemstones, crystals, and glass beads. Use thicker varieties, .018, .019, and .024, for heavy beads or nuggets. Use thinner wire, .010 and .012, for lightweight pieces and beads with very small holes, such as pearls. The thinnest wires can also be used for some bead-stitching projects.

flexible beading wire

nylon threads

parallel filament GSP

Tools & Materials

SEED BEADS

cube beads

triangle beads

drop beads

A huge variety of beads is available, but the beads most commonly used in the projects in this book are **seed beads**. Seed beads come in packages, tubes, and hanks. A standard hank (a looped bundle of beads strung on thread) contains 12 20-in. (51 cm) strands, but vintage hanks are often much smaller. Tubes and packages are usually measured in grams and vary in size.

Seed beads have been manufactured in many sizes ranging from the largest, 5º (also called "E beads"), which are about 5 mm wide, to tiny size 20º or 22º, which aren't much larger than grains of sand. (The symbol º stands for "aught" or "zero." The greater the number of aughts, e.g., 22º, the smaller the bead.) Beads smaller than Japanese 15ºs have not been produced for the past 100 years, but vintage beads can be found in limited sizes and colors. The most commonly available size in the widest range of colors is 11º.

Most round seed beads are made in Japan and the Czech Republic. **Czech seed beads** are slightly irregular and rounder than **Japanese seed beads**, which are uniform in size and a bit squared off. Czech beads give a bumpier surface when woven, but they reflect light at a wider range of angles. Japanese seed beads produce a uniform surface

Czech seed beads

and texture. Japanese and Czech seed beads can be used together, but a Japanese seed bead is slightly larger than the same size Czech seed bead.

Seed beads also come in sparkly cut versions. Japanese **hex-cut** or hex beads are formed with six sides. **2-** or **3-cut** Czech beads are less regular. **Charlottes** have an irregular facet cut on one side of the bead.

Japanese **cylinder beads**, otherwise known as Delicas (the Miyuki brand name), Toho Treasures (the brand name of Toho), and Toho Aikos, are extremely popular for peyote stitch projects. These beads are very regular and have large holes, which are useful for stitches requiring multiple thread passes. The beads fit together almost seamlessly, producing a smooth, fabric-like surface.

Bugle beads are thin glass tubes. They can be sized by number or length, depending on where they are made. Japanese size 1 bugles are about 2 mm long, but bugles can be made even longer than 30 mm. They can be hex-cut, straight, or twisted, but the selection of colors, sizes, shapes, and finishes is limited. Seed beads also come in a variety of other shapes, including **triangles, cubes,** and **drops.**

In stitches where the beads meet each other end to end or side by side — peyote stitch, brick stitch, and square stitch — try using Japanese cylinder beads to achieve a smooth, flat surface. For a more textured surface, use Czech or round Japanese seed beads. For right-angle weave, in which groups of four or more beads form circular stitches, the rounder the seed bead, the better; otherwise you risk having gaps. Round seed beads also are better for netting and strung jewelry.

twisted bugle beads

hex-cut beads

seed beads

Basics

THREAD AND KNOTS

Adding thread
To add a thread, sew into the beadwork several rows or rounds prior to the point where the last bead was added, leaving a short tail. Follow the thread path of the stitch, tying a few half-hitch knots (see "Half-hitch knot") between beads as you go, and exit where the last stitch ended. Trim the short tail.

Conditioning thread
Use beeswax or microcrystalline wax (not candle wax or paraffin) or Thread Heaven to condition nylon beading thread and Fireline. Wax smooths nylon fibers and adds tackiness that will stiffen your beadwork slightly. Thread Heaven adds a static charge that causes the thread to repel itself, so don't use it with doubled thread. Both conditioners help thread resist wear. To condition, stretch nylon thread to remove the curl (Fireline doesn't stretch). Lay the thread or Fireline on top of the conditioner, hold it in place with your thumb or finger, and pull the thread through the conditioner.

Ending thread
To end a thread, sew back through the last few rows or rounds of beadwork, following the thread path of the stitch and tying two or three half-hitch knots (see "Half-hitch knot") between beads as you go. Sew through a few beads after the last knot, and trim the thread.

Half-hitch knot
Pass the needle under the thread bridge between two beads, and pull gently until a loop forms. Cross back over the thread between the beads, sew through the loop, and pull gently to draw the knot into the beadwork.

Overhand knot
Make a loop with the thread. Pull the tail through the loop, and tighten.

Square knot
[1] Cross one end of the thread over and under the other end. Pull both ends to tighten the first half of the knot.
[2] Cross the first end of the thread over and under the other end. Pull both ends to tighten the knot.

Stop bead
Use a stop bead to secure beads temporarily when you begin stitching. Choose a bead that is different from the beads in your project. Pick up the stop bead, leaving the desired-length tail. Sew through the stop bead again in the same direction, making sure you don't split the thread. If desired, sew through it one more time for added security.

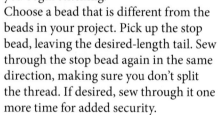

Surgeon's knot
[1] Cross one end of the thread over and under the other twice. Pull both ends to tighten the first half of the knot.
[2] Cross the first end of the thread over and under the other end. Pull both ends to tighten the knot.

Crochet
Slip knot and chain stitch
[1] Make a slip knot: Leaving the desired length tail, make a loop in the cord, crossing the spool end over the tail. Insert the hook in the loop, yarn over, and pull the cord through the loop.
[2] Yarn over the hook, and draw through the loop. Repeat this step for the desired number of chain stitches.

Beaded backstitch
To stitch a line of beads, come up through the fabric from the wrong side, and pick up three beads. Place the thread where the beads will go, and sew through the fabric right after the third bead. Come up between the second and third beads, and go through the third bead again. Pick up three more beads, and repeat. For a tighter stitch, pick up only one or two beads at a time.

Basics

STITCHES

Brick stitch

[1] To work the typical method, which results in progressively decreasing rows, work the first row in ladder stitch (see "Ladder stitch") to the desired length, exiting the top of the last bead added.

[2] Pick up two beads, sew under the thread bridge between the second and third beads in the previous row, and sew back up through the second bead added. To secure this first stitch, sew down through the first bead and back up through the second bead.

[3] For the remaining stitches in the row, pick up one bead per stitch, sew under the thread bridge between the next two beads in the previous row, and sew back up through the new bead. The last stitch in the new row will be centered above the last two beads in the previous row, and the new row will be one bead shorter than the previous row.

Increasing

To increase at the start of the row, repeat step 1 above, then repeat step 2, but sew under the thread bridge between the first and second beads in the previous row. To increase at the end of the row, work two stitches off of the thread bridge between the last two beads in the previous row.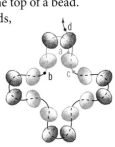

Tubular

[1] Begin with a ladder of beads, and join the ends to form a ring (see "Ladder stitch: Forming a ring"). Position the thread to exit the top of a bead.

[2] Following the instructions for flat brick stitch, pick up two beads to begin the row. Stitch around the ring in brick stitch.

[3] Join the first and last beads of the round by sewing down through the first bead and up through the last bead.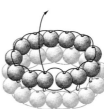

Herringbone stitch
Flat

[1] Work the first row in ladder stitch (see "Ladder stitch") to the desired length, exiting the top of an end bead in the ladder.

[2] Pick up two beads, and sew down through the next bead in the previous row (a–b). Sew up through the following bead in the previous row, pick up two beads, and sew down through the next bead (b–c). Repeat across the first row.

[3] To turn to start the next row, sew down through the end bead in the previous row and back through the last bead of the pair just added (a–b). Pick up two beads, sew down through the next bead in the previous row, and sew up through the following bead (b–c). Continue adding pairs of beads across the row.

Tubular

[1] Work a row of ladder stitch (see "Ladder stitch") to the desired length using an even number of beads. Form it into a ring to create the first round (see "Ladder stitch: Forming a ring"). Your thread should exit the top of a bead.

[2] Pick up two beads, sew down through the next bead in the previous round (a–b), and sew up through the following bead. Repeat to complete the round (b–c).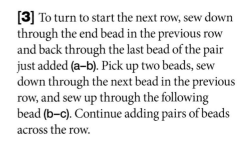

[3] You will need to step up to start the next round. Sew up through two beads — the next bead in the previous round and the first bead added in the new round (c–d).

[4] Continue adding two beads per stitch. As you work, snug up the beads to form a tube, and step up at the end of each round until your rope is the desired length.

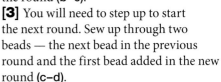

14

Twisted tubular

[1] Work a ladder and two rounds of tubular herringbone as explained above.

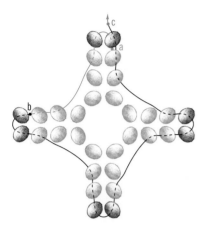

[2] To create a twist in the tube, pick up two beads, sew down through one bead in the next stack, then sew up through two beads in the following stack (a–b). Repeat around, adding two beads per stitch. Step up to the next round through three beads (b–c). Snug up the beads. The twist will begin to appear after the sixth round. Continue until your rope is the desired length.

Ladder stitch

Making a ladder

[1] Pick up two beads, and sew through them both again, positioning the beads side by side so that their holes are parallel (a–b).

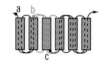

[2] Add subsequent beads by picking up one bead, sewing through the previous bead, then sewing through the new bead (b–c). Continue for the desired length.

This technique produces uneven tension, which you can correct by zigzag-ging back through the beads in the oppo-site direction or by choosing the "Cross-weave method" or "Alternative method."

Crossweave technique

[1] Thread a needle on each end of a length of thread, and center a bead.
[2] Working in crossweave technique, pick up a bead with one needle, and cross the other needle through it (a–b and c–d). Add all subsequent beads in the same manner.

Alternative method

[1] Pick up all the beads you need to reach the length your project requires. Fold the last two beads so they are parallel, and sew through the second-to-last bead again in the same direction (a–b).

[2] Fold the next loose bead so it sits parallel to the previous bead in the ladder, and sew through the loose bead in the same direction (a–b). Continue sewing back through each bead until you exit the last bead of the ladder.

Forming a ring

With your thread exiting the last bead in the ladder, sew through the first bead and then through the last bead again. If using the "Crossweave method" or "Alternative method" of ladder stitch, cross the threads from the last bead in the ladder through the first bead in the ladder.

Basics

Peyote stitch

Flat even-count

[1] Pick up an even number of beads, leaving the desired length tail **(a–b)**. These beads will shift to form the first two rows as the third row is added.

[2] To begin row 3, pick up a bead, skip the last bead  added in the previous step, and sew back through the next bead, working toward the tail **(b–c)**. For each stitch, pick up a bead, skip a bead in the previous row, and sew through the next bead until you reach the first bead picked up in step 1 **(c–d)**. The beads added in this row are higher than the previous rows and are referred to as "up-beads."

[3] For each stitch in subsequent rows, pick up a bead, and sew through the next up-bead in the previous row **(d–e)**. To count peyote stitch rows, count the total number of beads along both straight edges.

Flat odd-count

Odd-count peyote is the same as even-count peyote, except for the turn on odd-numbered rows, where the last bead of the row can't be attached in the usual way because there is no up-bead to sew through.

Work the traditional odd-row turn as follows:

[1] Begin as for flat even-count peyote, but pick up an odd number of beads. Work row 3 as in even-count, stopping before adding the last bead.

[2] Work a figure-8 turn at the end of row 3: Pick up the next-to-last bead (#7), and sew 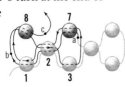 through #2, then #1 **(a–b)**. Pick up the last bead of the row (#8), and sew through #2, #3, #7, #2, #1, and #8 **(b–c)**.

[3] In subsequent odd-numbered rows, pick up the last bead of the row, sew under the thread bridge between the last two edge beads, 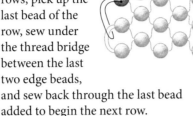 and sew back through the last bead added to begin the next row.

Tubular even-count

Tubular peyote stitch follows the same stitching pattern as flat peyote, but instead of sewing back and forth, you work in rounds.

[1] Start with an even number of beads tied into a ring (see "Square knot").

[2] Sew through the first bead in the ring. Pick up a bead, skip a bead in the ring, and sew through the next bead. Repeat to complete the round.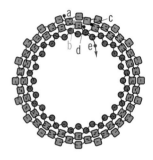

[3] To step up to start the next round, sew through the first bead added in round 3 **(a–b)**. Pick up a bead, and sew through the next bead in round 3 **(b–c)**. Repeat to complete the round.

[4] Repeat step 3 to achieve the desired length, stepping up after each round.

Tubular odd-count

[1] Start with an odd number of bead tied into a ring (see "Square knot").

[2] Sew through the first bead into the ring. Pick up a bead, skip a bead in the ring, and sew though the next bead. Repeat to complete the round. At the end of the round, you will sew through the last bead in the original ring. Do not step up. Pick up a bead, and sew through the first bead in the previous round. You will be stitching in a continuous spiral.

Two-drop

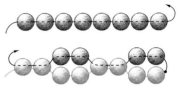

[1] Work two-drop peyote stitch the same as basic peyote, but treat pairs of beads as if they were single beads.

[2] Start with an even number of beads divisible by four. Pick up two beads (stitch 1 of row 3), skip two beads, and go through the next two beads. Repeat across the row.

Bezels

[1] Pick up enough seed beads to fit around the circumference of a rivoli or stone, and sew through the first bead again to form a ring **(a–b)**.

[2] Pick up a bead, skip the next bead in the ring, and sew through the following bead **(b–c)**. Continue working in tubular peyote stitch to complete the round, and step up through the first bead added **(c–d)**.

[3] Work the next two rounds in tubular peyote using beads one size smaller than those used in the previous rounds **(d–e)**. Keep the tension tight to decrease the size of the ring.

[4] Position the rivoli or stone in the bezel cup. Using the tail thread, repeat steps 2 and 3 to work three more rounds on the other side of the stone.

Increasing

[1] At the point of increase, pick up two beads instead of one, and sew through the next bead.

[2] When you reach the pair of beads in the next row, sew through the first bead, pick up a bead, and sew through the second bead.

Decreasing

[1] At the point of decrease, sew through two up-beads in the previous row.

[2] In the next row, when you reach the two-bead space, pick up one bead.

Zipping up or joining

To join two sections of a flat peyote piece invisibly, match up the two pieces so the end rows fit together. "Zip up" the pieces by zigzagging through the up-beads on both ends.

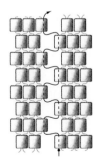

Right-angle weave
Flat strip

[1] To start the first row of right-angle weave, pick up four beads, and tie them into a ring (see "Square knot"). Sew through the first three beads again.

[2] Pick up three beads. Sew through the last bead in the previous stitch **(a–b)**, and continue through the first two beads picked up in this stitch **(b–c)**.

[3] Continue adding three beads per stitch until the first row is the desired length. You are stitching in a figure-8 pattern, alternating the direction of the thread path for each stitch.

Adding rows

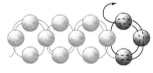

[1] To add a row, sew through the last stitch of row 1, exiting an edge bead along one side.

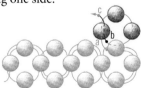

[2] Pick up three beads, and sew through the edge bead your thread exited in the previous step **(a–b)**. Continue through the first new bead **(b–c)**.

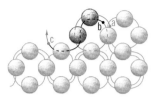

[3] Pick up two beads, and sew back through the next edge bead in the previous row and the bead your thread exited at the start of this step **(a–b)**. Continue through the two new beads and the following edge bead in the previous row **(b–c)**.

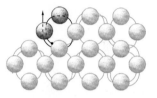

[4] Pick up two beads, and sew through the last two beads your thread exited in the previous stitch and the first new bead. Continue working a figure-8 thread path, picking up two beads per stitch for the rest of the row.

Square stitch

[1] String all the beads needed for the first row, then pick up the first bead of the second row. Sew through the last bead of the first row and the first bead of the second row again. Position the two beads side by side so that their holes are parallel.

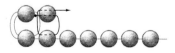

[2] Pick up the next bead of row 2, and sew through the corresponding bead in row 1 and the new bead in row 2. Repeat across the row.

Basics

Crimping

Use crimp beads to secure flexible beading wire. Slide the crimp bead into place over two strands of wire, and squeeze it firmly with chainnose pliers to flatten it. For a more finished look, use crimping pliers:

[1] Position the crimp bead in the hole that is closest to the handle of the crimping pliers.

[2] Holding the wires apart, squeeze the pliers to compress the crimp bead, making sure one wire is on each side of the dent.

[3] Place the crimp bead in the front hole of the pliers, and position it so the dent is facing the tips of the pliers. Squeeze the pliers to fold the crimp in half.

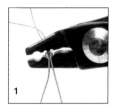

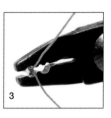

Opening and closing loops and jump rings

[1] Hold a loop or a jump ring with two pairs of pliers, such as chainnose, flatnose, or bentnose pliers.

[2] To open the loop or jump ring, bring the tips of one pair of pliers toward you, and push the tips of the other pair away from you.

[3] The open jump ring. Reverse the steps to close.

Plain loop

[1] Using chainnose pliers, make a right-angle bend in the wire directly above a bead or other component or at least ¼ in. (6 mm) from the end of a naked piece of wire. For a larger loop, bend the wire further in.

[2] Grip the end of the wire with roundnose pliers so that the wire is flush with the jaws of the pliers where they meet. The closer to the tip of the pliers that you work, the smaller the loop will be. Press downward slightly, and rotate the wire toward the bend made in step 1.

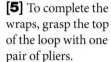

[3] Reposition the pliers in the loop to continue rotating the wire until the end of the wire touches the bend.

[4] The plain loop.

Wrapped loop

[1] Using chainnose pliers, make a right-angle bend in the wire about 2 mm above a bead or other component or at least 1¼ in. (3.2 cm) from the end of a naked piece of wire.

[2] Position the jaws of the roundnose pliers in the bend. The closer to the tip of the pliers that you work, the smaller the loop will be.

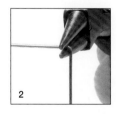

[3] Curve the short end of the wire over the top jaw of the roundnose pliers.

[4] Reposition the pliers so the lower jaw fits snugly in the loop. Curve the wire downward around the bottom jaw of the pliers. This is the first half of a wrapped loop.

[5] To complete the wraps, grasp the top of the loop with one pair of pliers.

[6] With another pair of pliers, wrap the wire around your stem two or three times. Trim the excess wire, and gently press the cut end close to the wraps with chainnose pliers.

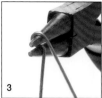

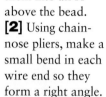

Loops, wrapped above a top-drilled bead

[1] Center a top-drilled bead on a 3-in. (7.6 cm) piece of wire. Bend each wire end upward, crossing them into an X above the bead.

[2] Using chain-nose pliers, make a small bend in each wire end so they form a right angle.

[3] Wrap the horizontal wire around the vertical wire as in a wrapped loop. Trim the excess wrapping wire.

Single-Stitch Projects

BEAD WEAVING

Crystal
blossoms
bracelet

Artfully arrange
chatons, crystals,
and pearls to create
a charming bracelet
of delicate posies.

designed by **Szidonia Petki**

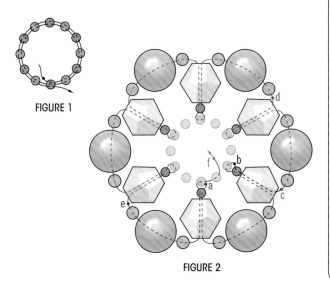

FIGURE 1

FIGURE 2

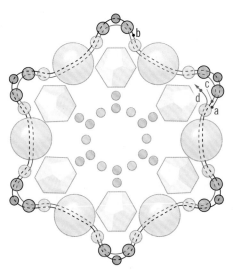

FIGURE 3

Difficulty rating

Legend

- ● 15º seed bead, color A
- ● 15º seed bead, color B
- ⬡ 6 mm bicone crystal
- ● 11º seed bead
- ● 6 mm pearl
- ● 8 mm chaton - top view
- ⬡ 3 mm bicone crystal
- ● 15º seed bead, color C

Materials

green bracelet 7½ in. (19.1 cm)

- **4** 8 mm (SS39) chatons (Swarovski 1088, erinite)
- **24** 6 mm glass pearls (Swarovski, iridescent green)
- bicone crystals (Swarovski)
  - **24** 6 mm bicone crystals (light smoked topaz)
  - **20** 3 mm bicone crystals (metallic light gold 2X)
- **1 g** 11º seed beads (Miyuki 2006, matte metallic dark bronze)
- 15º seed beads
  - **3 g** color A (Miyuki 2006, matte metallic dark bronze)
  - **1 g** color B (Miyuki 2008, matte metallic patina iris)
  - **1 g** color C (Toho 221, bronze)
- **1** toggle clasp
- **2** 6 mm jump rings
- Fireline, 6 lb. test
- beading needles, #12
- **2** pairs of chainnose, flatnose, and/or bentnose pliers

Information for the alternate colorway is listed at www. BeadAndButton.com/resources.

Components

1 On 1½ yd. (1.4 m) of thread, pick up a repeating pattern of a color A 15º seed bead and a color B 15º seed bead six times. Sew through the beads again to form a ring, leaving a 12-in. (30 cm) tail, and exiting the first A **(figure 1)**.

2 Pick up an A, a 6 mm bicone crystal, an 11º seed bead, a 6 mm pearl, an 11º, a 6 mm crystal, and an A. Skip the next B in the ring, sew through the following A to form a loop **(figure 2, a-b)**, and continue back through the last A and 6 mm crystal added **(b-c)**.

3 Pick up an 11º, a pearl, an 11º, a 6 mm crystal, and an A, skip the next B in the ring. Sew through the following A, and continue back through the last A and 6 mm added **(c-d)**. Repeat this stitch three times **(d-e)**.

4 Pick up an 11º, a pearl, and an 11º, and sew through the next 6 mm crystal and A in the first loop. Continue through the following A and B in the ring **(e-f)**. Set the working thread aside.

5 Thread a needle on the tail, and sew through the beadwork to exit an 11º in a loop, with the needle pointing toward the adjacent loop **(figure 3, point a)**. Pick up an 11º, a B, and an 11º, and sew through the next 11º, pearl, and 11º **(a-b)**. Repeat this stitch five times to complete the round **(b-c)**. Retrace the thread path, skipping the Bs just added **(c-d)**, and end the tail.

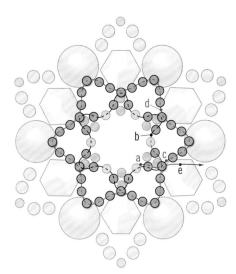

FIGURE 4

FIGURE 5

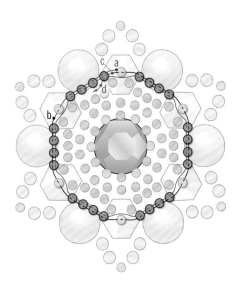

FIGURE 6

6 With the working thread, pick up three Bs, skip the next A in the inner ring, and sew through the following B to form a picot **(figure 4, a–b)**. Repeat this stitch five times to complete the round, and step up to exit the second B added in this round **(b–c)**.

7 Pick up five Bs, and sew through the center B in the next picot **(c–d)**. Repeat this stitch five times to complete the round **(d–e)**. Retrace the thread path, skipping the center B in each picot, and exit an A in the inner ring. This is the back of the component.

8 Turn the component over to the front surface. Pick up three As, skip the next B in the inner ring, and sew through the following A to form a picot **(figure 5, a–b)**. Repeat this stitch five times to complete the round, and step up to exit the second A added in this round **(b–c)**. Pick up two As, a B, and two As, and sew through the center A of the next picot **(c–d)**. Repeat this stitch five times to complete the round, and step up to exit the center B in the first picot **(d–e)**.

9 Pick up four As, and sew through the center B in the next picot **(figure 6, a–b)**. Repeat this stitch five times to complete the round **(b–c)**. Place the chaton in the ring of beads, face up. Skipping the Bs added in the previous round, retrace the thread path three times using a tight tension to secure the chaton **(c–d)**. The retracing of the thread path is shown only once in the figure for clarity. End the thread.

10 Work as in steps 1–9 to make a total of four components.

Assembly

1 Add 1 yd. (.9 m) of thread to a component, exiting a B in the outer picot and leaving a 12-in. (30 cm) tail to be used later for the clasp **(figure 7, point a)**. This sets up the tail to be in the proper position for adding the clasp. Sew through the beadwork as shown to exit the B in the opposite picot **(a–b)**. Place this component on the left side of your bead mat, and place another component on the right side.

2 With the working thread from the left component, pick up an A, a 3 mm crystal, an A, a color C 15º seed bead, an A, a 3 mm crystal, and an A, and sew down through the corresponding B on the right component **(b–c)**. Pick up the same pattern of beads, and sew up through the B on the left component that your thread exited at the start of this step **(c–d)**. Retrace the thread path, skipping the two Cs and two Bs **(d–e)**. Sew through the beadwork as needed to exit the B on the opposite picot of the right component.

3 Work as in steps 1–2 to attach the remaining components.

Clasp

1 With the working thread, pick up an A, a 3 mm crystal, an A, and a C three times, and then pick up an A, a 3 mm crystal, and an A. Sew through the B your thread exited at the start of this step, going in the same direction **(figure 8, a–b)**. Retrace the thread path, skipping the three Cs and the B **(b–c)**. Pull the thread tight, and sew through the beadwork as shown to exit the end C **(c–d)**.

2 Pick up an A and a C three times, and then pick up an A. Sew through the C your thread exited at the start of this step, going in the same direction **(d–e)**. Retrace the thread path twice, skipping the three Cs just added. End the working thread.

3 Open a jump ring, and attach one end of the clasp to the end loop of the bracelet.

4 Using the tail, work as in steps 1–3 on the other end of the bracelet. ◉

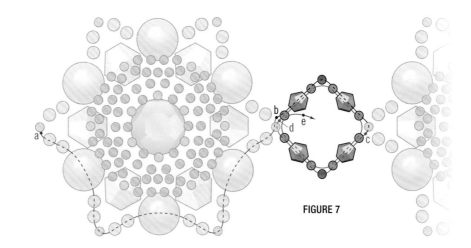

FIGURE 7

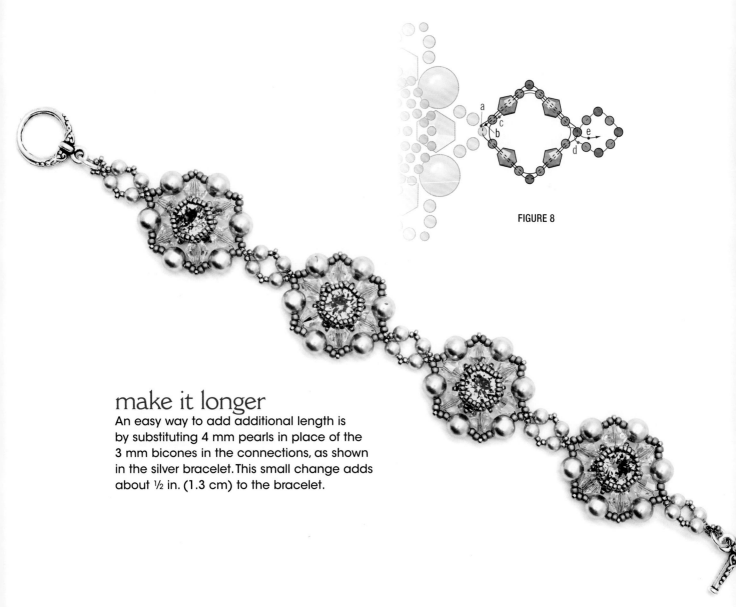

FIGURE 8

make it longer

An easy way to add additional length is by substituting 4 mm pearls in place of the 3 mm bicones in the connections, as shown in the silver bracelet. This small change adds about ½ in. (1.3 cm) to the bracelet.

BEAD WEAVING

Super cube beaded beads

Stitch up these cute and easy cube-shaped beaded beads,
and string them for an easy-to-wear necklace.

designed by **Zsuzsanna Veres**

Beaded bead

1 Attach a needle to each end of 4 ft. (1.2 m) of thread. With one needle, pick up a repeating pattern of a rondelle and an 8º seed bead four times. Sew through all the beads again to form a ring, and continue through the next rondelle, centering the beads on the thread **(figure 1)**.

2 With one needle, pick up an 8º, three SuperDuo beads, and an 8º, and sew through the rondelle your thread is exiting to form a loop **(figure 2, a–b)**. Retrace the thread path (not shown in the figure for clarity). Continue through the next 8º and rondelle in the ring **(b–c)**. Repeat these stitches three times to complete the round **(c–d)**, and continue through the next 8º and SuperDuo in the first loop added and through the open hole of the same SuperDuo **(d–e)**.

3 With the other needle, work as in step 2 to add another loop to each rondelle.

4 With the needle from the first set of loops, pick up a 15º seed bead, and sew through the open hole of the next SuperDuo in the following loop **(figure 3, a–b)**. Only the first round of loops is shown in the figure for clarity. Pick up two 15ºs, and sew through the open hole of the following SuperDuo **(b–c)**. Repeat just this stitch once more **(c–d)**. Repeat these three stitches three times to complete the round **(d–e)** using a tight tension. Continue through the next five beads to exit the center SuperDuo in the next loop **(e–f)**.

5 With the same thread, pick up a 3 mm fire-polished bead, and sew through the center SuperDuo in the next loop **(f–g)**. Repeat this stitch three times to complete the round using a tight tension. Continue through the following two 15ºs, SuperDuo, and 15º as shown **(g–h)**.

6 With the other needle, work as in steps 4–5 on the second round of loops.

7 With one needle, pick up a 15º, and sew through the next 8º along the side edge of the beaded bead **(figure 4, a–b)**. The side view of the beaded bead is shown in this figure for clarity. Repeat this stitch once more **(b–c)**. Pick up a 15º, and sew through the following 15º **(c–d)**. Repeat these three stitches to complete this edge **(d–e)**. Sew through the next eight beads along the top edge to exit the corresponding 15º on the following side edge **(e–f)**.

8 Work as in step 7 for the remaining side edges. To tighten up the bead, if needed, retrace the thread path through the fire-polished beads and center SuperDuos on each end, and end the threads.

9 Repeat steps 1–8 to make a total of three beaded beads.

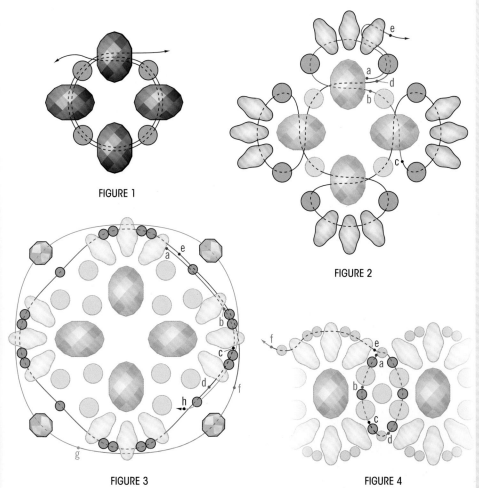

FIGURE 1

FIGURE 2

FIGURE 3

FIGURE 4

Materials

necklace 18 in. (46 cm)

- **16** 4.5 x 6 mm faceted rondelles (opaque teal)
- **72** 2.5 x 5 mm SuperDuo beads (chocolate bronze)
- **24** 3 mm fire-polished beads (ethereal halo azurite)
- **1 g** 8º seed beads (Japanese 460G, steel blue metallic)
- **1 g** 15º seed beads (Japanese P487, permanent galvanized silver sage)
- **2** 7-in. (18 cm) lengths of chain
- **1** lobster claw clasp
- **3** 6 mm jump rings
- **2** 2 x 2 mm crimp beads
- **2** wire guards
- **2** 3 mm crimp covers
- **10 in. (25 cm)** flexible beading wire, .019
- Fireline, 6 lb. test
- beading needles, #11 or #12
- crimping pliers
- wire cutters

raid your stash

Substitute a 6–8 mm bead or pearl for the rondelle used between the beaded beads to achieve a different look.

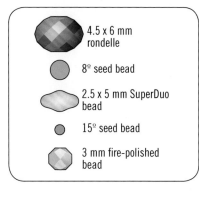

- 4.5 x 6 mm rondelle
- 8º seed bead
- 2.5 x 5 mm SuperDuo bead
- 15º seed bead
- 3 mm fire-polished bead

Assembly

1 On 10 in. (25 cm) of beading wire, center a repeating pattern of a rondelle and beaded bead three times, and then add one more rondelle.

2 On each end, string a crimp bead and a wire guard, and go back through the crimp bead. Use crimping pliers to compress the crimp bead, and trim the excess wire. Using crimping pliers, close a crimp cover over each crimp bead.

3 Using 6 mm jump rings, attach a 7 in. (18 cm) piece of chain to each wire guard, and attach a lobster claw clasp to the other end of one chain. ●

BEAD WEAVING

Vintage rosettes bracelet

Crystals and seed beads give this vintage-inspired bracelet loads of sparkle for a timeless look.

designed by **Szidonia Petki**

Rivoli component

1 On 2 yd. (1.8 m) of thread, pick up a repeating pattern of a SuperDuo and a color A 15º seed bead 12 times. Sew through the beads again to form a ring (not shown in figure for clarity), leaving a 6-in. (15 cm) tail. Retrace the thread path once more **(figure 1, a–b)**, and

sew through the open hole of the SuperDuo your thread is exiting **(b–c)**.
2 Pick up a 3 mm bicone crystal, and sew through the open hole of the next SuperDuo **(c–d)**. Repeat this stitch 11 times to complete the round. Retrace the thread path (not shown in figure for clarity), exiting the first 3 mm added **(d–e)**. End the tail.

3 Pick up two color B 15º seed beads, an A, and two Bs, and sew through the 3 mm your thread is exiting, going in the same direction, to form a picot **(figure 2, a–b)**. Continue through the next SuperDuo and 3 mm **(b–c)**. Repeat this stitch 11 times, and sew through the first three beads added in the first picot, exiting the A **(c–d)**.

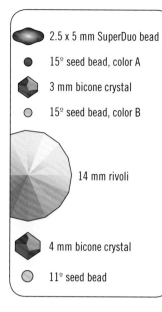

2.5 x 5 mm SuperDuo bead

15º seed bead, color A

3 mm bicone crystal

15º seed bead, color B

14 mm rivoli

4 mm bicone crystal

11º seed bead

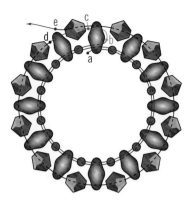

FIGURE 1

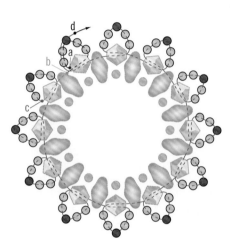

FIGURE 2

Difficulty rating

Materials
bracelet 7⅛ in. (18.1 cm)

- **3** 14 mm rivolis (Swarovski, crystal lilac shadow)
- **6 g** 2.5 x 5 mm SuperDuo beads (bronze)
- bicone crystals (Swarovski, crystal lilac shadow)
  - **54** 4 mm
  - **64** 3 mm
- **12** 11º seed beads (Miyuki 2006, matte metallic dark bronze)
- 15º seed beads
  - **1 g** color A (Miyuki 457, dark metallic bronze)
  - **3 g** color B (Miyuki 2006, matte metallic dark bronze)
- **1** ball and socket clasp (brass)
- **2** 4–6 mm jump rings (brass)
- Fireline, 4 lb. or 6 lb. test
- beading needles, #11 or #12

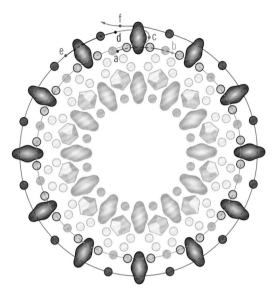

FIGURE 3

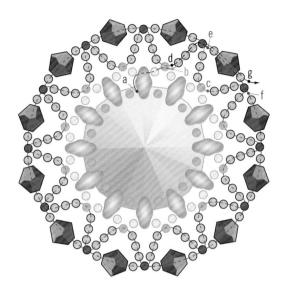

FIGURE 4

4 Pick up a B, a SuperDuo, and a B, and sew through the A in the next picot **(figure 3, a–b)**. Repeat this stitch 11 times to complete the round, and retrace the thread path (not shown in figure for clarity). Continue through the first B and SuperDuo added **(b–c)**, and sew through the open hole of the same SuperDuo **(c–d)**. Tighten the thread so the beadwork begins to cup.

5 Pick up an A, and sew through the open hole of the next SuperDuo **(d–e)**. Repeat this stitch 11 times to complete the round **(e–f)**, but do not pull the thread tight. Place the 14 mm rivoli face down in the beadwork. Pull the thread tight to close the beadwork around the rivoli, and retrace the thread path again to tighten. Exit a SuperDuo.

6 Sew through the other hole of the same SuperDuo, the next B, and the following A **(figure 4, a–b)**. The figure shows just the beads visible from the backside of the beadwork.

7 Pick up three Bs, an A, and three Bs, and sew through the next A to form a

picot **(b–c)**. Repeat this stitch 11 times to complete the round **(c–d)**. Continue through the first four beads in the first picot, exiting the A **(d–e)**.

8 Pick up a B, a 4 mm bicone crystal, and a B, and sew through the A in the next picot **(e–f)**. Repeat this stitch 11 times to complete the round, and retrace the thread path (not shown in figure for clarity). Sew through the first B, 4 mm, and B added **(f–g)**.

Crystal component

1 Continuing with the thread from the rivoli component, pick up a B, an A, and two Bs, and then pick up a repeating pattern of a 4 mm, two Bs, an A, and two Bs four times. Pick up a 4 mm, two Bs, an A, and a B, and sew through the B, 4 mm, and B your thread exited at the start of the step to form a ring **(figure 5, a–b)**. Continue through the first B and A added **(b–c)**.

2 Pick up three Bs, an A, and three Bs, and sew through the next A in the ring to form an arch **(c–d)**. Repeat this stitch five times to complete the round **(d–e)**. Continue through the first four beads added in the first arch to exit an A **(e–f)**.

3 Pick up a B, a 3 mm, and a B, and sew through the A in the next arch added in the previous round **(figure 6, a–b)**. Repeat this stitch five times to complete the round **(b–c)**, and continue through the beadwork as shown to exit the third A from the connection point on the outside edge and the next B **(c–d)**.

Clasp connection

1 Pick up two Bs, a 3 mm, an 11º seed bead, a 3 mm, and two Bs, skip the next B, 4 mm, and B, and sew through the following B **(figure 7)**.

2 Sew through the beadwork to exit the 11º just added **(figure 8, a–b)**. Pick up five 11ºs, and sew through the 11º your thread is exiting to form a loop **(b–c)**. Continue through the first 11º just added **(c–d)**.

3 Pick up an A, and sew through the next 11º in the loop **(d–e)**. Repeat this stitch three times, and sew through the next 11º **(e–f)**. Sew through the surrounding beadwork, and retrace the thread path through the loop. End the thread. This completes one end component.

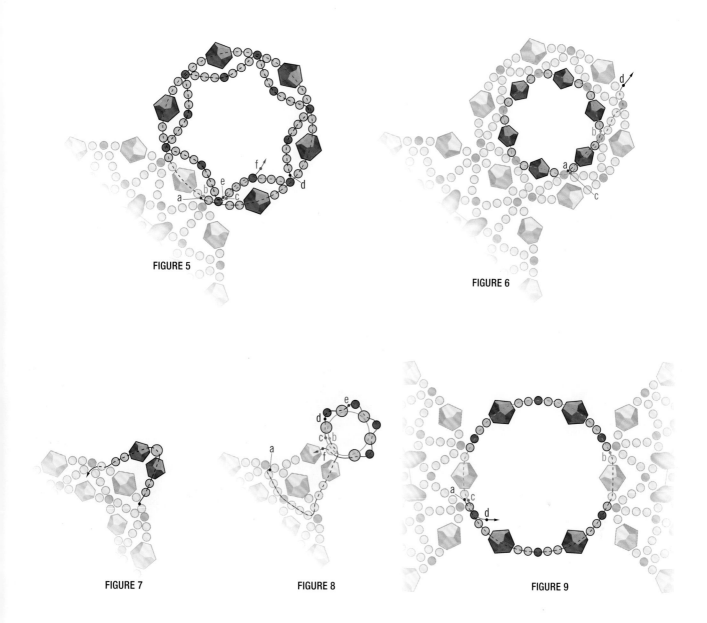

FIGURE 5

FIGURE 6

FIGURE 7

FIGURE 8

FIGURE 9

Do it all again
Repeat all the steps for "Rivoli component," "Crystal component," and "Clasp connection" to make another end section.

Center rivoli component
1 Repeat all the steps of "Rivoli component" to make a third component.
2 Pick up a B, an A, two Bs, a 4 mm, two Bs, an A, two Bs, a 4 mm, two Bs, an A, and a B. On the rivoli component of

an end section, sew through a B, 4 mm, and B on the opposite side from where the crystal component is attached **(figure 9, a–b)**. Pick up the same beads you just added, and sew through the B, 4 mm, and B your thread exited at the start of the step **(b–c)**. Continue through the next B and A **(c–d)**.
3 Repeat steps 2–3 of "Crystal component," and end the working thread.
4 Attach 1 yd. (.9 m) of thread to the center rivoli component, exiting the B,

4 mm, and B opposite the crystal component connection. Repeat steps 2–3 to attach the center rivoli component to the other end section.
5 Open a 6 mm jump ring, and attach one half of the clasp to the small loop on an end section. Repeat on the other end of the bracelet. ●

Gem of a spiral necklace

This unusual spiral uses an assortment of beads, including gemstones, and is stitched off a right-angle weave core.

designed by
Marcia Balonis

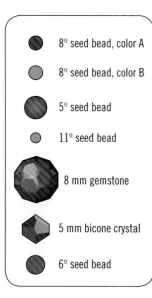

- 8º seed bead, color A
- 8º seed bead, color B
- 5º seed bead
- 11º seed bead
- 8 mm gemstone
- 5 mm bicone crystal
- 6º seed bead

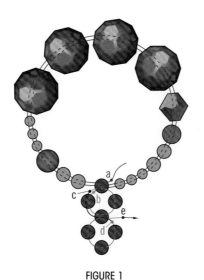

FIGURE 1

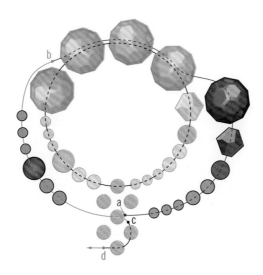

FIGURE 2

Materials

purple necklace 19 in. (48 cm)
- **46** 8 mm round faceted gemstones (amethyst)
- **47** 5 mm bicone crystals (Swarovski, lilac)
- **6 g** 5º seed beads (Miyuki 134FR, matte transparent dark topaz AB)
- **4 g** 6º seed beads (Toho 421, gold-lustered transparent pink)
- 8º seed beads
  - **6 g** color A (Toho 85F, matte metallic plum iris)
  - **6 g** color B (Miyuki 301, rose gold luster)
- **5 g** 11º seed beads (Miyuki 4220, Duracoat eggplant)
- **1** clasp
- Fireline, 10 lb. test
- beading needles, #10

green necklace colors
- 8 mm round faceted gemstones (green turquoise)
- 5 mm bicone crystals (Swarovski, Jet AB)
- 5º seed beads (Miyuki 146FR, matte transparent green AB)
- 6º seed beads (Miyuki 1255, metallic matte dark bronze)
- 8º seed beads
  - color A (Miyuki 2006, matte metallic dark bronze)
  - color B (Matsuno 605, green iris)
- 11º seed beads (Miyuki 4217, Duracoat seafoam)

Spiral

1 On a comfortable length of thread, pick up a color A 8º seed bead, two color B 8º seed beads, a 5º seed bead, three 11º seed beads, four 8 mm round gemstones, a 5 mm bicone crystal, a 6º seed bead, two Bs, and three 11ºs. Sew through the beads again to form a ring, leaving a 6-in. (15 cm) tail and exiting the first A **(figure 1, a–b)**.

note If your 11ºs slip inside the 5º, add a B between the 11ºs and the 5º in the ring just completed and for the remainder of the beadwork. Also, it is very important that you keep the beadwork in the position as illustrated and not flip the beadwork as the spiral is worked.

2 Working in right-angle weave (RAW), pick up three As, and sew through the A your thread exited at the start of this step **(b–c)**. Retrace the thread path (not shown in the figure for clarity), and continue through the next two As **(c–d)**.
3 Pick up three As, and sew through the A your thread exited at the start of this step **(d–e)**. Retrace the thread path (not shown in the figure for clarity).
4 Work a counterclockwise loop: Pick up three 11ºs, two Bs, a 6º, a crystal, and a gemstone, and sew through the adjacent three gemstones in the previous ring **(figure 2, a–b)**. Pick up three 11ºs, a 5º, and two Bs, and sew through the A your thread exited at the start of this step **(b–c)**, using a tight tension. Continue through the next two

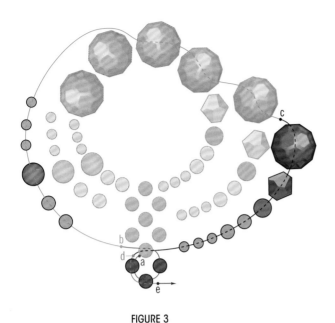

FIGURE 3

FIGURE 4

As **(c-d)**. Make sure this loop is positioned on top of the previous loop.
5 Work as in step 3 to add three As **(figure 3, a-b)**.
6 Work a clockwise loop: Pick up two Bs, a 5º, and three 11ºs, and sew through the last three gemstones added **(b-c)**. Pick up a gemstone, a crystal, a 6º, two Bs, and three 11ºs, and sew through the A your thread exited at the start of this step **(c-d)**. Continue through the next two As **(d-e)**. Make sure this loop is positioned on top of the previous loop.
7 Repeat steps 3–6 for approximately 8 in. (20 cm), skipping step 5 before the last loop of beads is added, and reserving four gemstones for the neck straps. Retrace the thread path through the last loop of beads added, and end the working thread and tail.

Neck strap

1 On the just-completed end of the spiral, add 2 ft. (61 cm) of thread, exiting the crystal in the last loop, with the needle pointing toward the gemstone. Work the neck strap as follows:
• Pick up five 11ºs, an A, five 11ºs, an A, a B, a 6º, a crystal, a 5º, a gemstone, a 5º, a crystal, a 6º, a B, and an A. Pick up this same pattern of beads again.
• Pick up a repeating pattern of five 11ºs and an A three times.
• Pick up half of the clasp, and sew back through the last A added **(figure 4, a-b)**.
• Pick up five 11ºs, and sew through the adjacent five 11ºs, A, and the clasp **(b-c)**. Retrace the thread path of the connection (not shown in the figure for clarity), and continue through the five

11ºs added in this step and the next A **(c-d)**.
• Pick up five 11ºs, an A, and five 11ºs, skip the next 11 beads, and sew through the following 11 beads. Repeat this stitch once more.
• Pick up five 11ºs, an A, and five 11ºs, sew through the next four gemstones in the last loop of the spiral, and end the thread.
2 Add 2 ft. (61 cm) of thread to the other end of the spiral, exiting the three 11ºs before the gemstone in the last loop, with the needle pointing toward the gemstone. Work the second strap as in step 1. ●

Dainty delight set

Embellish Silky beads with MiniDuos and seed beads for a stylish bracelet and necklace set.

designed by
Andrea Mazzenga

Difficulty rating

Materials

purple bracelet 7⅛ in. (18.1 cm)

- **14** 6 mm Silky beads (green opaque sliperit)
- **6 g** 2 x 4 mm MiniDuo beads (metallic suede purple)
- **15** 3 mm fire-polished beads (purple iris)
- **3 g** 11º seed beads (Miyuki 462, metallic gold iris)
- **1 g** 15º seed beads (Toho 332, gold luster raspberry)
- **1** clasp
- Fireline, 6 lb. test
- beading needles, #11 or #12

necklace 18 in. (46 cm)

- **38** 6 mm Silky beads (green opaque sliperit)
- **6 g** 2 x 4 mm MiniDuo beads (metallic suede purple)
- **39** 3 mm fire-polished beads (purple iris)
- **9 g** 11º seed beads (Miyuki 462, metallic gold iris)
- **2 g** 15º seed beads (Toho 332, gold luster raspberry)
- **1** clasp
- Fireline, 6 lb. test
- beading needles, #11 or #12

Information for the bracelets on p. 37 is listed at www.BeadAndButton.com/resources.

Picking up the Silky beads

The front of the Silky bead is the side with the bump, which should be facing up. With the holes running vertically, we will refer to the right hole (RH) or the left hole (LH).

Bracelet

Band

1 On a comfortable length of thread, attach a stop bead, leaving a 6-in. (15 cm) tail. Pick up a Silky bead (RH), two 11º seed beads, a 3 mm bead, and two 11ºs, and sew through the open hole of the Silky (LH) **(figure 1, a–b)**.

2 Pick up two 11ºs, a 3 mm, and two 11ºs, and sew through the Silky (RH) **(b–c)**. Continue through the next two 11ºs and 3 mm **(c–d)**.

3 Pick up two 11ºs, a Silky (LH), two 11ºs, a 3 mm, and two 11ºs, and sew through the open hole of the Silky (RH) **(d–e)**. Pick up two 11ºs, and sew through the adjacent 3 mm **(e–f)**. Continue through the following two 11ºs, Silky (LH), two 11ºs, and 3 mm **(f–g)**.

4 Pick up two 11ºs, a Silky (RH), two 11ºs, a 3 mm, and two 11ºs, and sew through the open hole of the Silky (LH) **(g–h)**. Pick up two 11ºs, and sew through the adjacent 3 mm **(h–i)**. Continue through the following two 11ºs, Silky (RH), two 11ºs, and 3 mm **(i–j)**.

5 Repeat steps 3–4 for the desired length (keeping in mind the length of your clasp), ending and adding thread as needed, and making sure the front of the Silkies are all facing up. You may end with step 3 or 4 depending on the desired length. A 7⅛-in. (18.1 cm) bracelet uses 14 Silkies.

Clasp and embellishment

1 Pick up a 15º seed bead, an 11º, and the loop of a clasp, and sew back through the 11º just added. Pick up a 15º, and sew through the 3 mm bead your thread exited at the start of this step **(figure 2, a–b)**. Retrace the thread path, and continue through the next two 11ºs **(b–c)**. If using a toggle clasp, attach the toggle ring on this end.

2 Pick up four MiniDuos, and sew through the next two 11ºs, 3 mm, and two 11ºs on the opposite edge **(c–d)**. Repeat this stitch to add MiniDuos on alternating edges for the remainder of

FIGURE 1   FIGURE 2

◇	6 mm Silky bead
⬤	11º seed bead
◯	3 mm bead
○	15º seed bead
⬭	2 x 4 mm MiniDuo

simple swap

Use 3 mm pearls instead of 3 mm fire-polished beads, as in the tourquoise/cream and copper/gold bracelets on p. 37.

the band, exiting the end 3 mm. End and add thread as needed.

3 Work as in step 1 to attach the other half of the clasp on this end of the band. If using a toggle clasp, make sure the toggle bar works properly before reinforcing. Add additional 15ºs equally on each side of the 11º if needed.

4 With your thread exiting the two 11ºs on the edge opposite the MiniDuos **(figure 3, point a)**, pick up four 11ºs, and sew through the next two 11ºs, 3 mm, and two 11ºs on the opposite edge **(a–b)**. Repeat this stitch on alternating edges for the remainder of the band, exiting the end 3 mm, and continuing through the next 11º **(b–c)**. End and add thread as needed.

5 Pick up a 15º, and sew through the open hole of the next MiniDuo **(c–d)**. Pick up a 15º, and sew through the following MiniDuo **(d–e)**. Repeat this last stitch twice **(e–f)**. Pick up a 15º, skip the next 11º, and sew through the following 11º, 3 mm, and 11º **(f–g)**. Repeat this step for the remainder of the band, exiting the end 3 mm, and sew through the next four 11ºs **(figure 4, a–b)**.

6 Pick up a 15º, an 11º and a 15º, and sew through the following four 11ºs, 3 mm, and four 11ºs on the opposite edge **(b–c)**. Repeat this stitch for the remainder of the band, remove the stop bead, and end the threads.

Necklace

The necklace instructions are for an 18 in. (46 cm) length. Increase or decrease the same number of Silkies on each end for the desired length.

1 Work as in "Bracelet: Band" to make a strip with 38 Silkies.
2 Work as in step 1 of "Clasp and embellishment" but pick up two 11ºs in place of each 15º.
3 With your thread exiting the second 11º on the end, pick up two 11ºs, a 15º, and two 11ºs, and sew through the next two 11ºs, 3 mm, and two 11ºs on the opposite edge. Repeat this stitch to embellish 12 Silkies.
4 Work as in step 2 of "Bracelet: Clasp and embellishment" for the next 14 Silkies.

FIGURE 3

FIGURE 4

5 Repeat step 3 to embellish the remaining Silkies. Attach the other half of the clasp as you did the first, and continue working as in step 3 for the 12 Silkies on this end.
6 Work as in step 4 of "Bracelet: Clasp and embellishment" to embellish the next 14 Silkies on the edges opposite the MiniDuos. After sewing through the 3 mm after the 14th Silky, sew through the first 11º on the opposite edge (sewing toward the MiniDuos).
7 Work as in step 5 of "Bracelet: Clasp and embellishment" to add 15ºs between the MiniDuos surrounding

the next 14 Silkies. After embellishing the 14th Silky, sew through the adjacent 3 mm, and continue through the next four 11ºs on the opposite edge.
8 Work as in step 6 of "Bracelet: Clasp and embellishment" for the next 14 Silkies. After embellishing the 14th Silky and sewing through the 3 mm, continue through the next two 11ºs on the opposite edge.
9 Work as in step 3 to embellish the remaining edge of the 12 Silkies on this end, and end the threads. ●

Delicate twist bangle

The beads may be small but they make a flexible, easy-to-wear bangle with a sparkly focal that's not overwhelming.

designed by **Ora Shai**

Twisted herringbone tube

1 On a comfortable length of thread, pick up four 15º seed beads leaving an 18-in. (46 cm) tail. Sew through all four beads again to form two stacks next to each other with their holes parallel **(figure 1)**.

2 Pick up two 15ºs, sew through the two 15ºs in the previous stack, and continue through the two 15ºs just added **(figure 2, a–b)**. Repeat this stitch three more time to make a ladder with six stacks **(b–c)**.

3 To form the ladder into a ring, sew up through the first stack, down through the last stack added, and up through the first stack again **(figure 3)**.

4 Work in twisted tubular herringbone stitch using 15ºs until the beadwork is ¾ in. (1.9 cm) shorter than the circumference of the widest part of your hand.

Embellishment

1 Pick up a 3 mm fire-polished bead, a 15º, and a 3 mm, and sew down through the next two 15ºs, and up through the following two 15ºs in the herringbone rope **(figure 4, a–b)**.

2 Pick up a 3 mm and a 15º, and sew down through the last 3 mm added and the two 15ºs below it **(b–c)**. Continue up through the next two 15ºs and the 3 mm just added **(c–d)**.

3 Pick up a 15º and a 3 mm, and sew down through the next two 15ºs in the following stack **(figure 5 a–b)**. Continue up through the two 15ºs in the previous stack, the 3 mm above it, the 15º and 3 mm just added, the next two 15ºs in the same stack, and up through the two 15ºs in the following stack **(b–c)**.

4 Repeat steps 2–3 once more.

5 Sew up through the first 3 mm added **(figure 6, a–b)**. Pick up a 15º, and sew down through the previous 3 mm and the next two 15ºs in the same stack **(b–c)**. Continue up through the next two 15ºs in the following stack, the first 3 mm, and the 15º just added **(c–d)**. This will form a ring of 15ºs on top of the fire-polished beads.

6 Pick up five 15ºs, skip the next 15º in the ring, and sew through the following 15º to form a picot **(figure 7, a–b)**. Repeat this stitch twice to complete the round, and sew through the next 15º in the ring, exiting on the inside of the tube **(b–c)**. *Note:* For clarity, the embellishment around the tube in **figures 7–8** is shown with only the last round of 15ºs.

7 Pick up five 15ºs, skip the next 15º in the ring, and sew through the following 15º **(figure 8, a–b)**. Repeat this stitch twice to complete the round, and step up through the first three 15ºs added in this round **(b–c)**. Make sure this round of beadwork sits inside the previous round.

8 Pick up a 3 mm bicone crystal, and sew through the center 15º in the next picot

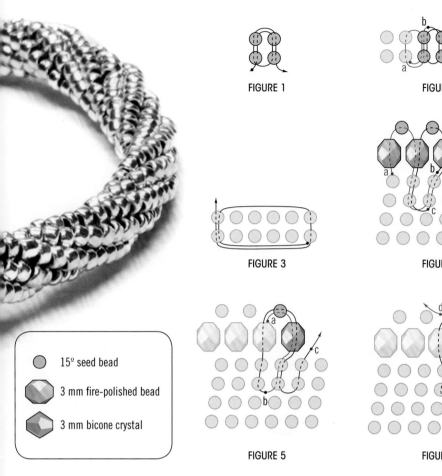

FIGURE 1

FIGURE 2

FIGURE 3

FIGURE 4

FIGURE 5

FIGURE 6

○ 15º seed bead

◆ 3 mm fire-polished bead

◆ 3 mm bicone crystal

Difficulty rating

◆ ◆ ◇ ◇ ◇

Materials
bangle 2½ in. (6.4 cm) inner diameter
- **3** 3 mm bicone crystals (Swarovski, turquoise AB2X)
- **12** 3 mm fire-polished beads (3FC854-F, full coated metallic gold)
- **6 g** 15º seed beads (Toho PF558, aluminum)
- Fireline, 4 lb. or 6 lb. test
- beading needles, #12 or #13

added in the previous round **(c–d)**. Repeat this stitch twice to complete the round **(d–e)**. Retrace the thread path, and end the thread.

9 Repeat steps 1–6 using the tail thread on the other end of the tube. *Note:* If your 15ºs are getting hard to sew through, sew under the nearest thread bridge instead.

10 Pick up two 15ºs, and sew through a center 15º from one of the picots added in step 7 on the other end of the tube **(photo a)**. Pick up two 15ºs, skip the next 15º in the ring, and sew through the following 15º in the ring on this end of the tube **(photo b)**. Repeat these stitches twice to complete the round, and end the threads. ●

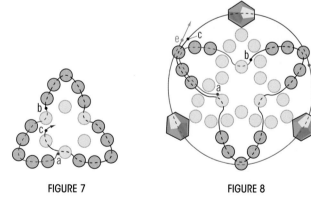

FIGURE 7

FIGURE 8

a

b

PEYOTE STITCH

Bed of roses
bracelet

Create a stunning peyote-stitched bracelet of blooming roses in lavish hues of red and pink.

designed by **Justyna Szlezak**

Materials
bracelet 7 x 1⅝ in. (18 x 4.1 cm)
- 11º Delica cylinder beads (Miyuki)
  - **4 g** color A (DB211, opaque alabaster luster)
  - **2 g** color B (DB070, rose-lined pink AB)
  - **2 g** color C (DB654, opaque maroon)
  - **3 g** color D (DB856, matte light red AB)
  - **1 g** color E (DB657, opaque olive)
  - **1 g** color F (DB734, opaque chocolate brown)
  - **1 g** color G (DB206, opaque salmon)
  - **1 g** color H (DB909, sparkling beige-lined chartreuse)
  - **1 g** color I (DB723, opaque dark cranberry)
  - **2 g** color J (DB105, dark cranberry gold luster)
  - **1 g** color K (DB769, matte transparent taupe)
  - **1 g** color L (DB1055, matte metallic rose green AB)
  - **1 g** color M (DB201, pearl white)
- **1 g** 11º seed beads (Miyuki 591, ivory pearl Ceylon)
- **2** 8 mm magnetic clasps
- Fireline, 6 lb. test
- beading needles, #11 or #12

Bracelet band

1 On a comfortable length of thread, attach a stop bead, leaving a 12-in. (30 cm) tail. Starting at the upper-right corner of the **pattern** (p. 42), pick up 10 color A 11º cylinder beads, one color L 11º cylinder bead, and 21 As for rows 1 and 2.
2 Following the **pattern**, work in flat even-count peyote stitch using the appropriate-color beads. End and add thread as needed, but do not end the working thread or tail when you complete the band.

make it longer
Use color A cylinders to work additional rows of peyote stitch evenly on each end of the base. Ten rows add approximately ⅜ in. (1 cm).

Clasp

1 With the tail thread, sew through the beadwork as shown to exit the second up-bead from the edge on the end row **(figure, a–b)**.
2 Pick up seven 11º seed beads, half of a magnetic clasp, and three 11ºs, and sew back through the fourth 11º just added. This forms a loop of beads through the clasp. Pick up three 11ºs, skip the next two up-beads in the end row, and sew through the following up-bead **(b–c)**. Pull the thread tight, and sew through the beadwork to retrace the clasp connection (not shown in figure for clarity).
3 Sew through the beadwork as shown to exit the seventh up-bead from where your thread just exited **(c–d)**. Work as in step 2 to add half of a second clasp to the band **(d–e)**. End the working thread.
4 Using the tail, work as in steps 1–3 to add the matching clasp halves to the opposite end of the band. ●

11º cylinder bead
- ⬜ color A
- ⬜ color B
- ⬛ color C
- ⬛ color D
- ⬜ color E
- ⬛ color F
- ⬜ color G
- ⬜ color H
- ⬛ color I
- ⬛ color J
- ⬜ color K
- ⬜ color L
- ⬜ color M
- ◯ 11º seed bead

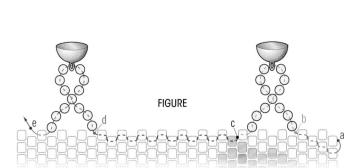

FIGURE

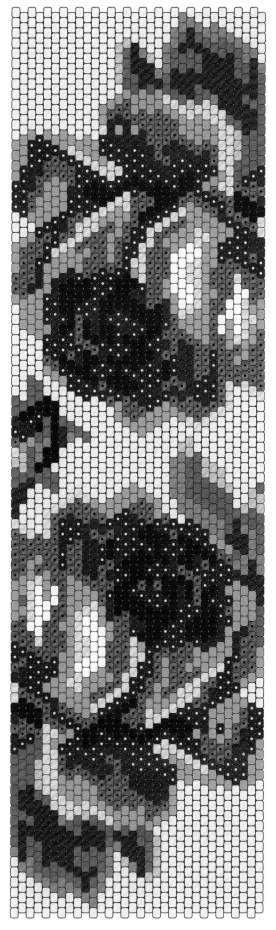

PATTERN

Picture
perfect
bracelet

Show off this charming
bracelet featuring decorative
frame-style components for
a sweet peek-a-boo look.

designed by **Debora Hodoyer**

Difficulty rating

Materials

bracelet 7 x 1½ in. (18 x 3.8 cm)
- **16** 6 mm fire-polished beads (blue iris)
- **10 g** 2.5 x 5 mm SuperDuo beads (metallic suede blue)
- **38** 4 mm glass pearls (aqua green)
- **4 g** 3.8 mm O-beads (pastel burgundy)
- **2 g** 8º seed beads (Toho 704, matte Andromeda)
- **2 g** 11º seed beads (Miyuki 4218, Duracoat dusty orchid)
- **1 g** 15º seed beads (Miyuki F4216, Duracoat steel blue matte)
- **2** magnetic clasps
- **4** 4 mm jump rings
- Fireline, 6 lb. test
- beading needles, #11 or #12
- **2** pairs of chainnose, flatnose, and/or bentnose pliers

Information for the green/teal pendant is listed at www.BeadAndButton.com/resources.

Component

1 On 4 ft. (1.2 m) of thread, pick up a repeating pattern of four SuperDuos, an O-bead, a 4 mm pearl, and an O-bead four times, leaving a 6-in. (15 cm) tail **(figure 1, a–b)**. Sew through all the beads again using a slightly loose tension, and continue through the first four SuperDuos and the open hole of the SuperDuo you exit last **(b–c)**. Your beads should lay flat and form a square, with the open holes of the SuperDuos positioned to the outside **(photo)**. Loosen the tension of the square if needed.

2 Pick up a SuperDuo, and sew through the open hole of the next SuperDuo **(c–d)**. Repeat this stitch two more times **(d–e)**. Pick up an O-bead, a 6 mm fire-polished bead, and an O-bead, and sew through the open hole of the next SuperDuo **(e–f)**. Repeat these four stitches three times to complete the round **(f–g)**, and continue through the open hole of the following SuperDuo

(g–h). Loosen or tighten the beadwork as needed for the beadwork to lay flat.
3 Pick up a SuperDuo, and sew through the open hole of the next SuperDuo **(figure 2, a–b)**. Repeat this stitch once **(b–c)**. Pick up two 11º seed beads, and sew through the following 6 mm **(c–d)**. Pick up two 11ºs, and sew through the open hole of the next SuperDuo **(d–e)**. Repeat these four stitches three times to complete the round **(e–f)** using an even tension so the beadwork remains flat, and continue through the open hole of the following SuperDuo **(f–g)**.
4 Pick up an O-bead, a 4 mm, and an O-bead, and sew through the open hole of the next SuperDuo **(g–h)**. Pick up three 15º seed beads, and sew through the next two 11ºs **(h–i)**. Pick up five 11ºs, skip the next 6 mm, and sew through the following two 11ºs **(i–j)**. Pick up three 15ºs, and sew through the open hole of the next SuperDuo **(j–k)**. Repeat these four stitches three times to complete the round **(k–l)**, and

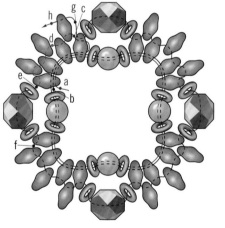

FIGURE 1

2.5 x 5 mm SuperDuo bead

3.8 mm O-bead

4 mm pearl

6 mm fire-polished bead

11º seed bead

15º seed bead

8º seed bead

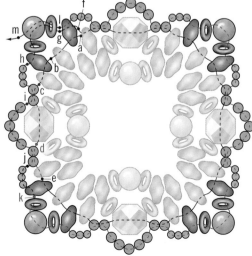

FIGURE 2

pendant option

Make one component, add a loop of five 11ºs off the center 11º on one corner, and attach an 8 mm jump ring.

continue through the following O-bead and 4 mm **(l–m)**.

5 Pick up five 11ºs, and sew through the 4 mm your thread is exiting to form a loop **(figure 3, a–b)**. Continue through the next O-bead, SuperDuo, and three 15ºs **(b–c)**. Pick up an 8º seed bead, skip the next two 11ºs, and sew through the following five 11ºs **(c–d)**. Pick up an 8º, skip the next two 11ºs, and sew through the following three 15ºs, SuperDuo, O-bead, and 4 mm **(d–e)**. Repeat these stitches three times to complete the round, but for the last stitch, sew through only the three 15ºs **(e–f)**.

6 Pick up a 15º and an 8º, and sew through the five 11ºs in the next loop **(f–g)**. Pick up an 8º and a 15º, and sew through the following three 15ºs, 8º, five 11ºs, 8º, and three 15ºs **(g–h)**. Repeat these stitches three times to complete the round **(h–i)**, and continue through the next 15º, 8º, five 11ºs, and 8º **(i–j)** to exit the second 8º added in this round. End the tail but not the working thread, and set the component aside.

7 Repeat steps 1–6 to make three more components for a 7-in. (18 cm) bracelet.

Connections

1 Position two components next to each other, with the working threads exiting on the top left. With the working thread of the component on the right **(figure 4, point a)**, pick up a 4 mm, skip the adjacent 8º on the left component, and sew through the following 8º on the left component **(a–b)**. Pick up a 15º, sew through the corresponding 8º on the right component **(b–c)**, and sew back through the 4 mm **(c–d)**. Continue through the top 8º on the left component **(d–e)**, pick up a 15º, and sew through the 8º your thread exited at the start of this step **(e–f)**. Retrace the thread path (not shown in the figure for clarity). Continue through the 4 mm and the next seven beads on the right component as shown to exit the next 8º **(f–g)**. Work as before to join this edge of the components **(g–h)**, and end this thread.

2 Repeat step 1 to attach the remaining components.

3 With the working thread on an end component, pick up eight 15ºs, and sew through the 8º your thread is exiting to form a clasp loop **(figure 5, a–b)**. Retrace the thread path, and continue through the beadwork to exit the corresponding 8º on the opposite edge **(b–c)**. Repeat this step to add another clasp loop **(c–d)**, and end the thread.

4 Add 12 in. (30 cm) of thread to the other end of the bracelet, and work as in step 3 to add clasp loops to this end.

5 Use jump rings to attach half of the clasp to each loop. ●

FIGURE 3

FIGURE 4

FIGURE 5

need it a bit longer?

To add a little more length, add more 15ºs equally to each clasp loop. You may also use larger or additional jump rings on each loop if necessary.

DiAMONDS
in the rough
set

Scatter sparkly crystals throughout a collection
of SuperDuos, pearls, and seed beads for simple,
yet fabulous, creations.

designed by **Cassie Donlen**

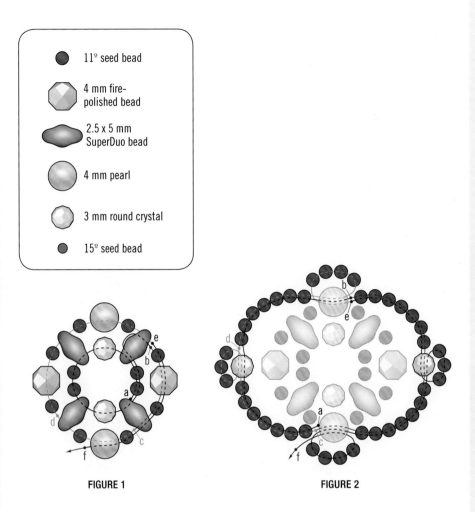

- 11º seed bead
- 4 mm fire-polished bead
- 2.5 x 5 mm SuperDuo bead
- 4 mm pearl
- 3 mm round crystal
- 15º seed bead

FIGURE 1

FIGURE 2

Difficulty rating

Materials

bracelet 8 in. (20 cm)
- **24** 2.5 x 5 mm SuperDuo beads (emerald alabaster pastel)
- **28** 4 mm pearls (Preciosa, bronze)
- **12** 4 mm fire-polished beads (azurite halo)
- **29** 3 mm round crystals (Preciosa, crystal golden flare)
- **4 g** 11º seed beads (Miyuki 462, metallic gold iris)
- **1 g** 15º seed beads (Toho 221, bronze)
- **1** toggle clasp
- Fireline, 6 lb. test
- beading needles, #11 or #12

earrings
1⅛ in. (2.9 cm)
- **8** 2.5 x 5 mm SuperDuo beads (emerald alabaster pastel)
- **6** 4 mm pearls (Preciosa, bronze)
- **4** 4 mm fire-polished beads (azurite halo)
- **8** 3 mm round crystals (Preciosa, crystal golden flare)
- **1 g** 11º seed beads (Miyuki 462, metallic gold iris)
- **1** pair of earring findings
- **2** pairs of chainnose, bentnose, and/or flatnose pliers

Bracelet
Components

1 On 1 yd. (.9 m) of thread, pick up two 11º seed beads, a SuperDuo, a 3 mm round crystal, a SuperDuo, two 11ºs, a SuperDuo, a crystal, and a SuperDuo, and tie the beads into a ring with a square knot, leaving a 6-in. (15 cm) tail. Sew through the next two 11ºs and SuperDuo, and continue through the open hole of the same SuperDuo **(figure 1, a–b)**.

2 Pick up an 11º, a 4 mm fire-polished bead, and an 11º, and sew through the open hole of the next SuperDuo **(b–c)**. Pick up an 11º, a 4 mm pearl, and an 11º, and sew through the open hole of the following SuperDuo **(c–d)**. Repeat these two stitches once to complete the round **(d–e)**. Sew through the outer ring again (not shown in the figure for clarity) to cinch up the beads to form a slight dome shape, and continue through the next six beads **(e–f)**.

3 Pick up seven 11ºs, a crystal, and seven 11ºs, skip the next seven beads in the outer ring, and sew through the following pearl **(figure 2, a–b)**. Repeat this step once **(b–c)**.

4 Sew through the next seven 11ºs and crystal, pick up three 11ºs, and sew through the crystal your thread is exiting, going in the same direction **(c–d)**. Sew through the following seven 11ºs and pearl, pick up four 11ºs, and sew through the pearl your thread is exiting, going in the same direction **(d–e)**. Repeat these two stitches once **(e–f)**.

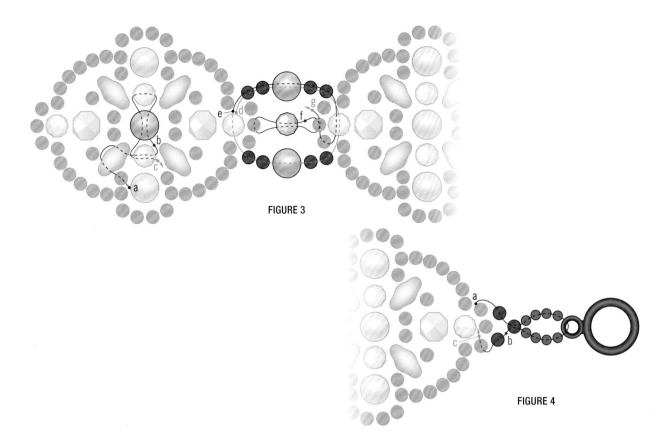

FIGURE 3

FIGURE 4

5 Sew through the beadwork as shown to exit a crystal in the inner ring **(figure 3, a–b)**. Pick up a pearl, sew through the corresponding crystal on the opposite side, and continue back through the pearl and the crystal your thread exited at the start of this step, going in the same direction **(b–c)**. End the tail, but not the working thread.

6 For an 8 in. (20 cm) bracelet, work as in steps 1–5 to make a total of six components.

Assembly

1 Place two components side by side on your bead mat with the pearls positioned at the top and bottom. With the working thread of the component on the left, sew through the beadwork as necessary to exit the edge crystal on the right side, with the needle pointing toward the top edge **(point d)**.

2 Pick up two 11ºs, a pearl, and two 11ºs, and sew down through the corresponding crystal on the other component. Pick up two 11ºs, a pearl, and two

11ºs, and sew up through the crystal your thread exited at the start of this step **(d–e)**. Retrace the thread path (not shown in the figure for clarity), and then sew through the beadwork as shown to exit the center 11º in the picot surrounding the crystal on the other component **(e–f)**. Pick up a crystal, sew through the center 11º in the adjacent picot on the first component, and continue back through the crystal and the 11º your thread exited at the start of this step, going in the same direction **(f–g)**. The connection point will also have a slight dome shape. End the working thread.

3 Work as in steps 1–2 to attach the remaining components, but do not end the working thread on the last component.

Clasp

1 With the working thread from the last component, sew through the beadwork as necessary to exit the first 11º in the picot surrounding the crystal on the

outer edge **(figure 4, point a)**. Pick up two 11ºs, eight 15º seed beads, and the loop of the toggle ring, and sew back through the last 11º added **(a–b)**. Pick up an 11º, skip the center 11º in the picot, and sew through the next 11º in the same picot **(b–c)**. Retrace the thread path several times to reinforce the connection, and end the thread.

2 Add 10 in. (25 cm) of thread to the opposite end of the bracelet, with the thread exiting the corresponding 11º of the end picot. Work as in step 1 to attach the other half of the clasp.

Earrings

1 Work as in steps 1–5 of "Components," except in step 4, pick up six 11ºs (instead of three 11ºs) when sewing through each crystal.

2 Open the loop of an earwire, attach it to the picot surrounding a crystal, and close the loop.

3 Make a matching earring. ●

BEAD WEAVING

Pyramids of Nubia
bracelet

Use Kheops beads to
stitch this patterned bracelet inspired by
jewelry from the ancient kingdoms of Nubia.

designed by **Marina Montagut**

Difficulty rating

Materials

bronze bracelet 7¾ in. (19.7 cm)
- **7 g** 6 x 6 mm Kheops beads (bronze red)
- **2 g** 4 x 6 mm pellet beads (amber)
- **3 g** 2.5 x 5 mm SuperDuo beads (chalk sliperit)
- **2 g** 3.8 x 1 mm O-beads (copper)
- **2 g** 8º seed beads (Miyuki 1052, galvanized gold)
- 11º seed beads
  - **1 g** color A (Miyuki 1052, galvanized gold)
  - **1 g** color B (Miyuki 4206, Duracoat galvanized pink blush)
- **1** toggle clasp
- Fireline, 4 or 6 lb. test
- beading needles, #11 or #12

purple bracelet colors
- 6 x 6 mm Kheops beads (blue luster)
- 4 x 6 mm pellet beads (light gray)
- 2.5 x 5 mm SuperDuo beads (alabaster pastel Bordeaux)
- 3.8 x 1 mm O-beads (magic purple)
- 8º seed beads (Miyuki 4220, Duracoat galvanized eggplant)
- 11º seed beads
  - color A (Toho 1204, purple marbled opaque sapphire)
  - color B (Toho 319K, sapphire purple luster)

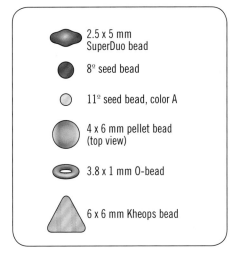

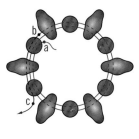

FIGURE 1

Components

How to pick up Kheops beads: With the side with two holes facing away from you, pick up the bead through the left hole (LH) or the right hole (RH), per the instructions.

1 On 1 yd. (.9 m) of thread, pick up a repeating pattern of a size 8º seed bead and a SuperDuo bead six times. Sew through the beads again to form a ring, leaving a 6-in. (15 cm) tail **(figure 1, a–b)**, and sew through the next 8º, SuperDuo, and 8º **(b–c)**.

2 Pick up a pellet bead, center it in the ring, skip the next five beads, and sew through the following 8º **(figure 2, a–b)**. Sew back through the pellet, the 8º your thread exited at the beginning of this step, and the following SuperDuo. Sew through the open hole of the same SuperDuo **(b–c)**.

design option
Use all 11º seed beads to form the picot as shown in the bronze bracelet.

3 Pick up an O-bead, a Kheops (LH), a color A 11º seed bead, an 8º, and an A, and sew through the open hole (RH) of the same Kheops **(c–d)** to form a picot. Pick up an O-bead, and sew through the open hole of the next SuperDuo **(d–e)**.

4 Pick up an O-bead and a Kheops (LH), and sew through the open hole (RH) of the same Kheops. Pick up an O-bead, and sew through the open hole of the following SuperDuo **(e–f)**.

5 Repeat step 3 twice **(f–g)**, step 4 once **(g–h)**, and step 3 once again **(h–i)**. Sew through the beadwork to exit a Kheops (LH) without a picot. End the tail but not the working thread.

6 Repeat steps 1–5 to make a total of seven components for a 7¾ in. (19.7 cm) bracelet. Each component measures ⅞ in. (2.2 cm) in width.

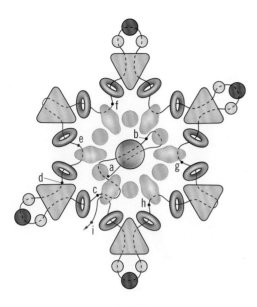

FIGURE 2

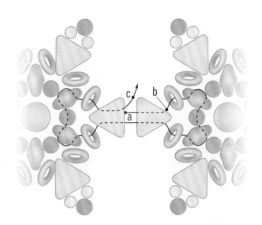

FIGURE 3

Assembly

1 Align a component with the working thread exiting a Kheops to a corresponding component where there is no picot or working thread on the Kheops. With the working thread, sew through the Kheops on the corresponding component **(figure 3, a–b)**. Sew through the beadwork as shown to join the components **(b–c)**. Retrace the thread path to reinforce the join, and end the thread.

2 Work as in step 1 to add the remaining components to the base using the working thread from each newly added component. Instead of ending the thread on the last component, sew through the beadwork to exit the end Kheops without a picot to get into position to add the clasp.

Clasp

1 With the working thread from an end component, pick up six color B 11º seed beads, the loop of the toggle ring, and six Bs, and sew back through the other hole of the same Kheops bead. Retrace the thread path to reinforce the join, and end the thread.

2 With the working thread from the component on the opposite end, work as in step 1, but pick up eight Bs on each side of the toggle bar. ◉

create a set
Make matching earrings by making a component, but add picots to every Kheops, and then make a loop to attach an earring finding.

NETTING
Snappy
safari
ring

Show off your wild side with animal print buttons
that snap into place on a netted ring band.

designed by **Kerrie Slade**

Ring band

The ring band is made to
measure and the instructions
include details to make a
1-in. (2.5 cm) tall band or a
shorter ⅝-in. (1.6 cm) band.

Tall band (1 in./2.5 cm)

1 On 2 yd. (1.8 m) of thread,
pick up 23 10º seed beads.
Leaving a 10-in. (25 cm) tail,
sew back through the 17th
bead to create a loop at the
end of the row **(figure 1, a–b)**.
2 Work in netting:
Row 2: Pick up three 10ºs,
skip the next three beads
in the strand, and sew back
through the next (the 13th)

bead in the previous row
(b–c). Repeat this stitch three
times, sewing back through
the ninth, fifth, and first beads
in the previous row **(c–d)**.
Row 3: Pick up four 10ºs, and
sew back through the middle
bead in the last group of
three beads added in the
previous step **(figure 2, a–b)**.
Pick up three 10ºs, and sew
through the middle bead
in the next group of three
beads **(b–c)**. Repeat this
stitch three times to complete the row **(c–d)**.
Row 4: Work as in row 3,
working in the opposite
direction **(figure 3)**.

3 Continue working as in
rows 3 and 4 until the band
fits around your finger. At the
end of the final row, the
working thread and tail
should be on the opposite
edges of the band.
4 To join the ends, pick up
two 10ºs, and sew through
the middle bead in the next
set of three beads on the
opposite end **(figure 4,
a–b)**. Pick up a 10º, and
sew through the next middle
bead on the other end **(b–c)**.
Repeat this stitch eight times
(c–d). Pick up two 10ºs,
and sew back through
the nearest middle bead

on the opposite edge **(d–e)**.
Retrace the thread path
through the connection.
5 Sew through the beadwork
to exit a pair of beads on
one edge. Pick up a 10º,
and sew through the next
pair of edge beads. Repeat
this stitch around the band
(figure 5). Using the tail,
repeat this step on the other
edge. End the tail but not
the working thread.
6 Sew through the beadwork
to exit near the center of the
band. Sew through a hole in
the female half of the snap,
and sew through an adja-
cent bead in the band.

Following the existing thread paths in the band, attach the snap half to the band by sewing through the remaining holes in the snap and adjacent beads in the band. Retrace the thread paths several times to secure, and end the thread.

Short band (⅝ in./1.6 cm)
To make a ⅝-in. (1.6 cm) band, work as in "Tall band" with the following changes:
• In step 1, begin by picking up 15 beads instead of 23, and sew back through the ninth bead instead of the 17th.
• In row 2, sew through the fifth bead instead of the 13th, and repeat the stitch once.
• In rows 3 and beyond, pick up four beads for the first stitch as before, and then work two three-bead stitches instead of four three-bead stitches.
• For the join, work the repeat four times instead of eight.

Interchangeable buttons

1 On 2 ft. (61 cm) of thread and leaving a 6-in. (15 cm) tail, sew through one hole of the male half of a snap (from front to back) and one hole of a button (from back to front). Pick up seven 10ºs, and sew through the opposite hole of the button and snap **(figure 6)**.
2 Sew up through an adjacent hole of the snap and the button, pick up three 10ºs, and sew through the middle 10º from the previous step **(figure 7, a–b)**. Pick up three 10ºs, and sew through the opposite hole of the button and snap **(b–c)**. Retrace the thread path through the button and snap several times, and end the working thread and tail.
3 Repeat steps 1 and 2 with the remaining buttons and male snap halves.
4 Press one of the buttons onto the snap on the ring base to wear your new ring. ●

FIGURE 1

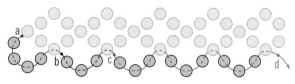
FIGURE 2

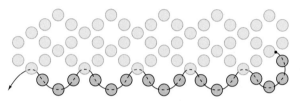
FIGURE 3

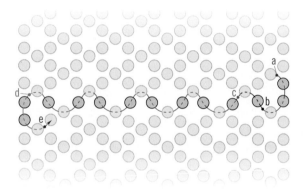
FIGURE 4

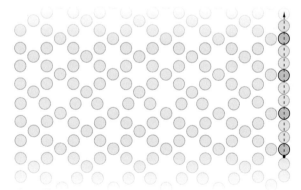
FIGURE 5

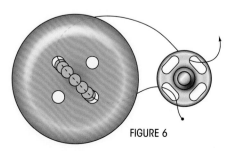
FIGURE 6

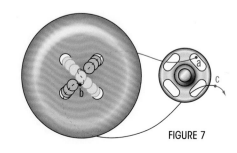
FIGURE 7

Difficulty rating

Materials
ring ⅝–1 in. (1.6–2.5 cm)
• **5** 18–20 mm Kazuri 4-hole ceramic buttons (elephant, lion, zebra, giraffe, cheetah)
• **3–4 g** 10º Czech seed beads (Preciosa, silver)
• **5** 7–8 mm snaps
• Fireline, 6 lb. test
• beading needles, #10–12

PEYOTE STITCH

Old Gl★ry
bracelet

Celebrate Independence Day in festive style with
this odd-count peyote-stitched bracelet that features
American flag motifs.

designed by **Andrea Mazzenga**

Base

1 On a comfortable length of thread, attach a stop bead, leaving a 10-in. (25 cm) tail. Starting at the lower-left corner of the **pattern**, pick up 13 color A 11º cylinder beads for rows 1 and 2 **(figure 1, a–b)**.

2 Work a pole embellishment stitch: Pick up an 11º seed bead and a 15º seed bead, and sew back through the 11º **(b–c)**.

3 Work the first six stitches of row 3 in flat odd-count peyote stitch using As **(c–d)**. Make a figure-8 turn to start the next row **(d–e)**, work a pole embellishment stitch **(e–f)**, and then sew through the bead added in the odd-count turn **(f–g)**.

4 Continue following the **pattern** for rows 4–75 while working in odd-count peyote stitch. Remember to work a pole embellishment stitch where indicated on the **pattern**.

easy embellishing

On odd-count rows that don't have a pole embellishment stitch, you can make the turn to start the next row by picking up the last bead of the row, sewing under the thread bridge between the last two edge beads, and sewing back through the last bead added.

PATTERN

Row 75
Row 39
Row 4

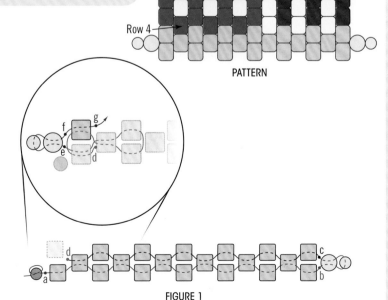

FIGURE 1

Difficulty rating

Materials

bracelet 7 x ⁷⁄₈ in. (18 x 2.2 cm)

- 11º Delica cylinder beads (Miyuki)
  - **2 g** color A (DB034, light 24kt gold-plated)
  - **3 g** color B (DB602, silver-lined red)
  - **3 g** color C (DB201, white pearl Ceylon)
  - **3 g** color D (DB047, silver-lined sapphire)
  - **1 g** color E (DB035, galvanized silver)
- **1 g** 11º seed beads (Miyuki 4203, Duracoat galvanized yellow gold)
- **1 g** 15º seed beads (Miyuki 4203, Duracoat galvanized yellow gold)
- 1 2-strand tube clasp
- Fireline, 6 lb. test
- beading needles, #11 or #12

▨	11º cylinder bead, color A
○	11º seed bead
○	15º seed bead
■	11º cylinder bead, color B
□	11º cylinder bead, color C
■	11º cylinder bead, color D
▨	11º cylinder bead, color E

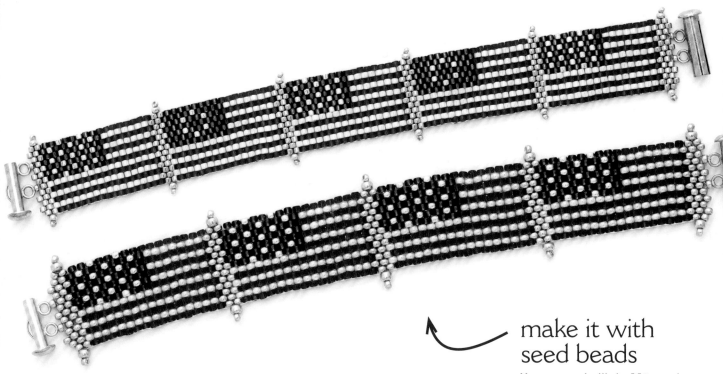

5 To make a 6¾ in. (17.1 cm) base, repeat the entire pattern starting on row 4 once, and then repeat rows 4–39 once again for a total of five flag motifs. End and add thread as needed.

Clasp

1 With the working thread, work two stitches using As **(figure 2, a–b)**.
2 Pick up a 15º, sew through the first loop of the clasp, continue back through the 15º just added, and sew through the next A. Work one stitch using an A **(b–c)**.

3 Work as in step 2, but sew through the other loop of the clasp **(c–d)**. Retrace the thread path of the clasp connection, and end the working thread.
4 Remove the stop bead from the tail. Sew under the thread bridge next to the edge of the nearest pole embellishment, and continue back through the A your thread was exiting at the start of this step. Repeat steps 1–3 to add the other half of the clasp to this end of the base. End the tail. **○**

make it with seed beads

You can substitute 11º seed beads for the 11º cylinder beads. This will slightly increase the size of each flag motif. A four-flag bracelet made with seed beads will measure about 6¼ in. (15.9 cm) long without the clasp.

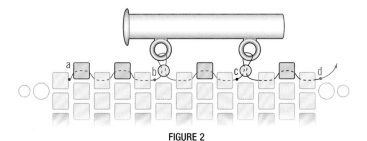

FIGURE 2

go long

To add a small amount of length, use As to work additional rows evenly on each end of the base, ending on an odd-numbered row and allowing ½ in. (1.3 cm) for the clasp.

To add an even greater length, continue repeating the pattern to make more flag motifs.

SYMPHONY OF PEARLS
necklace

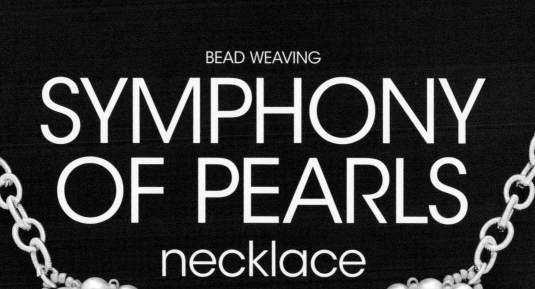

Create a beautiful pearl and seed bead
necklace that will have you singing with delight.

designed by **Alicia Campos**

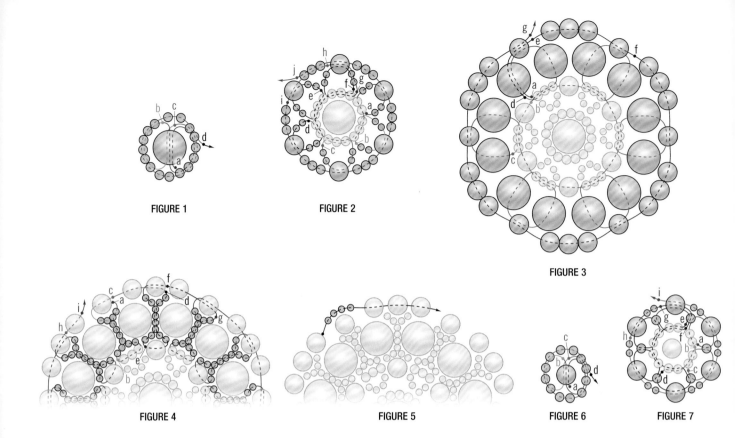

FIGURE 1

FIGURE 2

FIGURE 3

FIGURE 4

FIGURE 5

FIGURE 6

FIGURE 7

Center component

1 On 2 yd. (1.8 m) of thread, pick up a 6 mm pearl and six 11ºs seed beads. Sew through the pearl again in the same direction, leaving a 6-in. (15 cm) tail **(figure 1, a–b)**. This forms a loop of 11ºs around one side of the pearl. Pick up six 11ºs, and sew through the pearl again to form a loop on the other side of the pearl **(b–c)**. Sew through the first six 11ºs. Pick up two 11ºs, and sew through the next six 11ºs. Pick up two 11ºs, and sew through all the beads in the ring around the pearl (retrace not shown in the figure for clarity). Continue through the next two 11ºs **(c–d)**.

2 Pick up two 15ºs, a 4 mm pearl, and two 15ºs, and sew through the two 11ºs in the ring your thread just exited and the next three 11ºs to add a picot **(figure 2, a–b)**. Work five more picots with two 15ºs, a 4 mm, and two 15ºs in each, altering the thread path as follows:

Picot 1: Pick up the beads, and sew through the three 11ºs your thread just exited and the next three 11ºs in the ring **(b–c)**.

Picot 2: Pick up the beads, and sew through the three 11ºs your thread just exited and the next two 11ºs

in the ring **(c–d)**.

Picot 3: Pick up the beads, and sew through the two 11ºs your thread just exited and the next three 11ºs in the ring **(d–e)**.

Picot 4: Pick up the beads, and sew through the three 11ºs your thread just exited and the next three 11ºs in the ring **(e–f)**.

Picot 5: Pick up the beads, sew through the three 11ºs your thread exited **(f–g)**, and continue through the first two 15ºs and pearl added in this picot **(g–h)**.

3 Pick up three 11ºs, and sew through the pearl in the next picot **(h–i)**. Repeat this stitch five times to complete the round, and continue through the first three 11ºs added in this round **(i–j)**.

4 Pick up a 6 mm, a 4 mm, and a 6 mm, and sew through the three 11ºs your thread exited at the start of this step **(figure 3, a–b)**. Retrace the thread path (not shown in the figure for clarity), and continue through the next 4 mm and three 11ºs **(b–c)**. Repeat these stitches five times to complete the round **(c–d)**, and sew through the adjacent 6 mm and 4 mm as shown **(d–e)**.

5 Pick up three 4 mms, and sew through the next 4 mm **(e–f)**. Repeat this stitch five times to complete the round **(f–g)**,

and retrace the thread path using a tight tension so the beadwork begins to dome.

6 Pick up eight 15ºs, skip the 6 mm, and sew through the adjacent three 11ºs **(figure 4, a–b)**. Pick up two 15ºs, skip the last two 15ºs just added, and sew back through the next four 15ºs. Pick up two 15ºs, and sew through the 4 mm your thread exited at the start of this step **(b–c)**. Continue through the next two 4 mms **(c–d)**.

7 Pick up eight 15ºs, skip the 6 mm, and sew through the adjacent 4 mm **(d–e)**. Pick up two 15ºs, skip the last two 15ºs just added, and sew back through the next four 15ºs. Pick up two 15ºs, and sew through 4 mm pearl your thread exited at the start of this step **(e–f)**. Continue through the next two 4 mms **(f–g)**.

8 Repeat steps 6 and 7 five times to complete the round **(g–h)**, but after completing the last stitch, only sew through one 4 mm **(h–i)**.

9 Pick up four 15ºs, skip the next 4 mm, which sits slightly inward, and sew through the next three 4 mms **(figure 5)**. Repeat this stitch five times to complete the round, and end the threads.

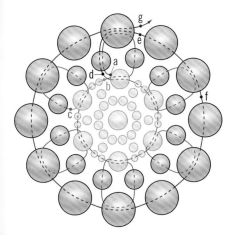

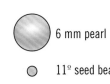

FIGURE 8

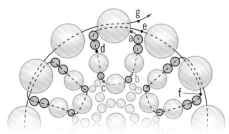

FIGURE 9

Difficulty rating

Materials
necklace 23 in. (58 cm)
- crystal pearls (Swarovski, white)
  - **37** 6 mm pearls
  - **72** 4 mm pearls
- seed beads (Toho PF478F, permanent finish matte galvanized lavender)
  - **2 g** 11º
  - **2 g** 15º
- **18 in. (46 cm)** chain, cut into two 9-in. (23cm) pieces
- **1** lobster clasp
- **3** 6 mm jump rings
- Fireline, 6 lb. test
- beading needles, #11 or #12
- **2** pairs of chainnose, bentnose, and/or flatnose pliers

Legend:
- 6 mm pearl
- 11º seed bead
- 15º seed bead
- 4 mm pearl

Side components

1 On 2 yd. (1.8 m) of thread, pick up a 4 mm pearl and four 11ºs. Sew through the pearl again in the same direction, leaving a 6-in. (15 cm) tail **(figure 6, a–b)**. This forms a loop of 11ºs around one side of the pearl. Pick up four 11ºs, and sew through the pearl again to form a loop on the other side of the pearl **(b–c)**. Sew through the first four 11ºs. Pick up two 11ºs, and sew through the next four 11ºs. Pick up two 11ºs, and sew through all the beads in the ring around the pearl (retrace not shown in the figure for clarity), and continue through the next two 11ºs **(c–d)**.

2 Pick up an 11º, a 4 mm, and an 11º, and sew through the two 11ºs your thread just exited to form a picot **(figure 7, a–b)**. Continue through the next two 11ºs in the ring **(b–c)**.

3 Pick up an 11º and a 4 mm, and sew through the adjacent 11º in the previous picot, the two 11ºs in the ring your thread just exited, and the next two 11ºs **(c–d)**. Repeat this stitch three times **(d–e)**.

4 For the last stitch in the round, sew through the adjacent 11º in the first picot, pick up a 4 mm, and sew through the adjacent 11º in the last picot added and the two 11ºs in the ring your thread

just exited **(e–f)**. Continue through the next 11º and pearl in this picot **(f–g)**.

5 Pick up two 15ºs, and sew through the next 4 mm **(g–h)**. Repeat this stitch five times to complete the round **(h–i)**.

6 Pick up a 4 mm, a 6 mm, and a 4 mm, and sew through the 4 mm your thread just exited to form a picot **(figure 8, a–b)**. Retrace the thread path (not shown in the figure for clarity). Continue through the next two 15ºs and 4 mm **(b–c)**. Repeat these stitches five times to complete the round **(c–d)**. Continue through the next 4 mm and 6 mm **(d–e)**.

7 Pick up a 6 mm, and sew through the next 6 mm **(e–f)**. Repeat this stitch five times to complete the round **(f–g)**, and retrace the thread path.

8 Pick up two 11ºs, and sew through the adjacent 4 mm in the first picot added in step 6 **(figure 9, a–b)**. Pick up a 15º, and sew through the next 4 mm **(b–c)**. Pick up a 15º, and sew through the following 4 mm in this picot **(c–d)**. Pick up two 11ºs, and sew through the pearl your thread exited at the start of this step **(d–e)**. Continue through the next two 6 mms **(e–f)**. Repeat these stitches five times to complete the round **(f–g)**. End the tail, but not the working thread.

9 Work as in steps 1–8 to make a second side component.

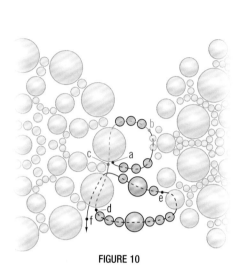

FIGURE 10

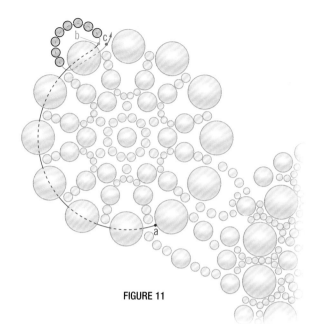

FIGURE 11

Connection

1 With the working thread exiting a 6 mm on a side component, pick up three 11ºs, and sew through the center two 15ºs in a set of four 15ºs on the outside edge of the center component **(figure 10, a–b)**. Pick up three 11ºs, and sew through the 6 mm your thread exited at the start of this step **(b–c)**. Retrace the thread path (not shown in figure for clarity), and continue through the next 6 mm in the side component **(c–d)**.

2 Pick up three 11ºs, a 4 mm, and three 11ºs, skip the next edge 4 mm on the center component, and sew up through the following 4 mm **(d–e)**. Pick up an 11º, a 4 mm, and an 11º, and sew down through the 6 mm your thread exited at the start of this step **(e–f)**. Retrace the thread path.

3 Sew clockwise through the next six 6 mms on the bottom outside edge of the side component **(figure 11, a–b)**. There should be four 6 mms between

the connection on the top edge and the point where your thread is exiting. Pick up eight 11ºs, and sew through the same 6 mm to form a loop **(b–c)**. Retrace the thread path, and end the thread.

4 Open a 6 mm jump ring, slide it through the loop just added and the end of a 9-in. (23 cm) piece of chain. Close the jump ring. Use a jump ring to attach the lobster clasp to the other end of the chain.

5 With the working thread from the other side component, attach it to the center component as before, making sure there is one set of four 15ºs (or seven pearls) between connection points on the top outer edge of center component. There should be three sets of four 15ºs along the bottom outer edge of the center component.

6 Work as in steps 3–4 to attach the other chain. ○

BEAD WEAVING

TRIBAL QUEEN
necklace

An inspiring combination of
dagger beads, SuperDuos,
and QuadraTiles enhances
a leather cord to create a
noble design.

designed by **Yasmin Sarfati**

Difficulty rating

Materials

gold/brown necklace
18 in. (46 cm)
- **48** 6 mm CzechMates four-hole QuadraTile beads (dark bronze)
- **15 g** 2.5 x 5 mm SuperDuo beads (opaque luster Picasso)
- dagger beads (Czech)
  - **48** 5 x 16 mm (smoked topaz)
  - **48** 3 x 10 mm (iris brown)
- **5 g** 11º seed beads (Toho PF557, galvanized starlight)
- **17 in. (43 cm)** 5 mm round leather cord (brown)
- 1 5 mm inner diameter round magnetic end clasp
- Fireline, 6 lb. test
- beading needles, #11 or #12
- Super New Glue or 2-part epoxy

Information for the alternate colorway is listed at www. BeadAndButton.com/resources.

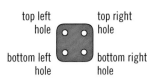

FIGURE 1

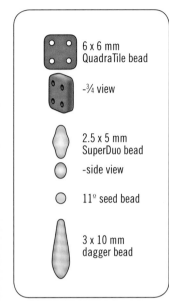

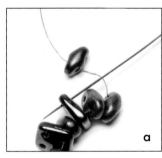

a

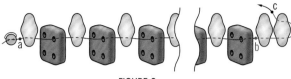

FIGURE 2

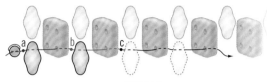

FIGURE 3

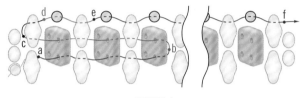

FIGURE 4

Base

For the purposes of these instructions, the holes of the QuadraTile will be referred to as top left hole (TL), top right hole (TR), bottom left hole (BL), and bottom right hole (BR) **(figure 1)**.
1 On 5 ft. (1.5 m) of thread, attach a stop bead, leaving a 6-in. (15 cm) tail. Pick up a repeating pattern of a SuperDuo and a QuadraTile (TR) 48 times **(figure 2, a–b)**.
2 Pick up two SuperDuos, and sew through the open hole of the last SuperDuo added **(b–c)**. The end SuperDuo will sit horizontally after the next step because it will be connected to both

the front and back row.
3 Working in the reverse direction, pick up a Super-Duo, and sew back through the next QuadraTile (TL) **(photo a)**. Repeat this stitch 47 times to complete the row.
4 Repeat step 2 on this end of the base, and pull the thread tight. Move the stop bead out of the way by sliding it about ¼ in. (6 mm) away from the end SuperDuo in the front row. With the working thread, sew through the end SuperDuo (the same hole the tail with the stop bead is exiting), with the needle facing toward the beadwork. This thread connection will make the last SuperDuo added sit horizontally. Continue through the next QuadraTile (TR), remove the stop bead, and end the working thread and tail.
5 On 2 yd. (1.8 m) of thread, attach a stop bead, leaving a 6-in. (15 cm) tail. Pick up a SuperDuo, and sew through the BR hole of the first QuadraTile picked up in step 1 **(figure 3, a–b)**. Pick up a SuperDuo, and sew

through the next QuadraTile (BR) **(b–c)**. Repeat this stitch 46 times to complete the front row, and then repeat step 2 once.
6 Working in the reverse direction, pick up a Super-Duo, and sew back through the open hole of the next QuadraTile (BL). Repeat this stitch 47 times to add SuperDuos to the back row. Pull the thread tight, and then repeat step 2 once. End and add thread as needed.
7 As before, slide the stop bead ¼ in. (6 mm) away from the end SuperDuo in the front row. With the working thread, sew through the end SuperDuo in the front row (the same hole the tail with the stop bead is exiting) with the needle facing toward the beadwork (only the front of the beadwork is shown in figure for clarity) **(figure 4, point a)**. Sew through the next five beads as shown **(a–b)**.
8 To get into position to start adding 11º seed beads, sew through the (TR) hole of the same

QuadraTile your thread is exiting, and continue back through the next five beads as shown **(b–c)**. Sew back through the open hole of the SuperDuo your thread is exiting **(c–d)**.

9 Pick up an 11º seed bead, and sew through the open hole of the next SuperDuo **(d–e)**. Repeat this stitch 47 times to complete the front row **(e–f)**. Sew through the open hole of the adjacent SuperDuo in the back row.

10 Work as in step 8 to add 11ºs to the top edge of the back row. After the last stitch, sew through the nearest hole of the adjacent SuperDuo in the front row with the needle facing toward the beadwork (only the front view is shown in the figure for clarity) **(figure 5, point a)**.

11 To get into position to add the first row of 3 x 10 mm dagger beads:

• Sew through the next 11º, and continue back through the adjacent QuadraTile (TR) (positioned below the same 11º), with the needle facing away from the beadwork.

• Sew around the closest thread bridge, and sew back through the hole of the same QuadraTile (TR) your thread just exited **(a–b)**.

• Sew back through the adjacent hole of the same QuadraTile (BR), and continue through the nearest hole of the next SuperDuo. Sew through the open hole of the same SuperDuo your thread is exiting **(b–c)**.

12 Pick up a 3 x 10 mm dagger bead, and sew through the open hole of the next SuperDuo **(c–d)**. Repeat this stitch 47 times to complete the front row **(d–e)**.

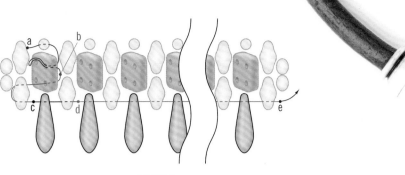

FIGURE 5

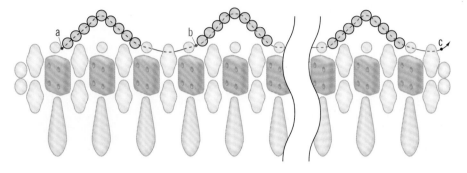

FIGURE 6

13 Sew through the open hole of the adjacent SuperDuo in the back row **(photo b)**.

14 Working in the reverse direction, pick up a 5 x 16 mm dagger bead, and sew through the open hole of the next SuperDuo. Repeat this stitch 47 times to add daggers to the back row.

15 Sew through the nearest hole of the adjacent Super-Duo in the front row. Remove the stop bead, and end the working thread and tail.

Assembly

1 Add 1 yd. (.9 m) of thread to the front row of the base, with the needle exiting the first 11º **(figure 6, point a)**.

2 Pick up nine 11ºs, skip the next SuperDuo, 11º, and SuperDuo in the front row, and sew through the following 11º, SuperDuo, and 11º to create a picot **(a–b)**. Repeat this stitch 15 times to complete the front row, but for the last stitch, sew through only the end 11º and Super-Duo **(b–c)**.

3 Sew through the bead-work to exit the adjacent end 11º in the back row, with the needle facing toward the beadwork.

4 Pick up four 11ºs, sew through the center 11º in the corresponding picot on the front row **(photo c)**. Slide the leather cord under the loop just created, center it

over the beadwork, and pull the thread tight. Pick up four 11ºs, skip over the leather cord and the next three beads in the back row, and sew through the follow-ing 11º, SuperDuo, and 11º to create a mirror image picot on the back row **(photo d)**. Pull the thread tight. Repeat these two stitches 15 times, but on the last stitch, sew through only the end 11º and SuperDuo. End the working thread and tail. If necessary, re-center the leather cord over the beadwork.

5 Use Super New Glue or 2-part epoxy to glue an end cap or magnetic clasp to each end of the cord. ●

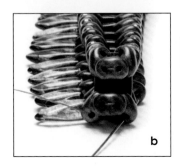

b

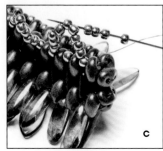

c

d

BEAD WEAVING

FEATHERED EDGE bracelet

Highlight rows of tile beads with two layers of triangles along the edges for a fun and feathery look.

designed by **Agnieszka Watts**

Picking up the two- and four-hole beads

QuadraTiles: In the position shown **(figure 1)**, the holes will be referred to as top left hole (TL), top right hole (TR), bottom left hole (BL), and bottom right hole (BR).

Tiles: With the holes running vertically, we will refer to the right hole (RH) or the left hole (LH) as needed.

Triangles: With the point with no hole pointing away from you, pick up the bead through the right hole (RH) or the left hole (LH).

Base

1 On a comfortable length of thread, attach a stop bead, leaving a 6-in. (15 cm) tail. Pick up two tile beads, and sew through the first tile again **(figure 2, a–b)**, positioning the tiles side-by-side. Continue through the second tile and the open hole of the same tile **(b–c)**.
2 Pick up a tile, and sew through the previous tile (RH), the tile just added **(c–d)**, and the open hole of the same tile **(d–e)**. Repeat these stitches, using a tight tension, to add a total of 25 tiles for a 6¾-in. (17.1 cm) bracelet

(including ½ in./1.3 cm for the clasp). Add or omit tiles for the desired length. Remove the stop bead, and end the tail.
3 Repeat steps 1–2 to make another strip the same length.
4 Position one strip horizontally on your bead mat with your needle exiting the right, upper hole **(figure 3, point a)**. Pick up a QuadraTile (BR) going from top to bottom, and sew back through the tile

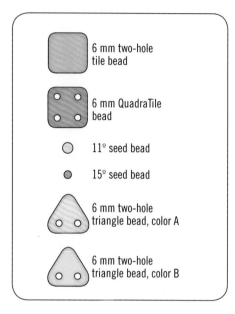

6 mm two-hole tile bead

6 mm QuadraTile bead

11º seed bead

15º seed bead

6 mm two-hole triangle bead, color A

6 mm two-hole triangle bead, color B

Materials
green and purple bracelet
6¾ x 1¼ in. (17.1 x 3.2 cm)
- **50** 6 mm CzechMates two-hole tile beads (Persian turquoise moon dust)
- **25** 6 mm CzechMates four-hole QuadraTile beads (purple opaque)
- 6 mm CzechMates two-hole triangle beads
  - **50** color A (matte metallic flax)
  - **48** color B (opaque luster Picasso)
- **1 g** 11º seed beads (Toho PF557F, matte galvanized starlight)
- **3 g** 15º seed beads (Toho 221, bronze)
- **1** 3-strand tube clasp
- Fireline, 4 lb. test, or Nymo size B
- beading needles, #11 or #12

Information for the alternate colorways is listed at www.BeadAndButton.com/resources.

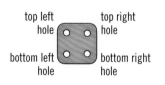

top left hole top right hole
bottom left hole bottom right hole

FIGURE 1

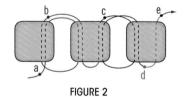

FIGURE 2

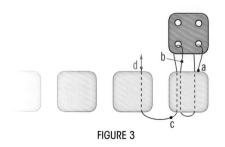

FIGURE 3

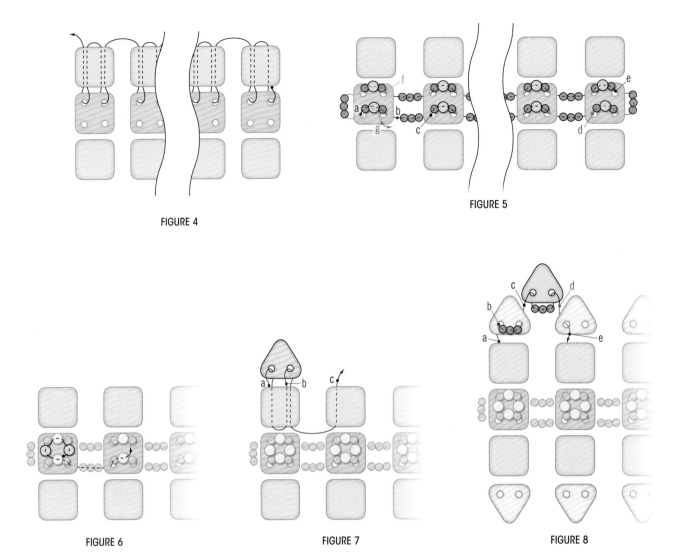

FIGURE 4

FIGURE 5

FIGURE 6

FIGURE 7

FIGURE 8

(RH) and the other hole of the same tile (LH) **(a–b)**. Sew through the QuadraTile (BL) from top to bottom, and continue back through the same hole of the tile (LH) **(b–c)**. Sew through the next tile (RH) **(c–d)**.

5 Work as in step 4 to add the 24 remaining QuadraTiles to this strip using a tight tension. End and add thread as needed, and set this working thread aside.

6 Using the working thread on the other tile strip, sew through the beadwork to exit the end hole. Attach this strip as before, sewing through the open holes of the existing QuadraTile beads **(figure 4)**. End and add thread as needed, and set this working thread aside.

Center embellishment

1 With the working thread from the lower strip, sew through the beadwork

to exit the QuadraTile (BL) going from bottom to top **(figure 5, point a)**. Pick up a 15º seed bead, an 11º seed bead, and a 15º, and sew down through the same QuadraTile (BR) **(a–b)**. Pick up three 15ºs, and sew up through the next QuadraTile (BL) **(b–c)**. The three 15ºs will be on the backside of the base (in the figure, the tiles are spread apart so you can see the beads being added to the bottom surface, but in actuality, the tiles are close together). Repeat these stitches for the remainder of the base using a tight tension **(c–d)**. When you reach the end QuadraTile, embellish the top as before. Pick up three 15ºs, and sew up through the same QuadraTile (TR) **(d–e)**.

2 Work as in step 1 to embellish the top holes of the QuadraTiles **(e–f)**. End and add thread as needed. When you reach the end QuadraTile, embellish

the top as before, pick up three 15ºs, sew up through the same QuadraTile (BL), and continue through the next 15º and 11º **(f–g)**.

3 Pick up an 11º, and sew through the opposite 11º. Pick up an 11º, and sew through the 11º your thread exited at the start of this step. Continue through the adjacent 15º, QuadraTile (BR), three 15ºs on the bottom surface, the following QuadraTile (BL), and the next 15º and 11º **(figure 6)**. Repeat these stitches for the remainder of the base, and end this thread.

Triangle embellishment

1 With the other working thread exiting the end hole in the top strip of tiles **(figure 7, point a)**, pick up a color A triangle (LH) going from top to bottom. Sew back through the same hole of the tile (LH), and continue through the

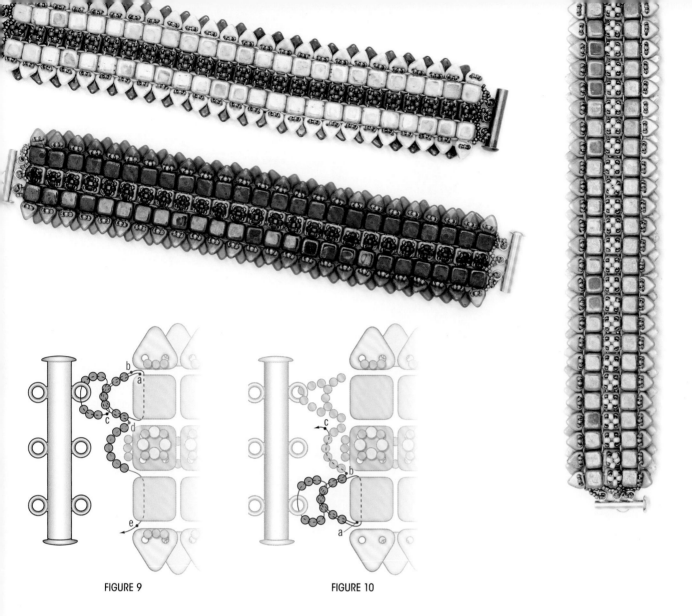

FIGURE 9   FIGURE 10

other hole of the same tile (RH) **(a–b)**.
Sew through the A (RH) going from top
to bottom, and continue back through
the same hole of the tile (RH) and the
adjacent tile (LH) **(b–c)**. Repeat these
stitches for the remainder of the top
edge. Sew through the beadwork to
exit the bottom edge, and add As as
before to this edge. End and add thread
as needed.

2 Sew through the beadwork to exit
the end tile (LH) in the top strip **(figure 8,
point a)**, and sew through the adjacent
A going from back to front **(a–b)**. Pick
up three 15ºs, and sew through the
same A (RH) going from front to back
(b–c). Pick up a color B triangle (LH)
going from front to back, pick up three
15ºs, and sew through the same B (RH)
going from back to front **(c–d)**. Continue
through the next A (LH) going from back
to front **(d–e)**. Repeat these stitches for

the remainder of the top edge. When
you get to the last A on this edge, add
three 15ºs to the top surface as before,
and sew through the beadwork to the
bottom edge. Work as before to add
Bs to this edge. End and add thread
as needed.

Clasp

1 Sew through the beadwork to exit the
end tile (LH) on the top strip **(figure 9,
point a)**. Pick up seven 15ºs, and sew
through the same tile (LH) going in the
same direction to form a loop **(a–b)**.
Continue through the next five 15ºs
(b–c). Pick up three 15ºs, the end ring
of half of the clasp, and three 15ºs, and
sew through the center three 15ºs in the
loop. Retrace the thread path of the
beads just added (not shown in the
figure for clarity), and continue through
the next two 15ºs **(c–d)**.

2 Pick up seven 15ºs, and sew through
the end tile (LH) on the bottom
strip **(d–e)**.

3 Work as in step 1 to attach the third
ring of the clasp **(figure 10, a–b)**.

4 Sew through the next five 15ºs in the
center loop **(b–c)**. Pick up three 15ºs,
the center ring of the clasp, and three
15ºs, and sew through the center three
15ºs in the adjacent loop. Retrace the
thread path, and end the thread.

5 Add 2 ft. (61 cm) of thread to the
other end of the bracelet, and attach
the remaining half of the clasp as
before. End the thread. ⦿

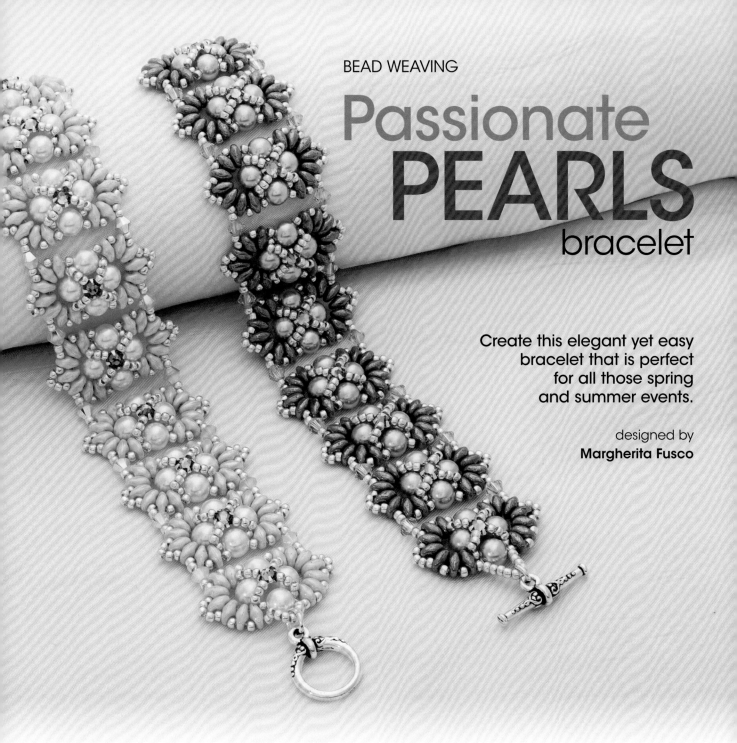

Passionate
PEARLS
bracelet

Create this elegant yet easy
bracelet that is perfect
for all those spring
and summer events.

designed by
Margherita Fusco

Components

1 On 2 ft. (61 cm) of thread,
pick up a repeating pattern
of a 6 mm pearl and an 11º
seed bead four times, and
tie the beads into a ring with
a square knot, leaving a 6-in.
(15 cm) tail. Sew through the
next pearl and 11º **(figure 1)**.
2 Pick up three 11ºs, a 4 mm
rose montée, and three 11ºs.
Cross the center of the ring
diagonally, and sew down
through the opposite 11º
(figure 2, a–b). Continue
through the next pearl and
11º **(b–c)**.
3 Pick up three 11ºs, and sew
through the open channel
of the montée. Pick up three
11ºs, and sew through the
adjacent 11º **(c–d)**.
4 Pick up seven SuperDuos,
skip the next pearl, and sew
through the following 11º
in the ring **(figure 3, a–b)**.
Continue through the
next pearl and 11º in the
ring **(b–c)**. Pick up seven
SuperDuos, skip the pearl,
and sew through the following 11º and pearl **(c–d)**.
5 Pick up an 11º, and sew
through the open hole of
the next SuperDuo **(figure 4,
a–b)**. Repeat this stitch six
times **(b–c)**. Pick up an 11º,
and sew through the following pearl **(c–d)**. Repeat
these stitches for the other
side of the component
(d–e). End the working
thread and tail, and set the
component aside.
6 Repeat steps 1–5 to make
8 more components for a
7½ in. (19.1 cm) bracelet.

Assembly

1 Add 4 ft. (1.2 m) of thread
to a component, exiting an
end 11º as shown **(figure 5,
point a)** with the needle
pointing toward the other
edge. Pick up seven 11ºs,
skip the pearl, and sew

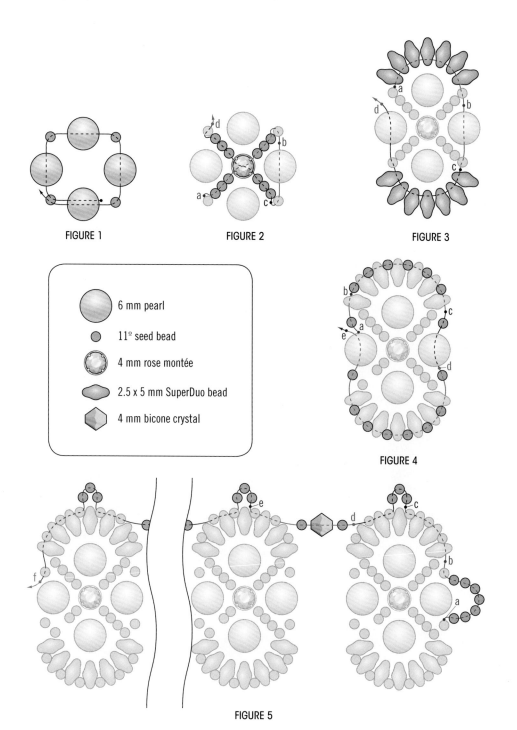

FIGURE 1

FIGURE 2

FIGURE 3

6 mm pearl

11º seed bead

4 mm rose montée

2.5 x 5 mm SuperDuo bead

4 mm bicone crystal

FIGURE 4

FIGURE 5

Difficulty rating

Materials

green bracelet 7½ x 1¼ in. (19.1 x 3.2 cm)

- **36** 6 mm pearls (Swarovski, white)
- **9** 4 mm (SS16) rose montées (Swarovski, black diamond)
- **16** 4 mm bicone crystals (Swarovski, chrysolite opal AB2X)
- **9 g** 2.5 x 5 mm SuperDuos (503000-14457, chalk green luster light)
- **4 g** 11º seed beads (Toho PF558, permanent finish galvanized aluminum)
- **1** toggle clasp
- **2** 6 mm jump rings
- Fireline, 6 lb. test
- beading needles, # 11 or #12
- **2** pairs of chainnose, flatnose, and/or bentnose pliers

Information for the purple colorway is listed at www. BeadAndButton.com/resources.

through the corresponding 11º to form a clasp loop **(a–b)**. Continue through the next six beads **(b–c)**.

note You may add 11ºs to the clasp loop if needed for length.

2 Pick up three 11ºs, skip the next SuperDuo, and sew through the following three beads to form a picot **(c–d)**. Pick up an 11º, a 4 mm

bicone crystal, and an 11º, and sew through the corresponding 11º, SuperDuo, and 11º in a new component **(d–e)**. Repeat these stitches for the remainder of this edge. For the last component, continue through the beadwork as shown to exit the end 11º between the pearl and SuperDuo **(e–f)**.
3 Work as in steps 1–2 to add a clasp loop with the same amount of 11ºs as used

on the opposite end, and embellish the other edge as before. Retrace the thread path of the clasp loops and edge embellishments, and end the thread.
4 Open a jump ring, and attach it to one half of the clasp and a clasp loop. Repeat on the other end. ●

BEAD WEAVING

Flowers
in
bloom
bracelet

A row of tiny Pip bead flowers adorns
your wrist on a base supported with
Kheops beads.

designed by **Stephanie Goff**

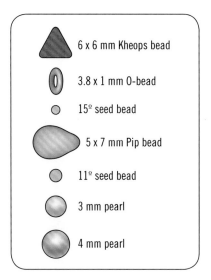

- 6 x 6 mm Kheops bead
- 3.8 x 1 mm O-bead
- 15º seed bead
- 5 x 7 mm Pip bead
- 11º seed bead
- 3 mm pearl
- 4 mm pearl

Materials

peach bracelet 7 in. (18 cm)
- **26** 6 x 6 mm Kheops beads (jet bronze)
- **48** 5 x 7 mm Pip beads (Preciosa, pink alabaster travertine)
- **5 g** 3.8 mm O-beads (matte metallic mix)
- pearls (Swarovski)
  - **12** 4 mm (powder almond)
  - **24** 3 mm (rose peach)
- **1 g** 11º seed beads (Toho PF552, sweet blush)
- **1 g** 15º seed beads (Toho PF551, rose gold)
- **1** clasp
- Fireline, 6 lb. test
- beading needles, #11 or #12

silver bracelet colors
- 6 x 6 mm Kheops beads (opaque light green luster)
- 5 x 7 mm Pip beads (Preciosa, silver graphite rainbow)
- 3.8 mm O-beads (graphite rainbow)
- 4 mm Druk beads (opaque luster amethyst; use in place of pearls)
- 3 mm pearl (Swarovski, pearl white)
- 11º seed beads (Toho PF552, sweet blush)
- 15º seed beads (Miyuki 551, gilt white opal)

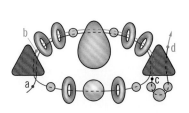

FIGURE 1

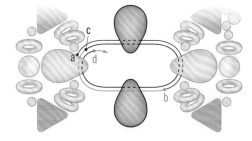

FIGURE 2

Strips

1 On a comfortable length of thread, pick up a Kheops bead through the right hole (RH) from bottom to top, leaving a 6-in. (15 cm) tail.

2 Pick up two O-beads, a 15º seed bead, a Pip bead, a 15º, two O-beads, a Kheops through the left hole (LH) from top to bottom, a 15º, an O-bead, a 3 mm pearl, an O-bead, and a 15º, and sew through the Kheops (RH) your thread exited at the start of this step, going from bottom to top **(figure 1, a–b)**. Continue through the next eight beads to exit the other Kheops (LH) from top to bottom **(b–c)** using a tight tension.

3 Pick up a 15º, an 11º seed bead, and a 15º, and sew through the open hole of the same Kheops, going from bottom to top **(c–d)**.

4 Repeat steps 2–3 ending with step 2, for the desired length, allowing approximately 1 in. (2.5 cm) for the clasp (depending on the clasp size and style). End the working thread and tail.

5 Repeat steps 1–4 to make another strip of equal length.

Joining the strips

1 Attach a comfortable length of thread to the beadwork, exiting an end Pip bead, with the needle pointing toward the other end of the beadwork **(figure 2, point a)**. Place the other strip next to the first so they mirror each other.

2 Pick up a Pip bead, and sew down through the corresponding Pip bead on the other strip **(a–b)**. Pick up a Pip bead, and sew up through the Pip bead your thread exited at the start of this step **(b–c)**. Retrace the thread path using a tight tension **(c–d)**.

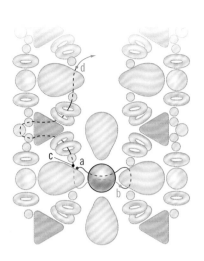

FIGURE 3

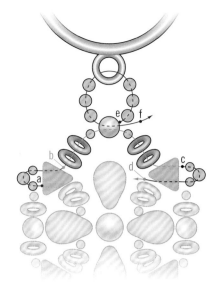

FIGURE 4

3 Pick up a 4 mm pearl, and sew through the corresponding Pip bead in the other strip **(figure 3, a–b)**. Sew back through the 4 mm pearl, and continue through the Pip bead your thread exited at the start of this step **(b–c)**. Sew through the beadwork as shown to exit the next Pip bead on this strip **(c–d)**.
4 Repeat steps 2–3 for the length of the strips. End the thread.

Clasp

1 Add 18 in. (46 cm) of thread to your beadwork, exiting the end Kheops as shown **(figure 4, point a)**. Pick up a 15º, an 11º, and a 15º, and sew through the open hole of the same Kheops **(a–b)**. Pick up two O-Beads, a 15º, a 3 mm pearl, a 15º, and two O-Beads, and sew through the open hole of the corresponding Kheops on the opposite side **(b–c)**. Pick up a 15º, an 11º, and a 15º, and sew through the other hole

of the same Kheops **(c–d)**.
2 Sew through the beadwork to exit the pearl added in the previous step **(point e)**. Pick up three 11ºs, the loop of a clasp, and three 11ºs, and sew through the pearl your thread exited at the start of this step **(e–f)**.
3 Retrace the thread path of steps 1–2 to reinforce, and end the thread.
4 Work as in steps 1–3 to attach the other half of the clasp to the other end of the bracelet. ●

Right **IN LINE** bracelet

The supple drape of this elegant
bracelet makes it very comfortable
to wear, and the embellished
QuadraTiles give it depth and bling.

designed by **Eileen Barker**

Difficulty rating

Materials

bracelet 6¾ x 1¼ in. (17.1 x 3.2 cm)
- **75** 6 x 6 mm CzechMates two-hole tile beads (dark bronze)
- **100** 6 mm CzechMates four-hole QuadraTile beads (dark bronze)
- **50** 4 mm fire-polished beads (metallic bronze)
- **25** 3.5 mm rose montées (Preciosa topaz AB)
- **50** 3.4 mm drop beads (Miyuki DP-374E, matte bronze)
- 11º seed beads
  - **2 g** color A (Miyuki F457N, matte dark chocolate brown)
  - **2 g** color B (Miyuki 457G, metallic brass)
- **2 g** 15º seed beads (Japanese 916E, topaz raspberry luster)
- **1** 3-strand clasp
- Fireline, 6 lb. test
- beading needles #11 or #12

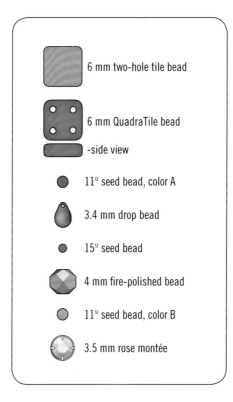

6 mm two-hole tile bead

6 mm QuadraTile bead

-side view

11º seed bead, color A

3.4 mm drop bead

15º seed bead

4 mm fire-polished bead

11º seed bead, color B

3.5 mm rose montée

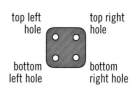

top left hole   top right hole

bottom left hole   bottom right hole

FIGURE 1

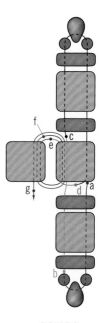

FIGURE 2

Base

For the purposes of these instructions, and with the QuadraTile in the position shown **(figure 1)**, the holes will be referred to as top left hole (TL), top right hole (TR), bottom left hole (BL), and bottom right hole (BR).

1 On a comfortable length of thread, pick up a tile bead, and sew through the open hole of the same tile, leaving a 6-in. (15 cm) tail. Tie the working thread and tail together with a square knot, and retrace the thread path **(figure 2, point a)**.

2 Pick up a QuadraTile (BR), a tile, a QuadraTile (BR), a color A 11º seed bead, a drop bead, and an A **(a–b)**. Sew back through the last QuadraTile added (BL), the open hole of the next tile, the following QuadraTile (BL), and the adjacent hole of the tile your thread exited at the start of this step **(b–c)**.

3 Pick up a QuadraTile (BL), a tile, a QuadraTile (BL), an A, a drop, and an A. Sew back through the last QuadraTile

added (BR), the open hole of the next tile, the following QuadraTile (BR), and the adjacent hole of the tile your thread exited at the start of this step **(c–d)**. Tighten the beadwork, and sew through the other hole of the same tile **(d–e)**.

4 Pick up a tile, and sew through the hole in the previous tile your thread exited at the start of this step **(e–f)**. Retrace the thread path using a tight tension, and continue through the same hole of the new tile **(f–g)**.

5 Repeat steps 2–4 for the desired length of bracelet (less ½ in./1.3 cm for the clasp), ending with step 3. End and add thread as needed, and end the threads when the base is complete. The base will be floppy until the top embellishment is added.

Top embellishment

1 Add a comfortable length of thread to the base, exiting an end drop with the needle pointing toward the other end of the beadwork **(figure 3, point a)**.

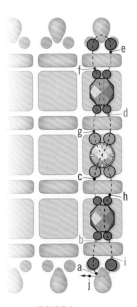

FIGURE 3

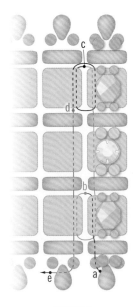

FIGURE 4

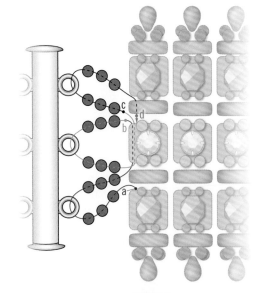

FIGURE 5

The top embellishment will be added to the top holes of the QuadraTiles in steps 2–7.

2 Pick up an A, and sew through the open hole of the adjacent QuadraTile (TL) **(a–b)**. Pick up a 15º seed bead, a 4 mm fire-polished bead, and a 15º, and sew through the next QuadraTile (TL) **(b–c)**.

3 Pick up a color B 11º seed bead, a 3.5 mm rose montée, and a B, and cross over to the other hole in the next QuadraTile (TR) **(c–d)**.

4 Pick up a 15º, a 4 mm fire-polished bead, and a 15º, and sew through the next QuadraTile (TR) **(d–e)**. Pick up an A, and sew through the adjacent drop. Pick up an A, and sew through the open hole of the same QuadraTile (TL) **(e–f)**.

5 Pick up a 15º, sew through the next fire-polished bead, pick up a 15º, and sew through the following QuadraTile (TL)**(f–g)**.

6 Pick up a B, sew through the open channel of the next rose montée, pick

up a B, and cross over to the other hole in the next QuadraTile (TR) **(g–h)**.

7 Pick up a 15º, sew through the next fire-polished bead, pick up an 15º, and sew through the following QuadraTile (TR) **(h–i)**. Pick up an A, and sew through next drop **(i–j)**.

8 Step 8 will be worked in the base using the bottom holes of the QuadraTiles: Sew through the following bottom A, QuadraTile (BL), and tile **(figure 4, a–b)**. Continue through the nearest hole of the adjacent tile, the previous tile, the next QuadraTile (BL), tile, QuadraTile (BL), and tile **(b–c)**.

note If you are having trouble sewing through the beads, flip the beadwork over so you can easily see and access the base layer.

Sew through the nearest hole of the adjacent tile, the previous tile, and the adjacent tile again **(c–d)**. Continue through the next QuadraTile (BR), tile, QuadraTile (BR), tile, QuadraTile (BR), A, and drop **(d–e)**.

9 Repeat steps 2–8 for the remainder of the base, ending with step 7. End and add thread as needed, and end the threads when the embellishment is complete.

Clasp

1 Add 12-in. (30 cm) of thread to the beadwork, exiting an end tile in an outer row with the needle pointing toward the center of the beadwork **(figure 5, point a)**. Pick up three Bs, sew through the first loop of the clasp, pick up three Bs, and continue through the next tile in the center row **(a–b)**.

2 Pick up three Bs, sew through the center loop of the clasp, pick up three Bs, and continue through the same tile, going in the same direction **(b–c)**.

3 Pick up three Bs, sew through the remaining loop of the clasp, pick up three Bs, and continue through the next QuadraTile (BL) with the needle pointing toward the center of the beadwork **(c–d)**. Retrace the thread path of the connection, and end the thread.

4 Repeat steps 1–3 to attach the other half of the clasp. ●

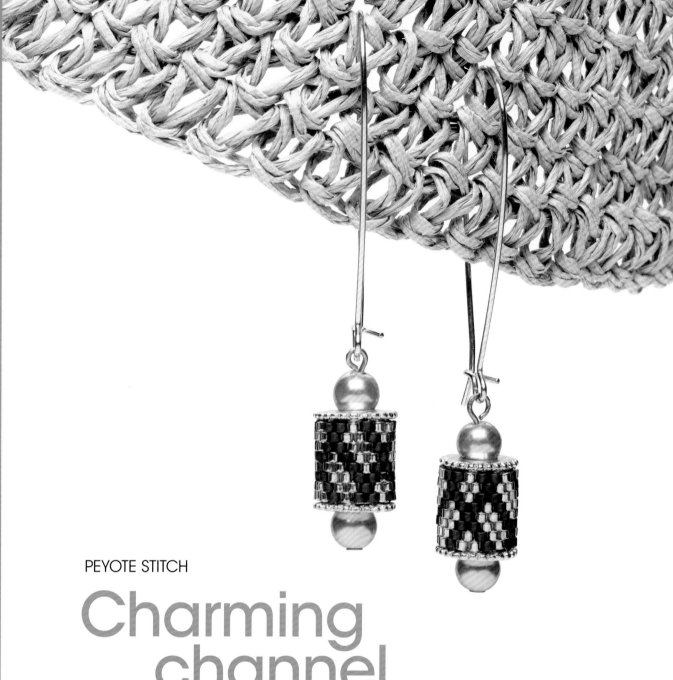

PEYOTE STITCH

Charming
channel
earrings

Stitch a lively peyote band around a
metal channel bead to create a pair
of snappy earrings.

designed by **Marla Salezze**

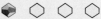

11° cylinder beads

color A

color B

PATTERN

Materials

black earrings 1¹⁄₁₆ in. (2.7 cm)

• 4 6 mm glass pearls (Swarovski, light gray)
• 11° Miyuki Delica cylinder beads
  - **1 g** color A (DB310, matte black)
  - **1 g** color B (DB1486, transparent luster squirrel gray)
• 2 13 x 11 mm channel beads (silver)
• 2 22-gauge 1½-in. (3.8 cm) head pins (silver)
• 1 pair of earring findings (silver)
• chainnose pliers
• roundnose pliers
• wire cutters

blue earring colors

• 6 mm glass pearls (Swarovski, bright gold)
• 11° Miyuki Delica cylinder beads
  - color A (DB1833, Duracoat galvanized bright gold)
  - color B (DB1782, white-lined rainbow gem turquoise)

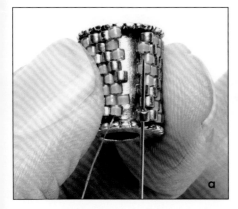

Earring band

1 On 1 yd. (.9 m) of thread, attach a stop bead, leaving a 6-in. (15 cm) tail. Starting at the lower-left corner of the **pattern**, pick up 11° cylinder beads for rows 1 and 2: one color A, four color Bs, and three As.

2 Following the **pattern**, work in flat even-count peyote stitch using the appropriate-color cylinders. End the tail, but not the working thread.

3 Make a second earring band.

Assembly

1 Wrap an earring band around the center of a channel bead, and zip up the ends **(photo a)**. End the working thread.

2 On a head pin, string a 6 mm pearl, the beaded channel bead, and a pearl. Make a plain loop: Trim the headpin ¼ in. (6 mm) from the top pearl, and using chainnose pliers, make a right-angle bend in the wire directly above the pearl **(photo b)**.

3 Grip the end of the wire with round-nose pliers so that the wire is flush with the jaws of the pliers where they meet. Rotate the wire toward the bend until the tip of the wire touches the bend, creating a loop **(photo c)**.

4 Slide the loop of the dangle onto a kidney ear wire.

5 Repeat steps 1–4 to complete the second earring. ●

Beaded fabric buttons

Make a fabric-covered button, and embellish it with beads for a stunning home accent or focal piece for your jewelry.

designed by
Lori Phillips

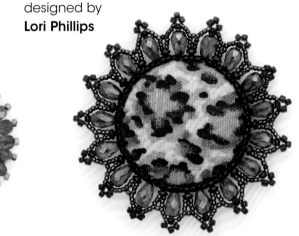

1 Following the manufacturer's instructions, cover the button form with fabric **(photo a)**.

2 Thread 2 yd. (1.8 m) of Fireline on your needle, and tie an overhand knot near the end. Sew through the fabric along the back of the button, exiting on the edge.

3 Using 8º seed beads, work a round of beaded backstitch around the perimeter of the button: Pick up two 8ºs, and line them up along the edge of the button. Sew down through the fabric after the second bead, come back up through the fabric between the two beads just added, and sew through the second bead again. Repeat this stitch to create a ring around the perimeter of the button **(photo b)**. It is important to end with a multiple of four beads so the embellishments will be evenly distributed. It is better to have this round of beads be a bit loose than too tight, as cramming in too many beads will cause the ring to buckle. Sew through all the beads in the ring again to snug them up.

4 Exiting any 8º in the ring, work a spike: Pick up a 4 mm rondelle, a 4 mm daisy spacer, a 10 x 7 mm teardrop (narrow end first), and an 11º seed bead. Skip the 11º, sew back through the teardrop, spacer, and rondelle, and then sew through the next four 8ºs in the ring **(photo c)**. Snug the beads to the button **(photo d)**. Repeat this stitch around the button, and then sew through the next three 8ºs to exit the middle pair of 8ºs between two spikes.

5 Pick up a 6 mm fire-polished bead and five 11ºs, and sew through the 11º at the tip of an adjacent spike **(photo e)**.

give or take

Adjust the number of 11ºs you pick up in step 5 as needed to fill the space.

6 Pick up five 11ºs and a 6 mm, sew through the two middle 8ºs between the next pair of spikes, and sew back through the 6 mm **(photo f)**. Pick up five 11ºs, and sew through the 11º at the tip of the next spike **(photo g)**.

7 Repeat step 6 to complete the round. After the final repeat, pick up five 11ºs, and sew through the first 6 mm and the two 8ºs in the ring below. Sew back through the 6 mm, the last five 11ºs added, and the 11º at the tip of the adjacent spike.

a

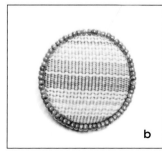

b

c

Materials

green/brown animal print button (below)
4 in. (10 cm)

- **1** size 100 (2½ in./6.4 cm) half-ball cover button (with teeth)
- cover button kit
- **4 in. (10 cm)** square of midweight fabric
- **26** 10 x 7 mm teardrop beads (olivine)
- **26** 6 mm fire-polished beads (rose gold topaz)
- **26** 4 mm rondelles (copper)
- **26** 4 mm daisy spacers (copper)
- **3 g** 8º seed beads (Miyuki 2013, matte olive)
- **3 g** 11º seed beads (Toho 221, bronze)
- beading needles, #10
- Fireline, 10 lb. test

make it your own!

This project can be varied in many ways. Mix and match these ideas — or come up with your own!

- Try different bead shapes and sizes.
- Omit the picots.
- Omit the seed bead outlines around the spikes.
- Work beaded backstitch only using fire-polished beads to make a modern bracelet (far left).
- Make short fringe using glass flower beads instead of teardrop beads (above).

8 Pick up three 11ºs, and sew through the same tip 11º and the next three 11ºs **(photo h)**. Pick up an 11º, and sew through the top four 11ºs to exit the tip 11º of the next spike **(photo i)**. Repeat this step to add a picot to each tip 11º. End the thread. ◗

cover button sizes

SIZE	MEASUREMENT
30	¾ in. (1.9 cm)
36	⅞ in. (2.2 cm)
45	1⅛ in. (2.9 cm)
60	1½ in. (3.8 cm)
75	1⅞ in. (4.8 cm)
100	2½ in. (6.4 cm)

Not sure what size cover button to use? Let this handy chart be your guide.

COSMIC
BURST
pendant

Capture a rivoli with a
collection of two-hole
and four-hole beads to
create a radiant pendant.

designed by **Hannah Rosner**

tight spaces

If you have difficulty sewing through the beadwork, it is helpful to use a #12 needle because it has a tendency to curve, thus making it easier to sew through the bead holes at an angle. It is also helpful to shift the beads with your fingers when trying to maneuver the needle.

Difficulty rating

Materials

lavender/plum/dark green pendant 1⁷⁄₈ in. (4.8 cm)

- **1** 14 mm rivoli (Swarovski, light amethyst)
- 6 mm CzechMates four-hole QuadraTile beads
  - **18** color A (metallic suede plum)
  - **9** color B (metallic suede light green)
- **9** 6 mm CzechMates two-hole triangle beads (metallic suede light green)
- **18** 4 mm fire-polished beads (matte purple AB)
- **27** 2.5 x 6 mm mini dagger beads (tanzanite iris)
- **1 g** 6º seed beads (Toho 166, transparent light amethyst)
- **1 g** 11º seed beads (Toho 82F, metallic blue iris)
- **1 g** 15º seed beads (Toho 702, matte soft brown)
- Fireline, 6 lb. test
- beading needles, #12

topaz/purple/light green pendant colors

- 14 mm rivoli (Swarovski, paradise shine)
- 6 mm CzechMates four-hole QuadraTile beads
  - color A (metallic suede purple)
  - color B (matte metallic leather)
- 6 mm CzechMates two-hole triangle beads (rosaline celsian)
- 2.5 x 6 mm Rizo beads (alabaster pastel olivine; in place of mini dagger beads)
- 6º seed beads (Toho Y301, antique amber hybrid Picasso)
- 11º seed beads (Miyuki 193, 24 kt gold light-plated)
- 15º seed beads (Toho 980, dark pink-lined aqua)

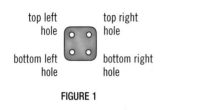

top left hole top right hole
bottom left hole bottom right hole

FIGURE 1

FIGURE 2

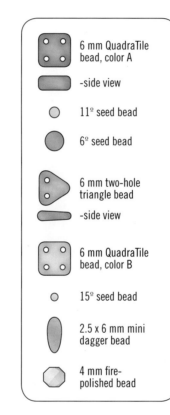

6 mm QuadraTile bead, color A

-side view

11º seed bead

6º seed bead

6 mm two-hole triangle bead

-side view

6 mm QuadraTile bead, color B

15º seed bead

2.5 x 6 mm mini dagger bead

4 mm fire-polished bead

With the QuadraTile in the position shown **(figure 1)**, the holes will be referred to as top left (TL), top right (TR), bottom left (BL), and bottom right (BR).

How to pick up triangle beads: With the point of the triangle with no hole facing to the right, pick up the bead through the top hole (TH) or the bottom hole (BH), per the instructions.

For clarity, figures 2, 3, 4, and 6 show the top view of the beadwork. Figures 5 and 7 show the side view of the beadwork.

Ring

1 On a comfortable length of thread, pick up a repeating pattern of an 11º seed bead and a color A QuadraTile bead (BL) 18 times. Tie a square knot to form the beads into a ring, leaving a 10-in. (25 cm) tail.

2 Sew through the (TL) hole of the nearest A QuadraTile **(figure 2, point a)**. Pick up an 11º seed bead, and sew through the closest hole (TL) of the next A **(a–b)**. Repeat this stitch 17 times to complete the round **(b–c)**. This will position the new 11ºs above the 11ºs in step 1.

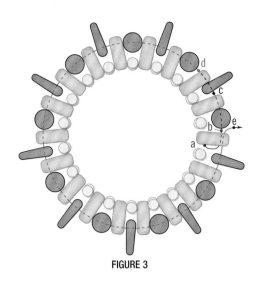

FIGURE 3

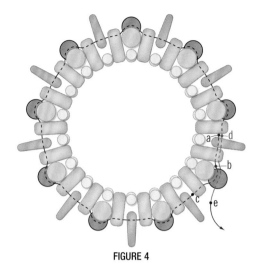

FIGURE 4

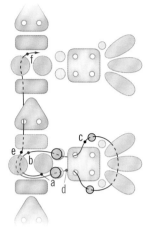

FIGURE 5

3 Working in the reverse direction, sew through the adjacent hole of the same A (TR) **(figure 3, a–b)**. Pick up a 6º seed bead, and sew through the next A (TR) **(b–c)**. Pick up a triangle bead (TH), and sew through the next A (TR) **(c–d)**. Repeat these two stitches eight times to complete the round **(d–e)**, making sure the point of each triangle faces away from the center of the ring.
4 Working in the reverse direction, sew through the remaining open hole of the same A (BR) **(figure 4, point a)**. Sew through the open hole of the next triangle (BH) and the open hole of the following A (BR) **(a–b)**. Pick up a 6º, and sew through the open hole of the following A (BR) **(b–c)**. This will position the new 6º to sit below the 6º in the previous round. Repeat these two stitches eight times to complete the round **(c–d)**, and continue through the next triangle (BH), A (BR), and 6º added in this round **(d–e)**.

Embellishment
1 Pick up an 11º, a color B QuadraTile (BR), a 15º seed bead, three dagger beads, and a 15º, and sew through the adjacent hole of the same B (BL) **(photo a)**. Pick up an 11º, and sew through the 6º your thread exited at the start of this step, going in the same direction **(photo b)** to form a picot set. Continue through the next A (BR), triangle (BH), A (BR), and 6º.
2 Repeat step 1 eight times to make a total of nine picot sets.
3 Sew through the adjacent 6º **(figure 5, a–b)**. Secure the picot set to the ring: Pick up an 11º, and sew up through the adjacent B (TL) **(b–c)**. Pick up a 15º, and sew through the next three daggers in the picot set. Pick up a 15º, and sew down through the same B (BL) **(c–d)**. Pick up an 11º, and sew through the 6º your thread exited at the start of this step **(d–e)**. Continue through the next A (TL),

a

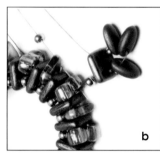

b

triangle (TH), A (TL), and 6º **(e–f)**.
4 Work as in step 3 to secure the remaining eight picot sets.

Rivoli setting
1 Sew through the next A (TR), triangle (TH), and A (TR) **(figure 6, a–b)**. Continue through the adjacent hole of the same A (TL) and the following 11º to reverse direction **(b–c)**.
2 Pick up a 15º seed bead, and sew through the 11º your thread exited at the start of this step, going in the same direction **(c–d)**.
3 Pick up a 4 mm fire-polished bead and a 15º. Skip the next three beads

in the inner ring, and make a square stitch by sewing back through the next 11º (sitting adjacent to the next triangle), going in the opposite direction with the needle facing toward the beads just added. Continue through the 15º just added, going in the same direction **(d–e)**. Pull the thread tight. Repeat this stitch seven times **(e–f)**. Pick up a fire-polished bead, and sew through the first 15º added to complete the round **(f–g)**. Sew through the ring of beads just added, and pull the thread tight to cinch up the beadwork.
4 Flip your work over, and sew through the beadwork

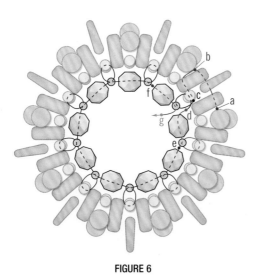

FIGURE 6

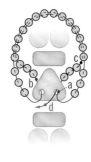

FIGURE 7

to exit an 11º that is adjacent to a triangle on the opposite surface.

5 Place a rivoli face-up in the center of the ring.

6 To secure the rivoli, work as in steps 2–3. End the working thread, but not the tail.

Bail

1 With the tail, sew through the beadwork to exit a triangle on the front side of the pendant **(figure 7, point a)**. Pick up 20 11ºs, and sew through the adjacent hole of the same triangle, with the thread exiting in the opposite direction **(a–b)**.

2 Pick up three 11ºs, skip the last three 11ºs added in the previous step, and sew through the next 14 11ºs **(b–c)**. Pick up three 11ºs, and sew through the adjacent hole of the same triangle **(c–d)**. Retrace the thread path several times to reinforce the connection, and end the thread. ●

change the look

For an open look, skip adding the rivoli in step 5 of "Rivoli setting."

CROSSWEAVE

Sweet
expressions
beaded bead

These beaded beads
are fun and quick to stitch
up, thanks in part to a few
lightweight and colorful
paper beads.

designed by **Cary Bruner**

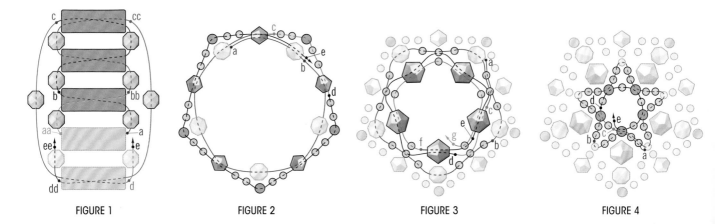

FIGURE 1   FIGURE 2   FIGURE 3   FIGURE 4

1 Thread a needle on each end of 2 yd. (1.8 m) of thread. With one needle, pick up a 3 mm fire-polished bead, a barrel bead, a fire-polished bead, and a barrel. Cross the other needle through the last barrel added, and center the beads on the thread. With both needles, retrace the thread path, exiting at **figure 1, points a and aa.**

2 With each needle, pick up a fire-polished bead. With one needle, pick up a barrel, and cross the other needle through it **(a–b and aa–bb)**. With each needle, retrace the thread path (not shown in the figure for clarity). Repeat this step twice **(b–c and bb–cc)**.

3 With each needle, pick up a fire-polished bead, and sew through the first barrel added to form a ring **(c–d and cc–dd)**. With each needle, retrace the thread path (not shown in the figure for clarity), and continue through the next fire-polished bead **(d–e and dd–ee)**.

4 With one needle, pick up a 3 mm bicone crystal, and sew through the next fire-polished bead **(figure 2, a–b)**. Repeat this stitch four times to complete the round, and sew through the first 3 mm crystal added **(b–c)**. Repeat this step with the other thread.

5 With one needle, pick up two 15º seed beads, an 11º seed bead, and two 15ºs, and sew through the next 3 mm crystal to form a picot **(c–d)**. Position these beads to the outside edge of the fire-polished beads. Repeat this stitch four times to complete the round, and sew through the next fire-polished bead **(d–e)**. Repeat this step with the other thread. The next five rounds will be positioned to the inside of the previous rounds of beads.

6 With one needle, pick up three 15ºs, and sew through the next fire-polished bead to form a picot **(figure 3, a–b)**. Repeat this stitch four times to complete the round, and sew the through first two 15ºs added **(b–c)**. Repeat this step with the other thread.

7 With one needle, pick up a 4 mm bicone crystal, and sew through the center 15º in the next picot in the previous round **(c–d)**. Repeat this stitch four times to complete the round, and sew through the first 4 mm added **(d–e)**. Repeat this step with the other thread.

8 With one needle, pick up a 15º, and sew through the next 4 mm **(e–f)**. Repeat this stitch four times to complete the round, and sew the through first 15º added **(f–g)**.

Repeat this step with the other thread.

9 With one needle, pick up two 15ºs, an 11º, and two 15ºs, and sew through the next 15º in the previous round **(figure 4, a–b)**. Repeat this stitch four times to complete the round, and sew through the first two 15ºs and 11º added in this step **(b–c)**. Repeat this step with the other thread.

10 With one needle, pick up a 15º, and sew through the next 11º **(c–d)**. Repeat this stitch four times to complete the round **(d–e)**, and retrace the thread path to tighten the beadwork. Sew through the beadwork to exit the 11º in a picot added in step 5 that sits on the outside edge of the beaded bead nearest the barrel beads **(figure 5, point a)**. Repeat this step with the other thread, making sure to exit the corresponding 11º on the other end, and exiting in the same direction **(point aa)**.

11 With one needle, pick up 10 15ºs, and sew through the corresponding 11º. With the other needle, cross through the 15ºs just added, and sew through the 11º from the start of the step **(a–b and aa–bb)**.

note Because 15ºs may vary slightly in size, you may need to adjust the number of 15ºs so they fit snugly between the 11ºs on each end.

Repeat these stitches to add 15ºs on the other side of the same 11ºs **(b–c and bb–cc)**. With each needle, sew through the next two 15ºs, 3 mm crystal, two 15ºs, and 11º **(c–d and cc–dd)**. Repeat this step four times to complete the round, and end the threads. ●

Difficulty rating

Materials
purple beaded bead
1¼ x ⅝ in. (3.2 x 1.6 cm)
- **5** Sweet Expressions paper barrel beads (purple mosaic)
- bicone crystals
  - **10** 4 mm (Preciosa, matte violet)
  - **10** 3 mm (Swarovski, turquoise AB2X)
- **10** 3 mm round fire-polished beads (orchid aqua polychrome)
- **20** 11º seed beads (Miyuki 4218, Duracoat dusty orchid)
- **2 g** 15º seed beads (Miyuki 4201, Duracoat galvanized silver)
- Fireline, 6 lb. test
- beading needles, #11 or #12

green beaded bead
- Sweet Expressions paper barrel beads (peridot green)
- bicone crystals
  - 4 mm (olivine AB2X)
  - 3 mm (Jonquil satin)
- 3 mm round fire-polished beads (green brown)
- 11º seed beads (Toho PF470, permanent galvanized matte silver)
- 15º seed beads (Miyuki 318J, light olive gold luster)

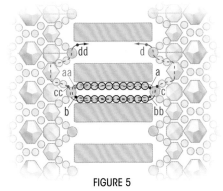

FIGURE 5

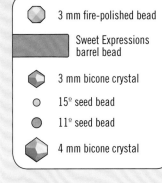

BEAD WEAVING
DYNAMIC DIAMONDS
bracelet

Connect X-shaped components using seed beads, crystals, and O-beads for a fun and easy-to-make bracelet of open diamonds.

designed by **Connie Whittaker**

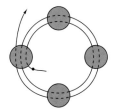

FIGURE 1

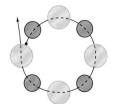

FIGURE 2

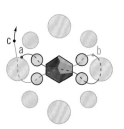

FIGURE 3

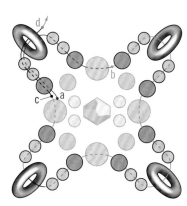

FIGURE 4

Components

1 On 2 ft. (61 cm) of thread, pick up four 8º seed beads, and sew through the beads again to form a ring, leaving a 6-in. (15 cm) tail **(figure 1)**. Retrace the thread path once more.

2 Pick up an 11º seed bead, and sew through the next 8º. Repeat this stitch three times to complete the round **(figure 2)**.

3 Pick up a 15º seed bead, a 3 mm bicone crystal, and a 15º, cross over the opening diagonally, and sew through the corresponding 8º, going in the same direction **(figure 3, a–b)**. Pick up a 15º, and sew back through the crystal. Pick up a 15º, and sew through the 8º your thread exited at the start of this step **(b–c)**.

4 Pick up an 11º, two 15ºs, an O-bead, two 15ºs, and an 11º, skip the next 11º in the ring, and sew through the next 8º **(figure 4, a–b)**. Repeat this stitch three times to complete the round **(b–c)**, and continue through the following 11º, two 15ºs, and O-bead **(c–d)**. Make sure your thread is exiting the O-bead in the upper-left corner and the crystal is in a horizontal position. End the tail, but not the working thread, and set the component aside.

5 Repeat steps 1–4 to make 13 more components for a 7½ in. (19.1 cm) bracelet (not including the clasp length).

Difficulty rating

Materials
green/purple bracelet
7¾ in. (19.7 cm)
- **14** 3 mm bicone crystals (Swarovski, amethyst)
- **3 g** 3.8 mm O-beads (pastel bordeaux)
- **2 g** 8º seed beads (Miyuki 2035, matte metallic khaki iris)
- **2 g** 11º seed beads (Toho 512F, matte sage pewter)
- **2 g** 15º seed beads (Toho 221, bronze)
- **1** toggle clasp
- Fireline, 6 lb. test
- beading needles, #11 or # 12

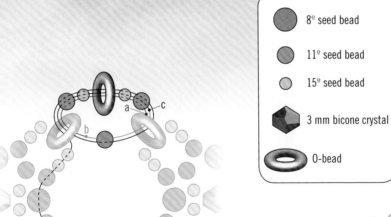

○ 8º seed bead

○ 11º seed bead

○ 15º seed bead

◆ 3 mm bicone crystal

○ O-bead

FIGURE 5

FIGURE 6

6 Place two components next to each other with the working threads in the top-left position. With the working thread from the right-hand component, pick up an 11º, a 15º, an O-bead, a 15º, and an 11º, and sew down through the top-right O-bead in the left component **(figure 5, a–b)**. Pick up an 11º, and sew up through the O-bead your thread exited at the start of this step **(b–c)**. Retrace the thread path using a tight tension, and continue through the 11º, 15º, O-bead, 15º, and 11º just added, and the next nine beads in the left-hand component to exit the lower-right O-bead **(c–d)**. Work as before to attach the bottom corners **(d–e)**, and end this thread.
7 Work as in step 6 to attach the remaining components, and end any remaining threads.

Clasp
1 Add 12 in. (30 cm) of thread to an end component, exiting an 11º as shown **(figure 6, point a)** with the needle pointing toward the top edge of the component. Pick up four 15ºs, the loop of a toggle ring, and four 15ºs, and sew back through the 11º your thread exited at the start of this step to form a loop **(a–b)**. Sew through the next 8º and the following 11º **(b–c)**. Pick up four 15ºs, sew through the loop on the toggle ring, pick up four 15ºs, and sew back through the 11º your thread just exited **(c–d)**. Retrace the thread path, and end the thread.
2 Repeat step 1 to attach the toggle bar to the other end of the bracelet, but pick up six seed beads instead of four for each side of each loop. Check to make sure the toggle works properly, and adjust the number of 15ºs in the loops if necessary.

PEYOTE STITCH

Doing donuts
pendant

Craft a cute donut pendant with seed beads
and a handful of fire-polished beads.

designed by **Justyna Szlezak**

Difficulty rating

Materials

**gold/aqua pendant
1⅞ in. (4.8 cm)**
- 4 mm fire-polished beads
  - **20** color E
  (stone blue luster)
  - **10** color F
  (matte metallic flax)
- **40** 3 mm fire-polished beads
  (moondust turquoise)
- 8º seed beads
  - **2 g** color B (Toho 4204,
  Duracoat galvanized
  Champagne)
  - **1 g** color C (Toho 460G,
  steel blue metallic)
- 11º seed beads
  - **3 g** color A (Toho Takumi
  989, gold-lined crystal)
  - **1 g** color D
  (Toho 920, seafoam)
- **1** bail
- **1** 4 mm jump ring
  (21- or 22-gauge)
- beading needles, #12
- Fireline, 6 lb. test
- cardboard or thread bobbin
- **2** pairs of chainnose, flatnose, and/or bentnose pliers
- polyester fiberfill or felt
  (optional)

**bronze/blue pendant
colors**
- 4 mm fire-polished beads
  - color E (capri blue luster)
  - color F (matte metallic flax)
- 3 mm fire-polished beads
  (capri blue luster)
- 8º seed beads
  - color B (Toho 509, bronze
  plum iris)
  - color C (Toho 1207, marbled
  opaque turquoise blue)
- 11º seed beads
  - color A (Toho 509, bronze
  plum iris)
  - color D (Toho 274, color-
  lined teal)

FIGURE 1

Side 1

1 On 3 yd. (2.7 m) of thread, pick up 40 color A 11º seed beads. Leaving a 1-yd. (.9 m) tail, tie the beads into a ring with a square knot. These beads will shift to form the first two rounds as the next round is added. Wrap the tail around a piece of card-board or a thread bobbin to keep it out of the way until needed.

2 Work rounds of tubular peyote stitch as follows, stepping up at the end of each round. Stitch using a tight tension throughout, and end and add thread if needed.

Rounds 3–9: Using As, work seven rounds (20 stitches per round) for a total of nine rounds.

Rounds 10–11: Using color B 8º seed beads, work 20 stitches per round **(figure 1, a–b and b–c)**.

Round 12: Work one stitch with a 3 mm fire-polished bead and one stitch with a B. Repeat these stitches nine times to complete the round **(c–d)**.

Round 13: Work 20 stitches using color C 8º seed beads **(d–e)**.

Round 14: Work one stitch with a 3 mm and one stitch with three color D 11º seed beads. Repeat these stitches nine times to complete the round **(e–f)**.

Round 15: Pick up two As, and sew through the middle D in the next trio of Ds. Pick up two As, and sew through the next 3 mm. Repeat these

stitches nine times to complete the round, stepping up through the first pair of As **(f–g)**.

Round 16: Pick up a color E 4 mm fire-polished bead, and sew through the next pair of As. Pick up two As, and sew through the next pair of As. Repeat these stitches nine times to complete the round **(g–h)**.

Round 17: Work 20 stitches with Bs, treating each pair of As as a single bead **(h–i)**.

Round 18: Pick up a color F 4 mm fire-polished bead, and sew through the next B. Pick up four Ds, and sew through the following B. Repeat these stitches nine times to complete the round **(i–j)**. Tie a half-hitch knot, but don't trim the working thread.

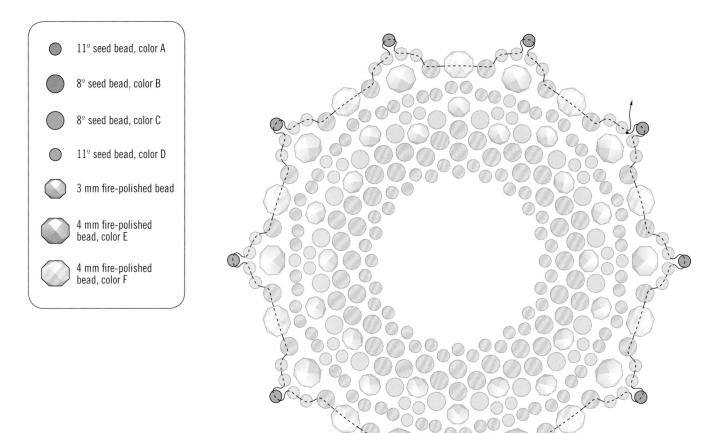

Key:
- 11º seed bead, color A
- 8º seed bead, color B
- 8º seed bead, color C
- 11º seed bead, color D
- 3 mm fire-polished bead
- 4 mm fire-polished bead, color E
- 4 mm fire-polished bead, color F

FIGURE 2

Side 2 and finishing

1 Unwind the tail from the cardboard or bobbin, and thread a needle on it.

2 Repeat rounds 10–17 on this side of the original nine rounds. When you get to round 12 and beyond, be sure to place the beads in the correct order (if you work around the ring opposite the direction you worked the first side, you will need to reverse the order in which you pick them up) so this side works up as a mirror image of side 1.

3 If desired, stuff the pendant with polyester fiberfill or a strip of felt.

4 Join the two sides by zipping up round 17 on side 2 with round 18 on side 1.

5 Using whichever thread is longest, sew through the beadwork to exit between the second and third D of a group of four Ds. Pick up a D, and sew through the next seven beads to exit between the second and third D in the next group of four Ds. Repeat this stitch nine times to complete the round **(figure 2)**. End the threads.

6 Open a 4 mm jump ring, slide it through an 11º added in the previous step and the loop of a bail. Close the jump ring. String your pendant as desired. ●

make it reversible

To create a second look for your pendant, use different colors for the fire-polished beads and color C 8º seed beads on side 2 — just make sure they coordinate with the color A 11ºs and color B 8ºs.

BEAD WEAVING

Elegance
with an
attitude

The monochromatic colors and spike
beads bring texture and dimension
to this sophisticated bracelet.

designed by **Nicole Vogt**

keep it together
If desired, use a 2-strand clasp
instead of a 4-strand clasp.

Difficulty rating

Materials
bracelet 7¼ in. (18.4 cm)

- **30** 5 x 8 mm baby spike beads (nickel silver)
- **44** 4 mm bicone crystals (Swarovski, crystal comet argent light 2X)
- **82** 2.5 x 5 mm SuperDuo beads (crystal Labrador full)
- seed beads (Miyuki 4201, Duracoat silver)
  - **2 g** 11º seed beads
  - **3 g** 15º seed beads
- **1** four-strand box clasp
- **8** 5 mm jump rings
- Fireline, 6 lb. test
- beading needles, #11 or #12
- **2** pairs of chainnose, flatnose, and/or bentnose pliers

did you know?
Filigree-style box clasps are sometimes referred to as pearl clasps because they are frequently used in multistrand pearl necklaces and bracelets.

Components

1 On 4 ft. (1.2 m) of thread, pick up a repeating pattern of a SuperDuo and an 11º seed bead four times. Sew through all the beads again to form a ring, leaving a 6-in. (15 cm) tail. Continue through the next SuperDuo, 11º, and SuperDuo **(figure 1, a-b)**, and the open hole of the same SuperDuo **(b-c)**.

2 Pick up a repeating pattern of an 11º and a SuperDuo three times, then pick up an 11º. Sew through the SuperDuo your thread exited at the start of this step, retrace the thread path (not shown in the figure for clarity), and continue through the next 11º and SuperDuo **(c-d)**. Sew through the open hole of the same SuperDuo **(d-e)**. Repeat this step once more **(figure 2, a-b)**.

3 Pick up an 11º, and sew through the open hole of the next SuperDuo from the first round **(b-c)**. Pick up an 11º, a SuperDuo, an 11º, a SuperDuo, and an 11º, and sew through the SuperDuo your thread exited at the start of this step **(c-d)**. Retrace the thread path (not shown in figure for clarity), sew through the next 11º and SuperDuo **(d-e)**, and continue through the other hole of the same SuperDuo **(e-f)**.

4 Pick up a baby spike bead, and sew through the corresponding SuperDuo on the other side of the center opening **(figure 3, a-b)**. With the tip of the spike pointing up, push the spike down into the center opening so the base of the spike sits below the surrounding beads. Sew through the other hole of the same SuperDuo **(b-c)** and back through the spike and the corresponding hole of the SuperDuo from the start of this step **(c-d)**. Sew through the other hole of the same SuperDuo and the next 11º **(d-e)**.

5 Pick up three 15º seed beads, skip the next SuperDuo, and continue through the following 11º **(figure 4, a-b)**. Repeat this stitch three times **(b-c)**, and sew through the beadwork as shown **(c-d)**.

6 Pick up a 15º, a 4 mm bicone crystal, and a 15º, and sew through the open

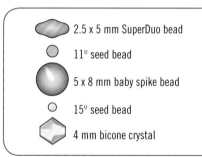

- 2.5 x 5 mm SuperDuo bead
- 11º seed bead
- 5 x 8 mm baby spike bead
- 15º seed bead
- 4 mm bicone crystal

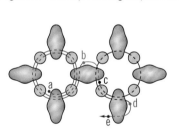

FIGURE 1

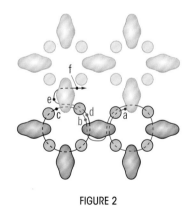

FIGURE 2

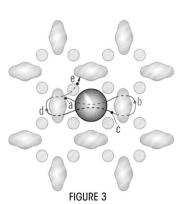

FIGURE 3

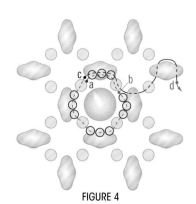

FIGURE 4

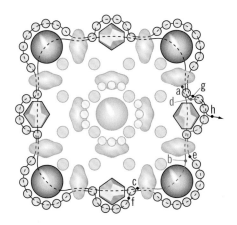

FIGURE 5

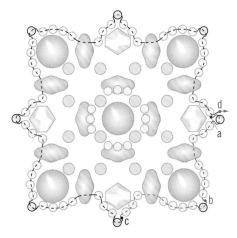

FIGURE 6

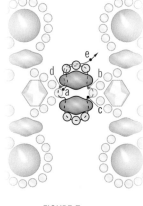

FIGURE 7

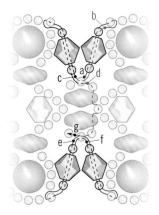

FIGURE 8

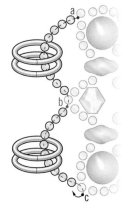

FIGURE 9

hole of the next SuperDuo **(figure 5, a–b)**. Pick up a spike (with the tip pointing up), and sew through the open hole of the following SuperDuo **(b–c)**. Repeat these stitches three times to complete the round using a medium tension, and continue through the first 15º added **(c–d)**. Stitching this round too tight may make sewing through the beadwork more difficult when adding the remaining beads.

7 Pick up four 15ºs, skip the adjacent crystal, and sew through the next 15º and SuperDuo **(d–e)**. Pick up eight 15ºs, skip the next spike, and sew through the following SuperDuo and 15º **(e–f)**. Repeat these stitches three times to complete the round **(f–g)**, and continue through the first two 15ºs added in this round **(g–h)**.

8 Pick up a 15º, and sew through the next three 15ºs, SuperDuo, and four 15ºs **(figure 6, a–b)**. Pick up a 15º, and sew through the next four 15ºs, SuperDuo, and three 15ºs **(b–c)**. Repeat these stitches three times to complete the round **(c–d)**, and end the working thread and tail.

9 Repeat steps 1–8 to make five more components for a 6½-in. (16.5 cm) bracelet (not including the clasp).

Connections

1 Add 2 ft. (61 cm) of thread to a component, exiting the middle 15º in the outside loop surrounding a crystal **(figure 7, point a)**. Pick up SuperDuo

and three 15ºs, and sew through the open hole of the same SuperDuo **(a–b)**. Sew through the corresponding 15º on a new component **(b–c)**. Pick up a SuperDuo and three 15ºs, and sew through the open hole of the same SuperDuo and the 15º your thread exited at the start of this step **(c–d)**. Continue through the next SuperDuo and two 15ºs **(d–e)**.

2 Pick up a 15º, a crystal, and a 15º, and sew through the middle 15º of the loop around a spike on the top right corner of the new component **(figure 8, a–b)**. Sew back through the three beads just added and the 15º your thread exited at the start of this step **(b–c)**. Repeat this stitch to connect the top left corner of the existing component **(c–d)**. Sew through the beadwork as shown **(d–e)**, and repeat these stitches to attach the bottom left corner

of the existing component **(e–f)** and the bottom right corner of the new component **(f–g)**. End the thread.

3 Repeat steps 1–2 to connect the remaining components.

4 Add 12 in. (30 cm) of thread to an end component, exiting the middle 15º in the top loop around a spike with the needle pointing away from the top edge **(figure 9, point a)**. Pick up 10 15ºs and two jump rings, and sew through the middle 15º in the loop around the crystal on the end of the bracelet **(a–b)**. Pick up 10 15ºs and two jump rings, and sew through the center 15º in the bottom loop **(b–c)**. Retrace the thread path through these loops twice, and end the thread. Repeat this step at the other end of the bracelet.

5 Attach the jump rings to the loops of the clasp at both ends of the bracelet. ●

PLAYFUL PINWH

Pendant

1 Cut a 2-in. (5 cm) square of beading foundation and two 2-in. (5 cm) squares of Ultrasuede. Apply a thin coat of E6000 around the perimeter of the beading foundation, and center a piece of Ultrasuede on top. Allow the glue to dry, and set the other piece of Ultrasuede aside for later.

2 Tie an overhand knot at the end of 1 yd. (.9 m) of conditioned thread. Center the enamel cabochon on the piece of glued Ultrasuede and foundation, and hold it in place. Sew up through the back of the foundation and Ultrasuede, exiting the center of an oval-shaped hole on the outer edge of the cab. Pick up a 3 mm crystal and a 15º seed bead **(photo a)**, and sew back through the crystal, Ultrasuede, and foundation. Pull the thread tight, and repeat this stitch seven times to add a crystal in each remaining oval-shaped hole. End the thread.

3 Tie an overhand knot at the end of 1 yd. (.9 m) of thread. Sew up through the back of the foundation and Ultrasuede, exiting near the outer edge of the cab. Work in beaded backstitch around the cab **(photo b)**: Pick up two 11º seed beads for each stitch, line them up next to the cab, and sew back down through the Ultrasuede and foundation. Sew up between the two beads and through the second bead just added. End with an even number of beads, and sew through the first 11º added in the round, the Ultrasuede, and the foundation. End the thread.

4 Carefully trim the foundation and Ultrasuede close to the 11ºs, being careful not to cut any threads. Apply a thin coat of E6000 to the back of the foundation, and center the other piece of Ultrasuede on it. Allow the glue to dry, and carefully trim the Ultrasuede around the perimeter of the beadwork using the edge of the foundation as a guide.

EEL

Use easy bead embroidery techniques to make a fun, enameled pendant that is perfect for jeans and a t-shirt!

designed by **Meg Mullen**

e

Materials
seafoam/tan pendant 2 in. (5 cm)
- 1 1¼ in. (3.2 cm) enamel cabochon (seafoam, www.gardannebeads.etsy.com)
- 20 4 mm bicone crystals (Swarovski, Pacific opal)
- 1 g 8º seed beads (Miyuki 536, turquoise Ceylon)
- 1 g 11º seed beads (Miyuki 351, peach-lined aqua)
- 1 g 15º seed beads (Miyuki 412, opaque turquoise green)
- 1 42-in. (1.4 m) silk ribbon
- nylon beading thread, size D
- beading needles, #10
- 1 2-in. (5 cm) piece of beading foundation
- 2 2-in. (5 cm) pieces of Ultrasuede (tan)
- E6000 adhesive
- scissors

green/blue pendant colors (in how-to photos)
- 1¼ in. (3.2 cm) enamel cabochon (bitter green)
- 4 mm bicone crystals (Swarovski, crystal satin AB)
- 8º seed beads (Toho 995, gold-lined rainbow aqua)
- 11º seed beads (Toho 513F, higher metallic frosted carnival)
- 15º seed beads (Toho 999, gold-lined rainbow black diamond)
- Ultrasuede (teal blue)

Embellishment and bail

1 Tie an overhand knot at the end of 1 yd. (.9 m) of conditioned thread, and sew up between the foundation layers with the needle exiting an 8º edge bead. Pick up a 15º seed bead, sew down through the adjacent 8º, and sew back up through the next 8º. Pick up a crystal and a 15º, and sew back through the crystal and the 8º your thread exited at the start of this step. Continue up through the next 8º **(photo d)**. Repeat these two stitches eleven times to add a total of 12 crystals, and then add another 15º in the same manner.

2 To determine the number of loops needed to make the bail, count the number of unembellished 8ºs. This number might vary, depending on how many 8ºs were used in the edging. An odd number of 8ºs will need three loops for the bail, and an even number of 8ºs will need two loops for the bail. Pick up 14 11ºs, sew back through the 8º your thread exited at the start of this step **(photo e)**, and continue up through the adjacent 8º. Repeat this stitch to make a total of two or three loops, and end the thread.

3 String the bail on a strand of silk ribbon. ●

d

5 Tie an overhand knot at the end of 1 yd. (.9 m) of conditioned thread, and trim the tail. Sew between the cab's foundation and Ultrasuede, hiding the knot between the two layers and exiting the back of the Ultrasuede about 1 mm from the edge.

6 Work a brick stitch edging: Pick up two 8º seed beads, sew up through the foundation layers one bead's width away from where the thread is exiting, and continue back through the second bead just added. For each subsequent stitch, pick up one 8º, sew up through the three layers one bead's width away from where the thread is exiting, and continue up through the new bead just added. Repeat this stitch around the perimeter **(photo c)**. After adding the final bead, sew down through the first bead in the edging, through the foundation layers, and back through the first bead again. End the working thread in the edging beads.

c

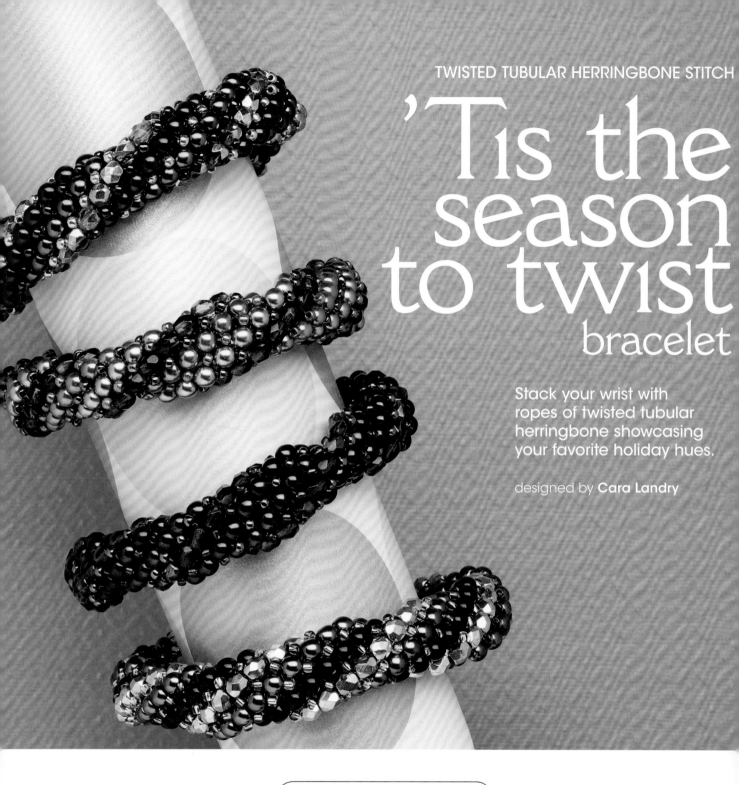

'Tis the season to twist
bracelet

Stack your wrist with ropes of twisted tubular herringbone showcasing your favorite holiday hues.

designed by **Cara Landry**

This project calls for three colors of 4 mm beads. I typically use two colors of pearls and one of fire-polished beads. I don't suggest using crystals, as their sharp ends can cut your thread. For a thinner tube, substitute 3 mm beads for the 4 mms and 15º seed beads for the 11ºs, as in the gold bracelet, p. 98.

Avoid using tight tension with this project, as your tube will be stiff. Instead, use just enough tension so that your thread doesn't show between beads.

 4 mm glass pearl, color A

 4 mm fire-polished bead, color B

 4 mm glass pearl, color C

 11º seed bead, color D

 11º seed bead, color E

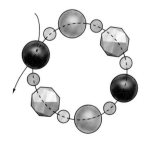

FIGURE 1

Twisted tubular rope

1 On a comfortable length of thread, pick up a color A 4 mm bead, a color D 11º seed bead, a color B 4 mm bead, a color E 11º seed bead, a color C 4 mm bead, a D, an A, an E, a B, a D, a C, and an E. Sew through the first A to form a ring, leaving a 12-in. (30 cm) tail **(figure 1)**.

2 Pick up an A, a D, and a B. Skip the next D in the ring, and sew through the following B, E, and C **(figure 2, a–b)**. Arrange the new beads so that they form a modified herringbone stitch, with the D centered at the top of the stitch.

3 Pick up a C, a D, and an A. Skip the next D in the ring, and sew through the following A, E, and B **(b–c)**. Arrange the new beads as before.

4 Pick up a B, a D, and a C. Skip the next D in the ring, and sew through the following C, E, and two As **(c–d)**.

5 Pick up an A, a D, and a B, and sew down through the next top two Bs **(figure 3, a–b)**.

6 Pick up an E, and sew up through the top C in the next column **(b–c)**.

7 Pick up a C, a D, and an A, and sew down through the next top two As **(c–d)**.

8 Pick up an E, and sew up through the top B in the next column **(d–e)**.

9 Pick up a B, a D, and a C, and sew down through the next top two Cs **(e–f)**.

10 Pick up an E, and step up through the top two As in the next column to complete the round **(f–g)**. Tighten the round to continue forming a tube shape.

11 Work as in steps 5–10 for the desired length bracelet (less the length of the clasp). The twist in the tube will appear after several rounds. End and add thread as needed. As you stitch, take note of any 11ºs that sit toward the inside of the tube, and push them to the outside with your needle or finger.

Materials

red/green/gold bracelet
9 in. (23 cm)
- 4 mm round beads
  - **140** color A glass pearls (Preciosa, bordeaux)
  - **140** color B fire-polished beads (Preciosa, light orange/gold half-coated)
  - **140** color C glass pearls (Preciosa, dark green)
- 11º seed beads
  - **3 g** color D (Toho 83, metallic bronze iris)
  - **3 g** color E (Toho PF557, permanent finish galvanized starlight)
- Fireline, 6 lb. test
- beading needles, #12
- **1** clasp

blue/green/hematite bracelet colors
- 4 mm round beads
  - color A glass pearls (Preciosa, dark Montana)
  - color B fire-polished beads (Preciosa, two-tone gray/black)
  - color C glass pearls (Preciosa, light green)
- 11º seed beads
  - color D (Toho 1703, gilded marble turquoise)
  - color E (Toho 81, metallic hematite)

purple/bronze/fuchsia bracelet colors
- 4 mm round beads
  - color A glass pearls (Preciosa, dark amethyst on crystal)
  - color B fire-polished beads (Preciosa, dark amethyst with sapphire/gold)
  - color C glass pearls (Preciosa, dark fuchsia)
- 11º seed beads
  - color D (Toho 221, bronze)
  - color E (Toho 2223, Takumi silver-lined dragonfruit)

silver/gray/black bracelet colors
- 4 mm round beads
  - color A glass pearls (Preciosa, dark gray)
  - color B fire-polished beads (Preciosa, full-coated silver)
  - color C glass pearls (Preciosa, black)
- 11º seed beads
  - color D (Toho 21, silver-lined crystal)
  - color E (Toho 29B, silver-lined gray)

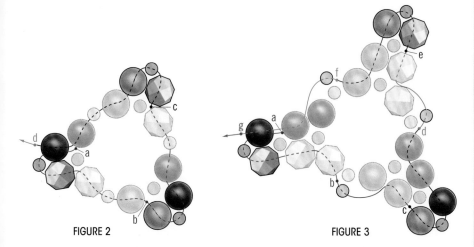

FIGURE 2   FIGURE 3

stepping up At the end of each round, sew through two As to step up to get into position to begin the next round.

gold/cream bracelet colors
7¾ in. (19.7 cm)

- 3 mm round beads
  - **160** color A glass pearls (Preciosa, light gold)
  - **160** color B fire-polished beads (Preciosa, light gold metallic half-coat)
  - **160** color C glass pearls (Preciosa, parchment)
- 15º seed beads
  - **1 g** color D (Toho 558, galvanized aluminum)
  - **1 g** color E (Toho 557, galvanized starlight)

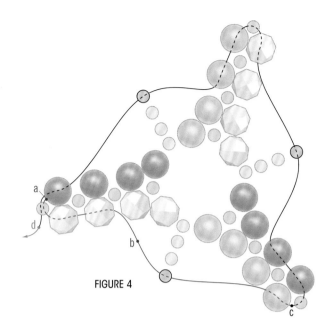

FIGURE 4

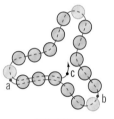

FIGURE 5

FIGURE 6

the size of it
Because of the diameter of the tube, your beadwork will need to be longer than your normal bracelet length. Check the fit of the tube around your wrist to determine the right length.

Closing rounds and clasp

With your thread exiting the column of As and Bs, work several modified rounds to close the end of the tube:

1 Without adding any beads, sew through the next D and the top two 4 mms in this column **(figure 4, a–b)**. Pick up an E, and sew up through the top 4 mm in the next column **(b–c)**. Repeat these stitches twice, and sew through the top D in the first column **(c–d)**.

2 Pick up five Es, and sew through the D in the next column **(figure 5, a–b)**. Repeat this stitch twice, and exit the first three Es added in this step **(b–c)**.

3 Pick up a D, and sew through the middle E in the next set of five Es. Repeat this stitch twice **(figure 6)**.

4 With your thread exiting an end E, pick up half of the clasp, and sew through the opposite D. Sew back through the clasp and the starting E. Retrace the thread path of the clasp connection, and end the working thread.

5 With your tail exiting an A at the other end of the bracelet, sew through the next E. Pick up five Es, and sew through the E in the next column. Repeat this stitch twice, and continue through the first three Es added in this step.

6 Repeat steps 3–4. ●

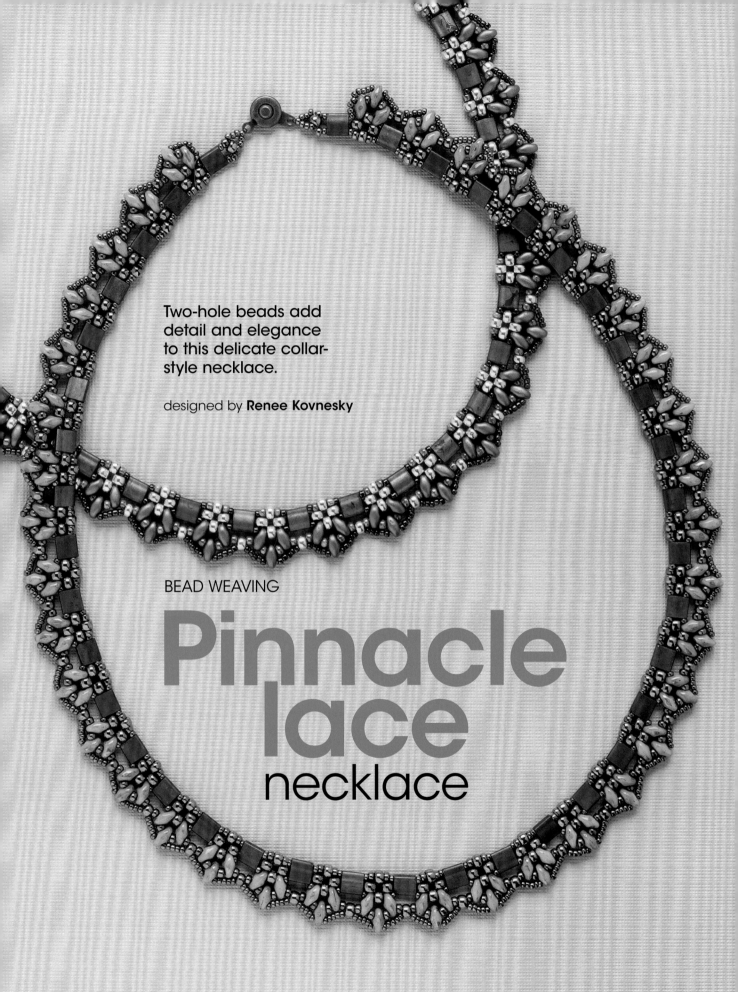

Two-hole beads add
detail and elegance
to this delicate collar-
style necklace.

designed by **Renee Kovnesky**

BEAD WEAVING

Pinnacle
lace
necklace

Difficulty rating

Materials

turquoise necklace 19 in. (48 cm)
- **39** 5 x 5 mm Tila beads (Miyuki 2006, metallic matte bronze)
- **8 g** 2.5 x 5 mm SuperDuo beads (opaque turquoise Picasso)
- seed beads (Miyuki 457, metallic dark bronze)
  - **5 g** 8º seed beads
  - **2 g** 11º seed beads
  - **3 g** 15º seed beads
- **1** clasp
- Fireline, 4 or 6 lb. test
- beading needles, #11

copper necklace colors
- Tila beads (Miyuki 2002, metallic matte silver gray)
- 2.5 x 5 mm SuperDuo beads (matte metallic copper)
- 8º seed beads (Miyuki 4201, Duracoat galvanized silver)
- 11º seed beads (Toho 1208, marbled turquoise Ceylon gray)
- 15º seed beads (Toho 222, dark bronze)

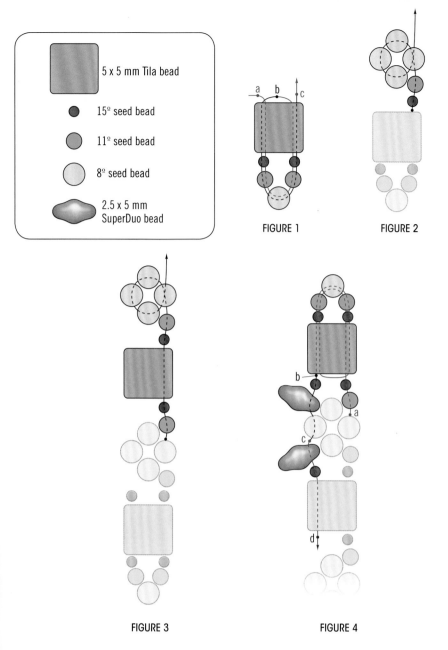

5 x 5 mm Tila bead	
15º seed bead	
11º seed bead	
8º seed bead	
2.5 x 5 mm SuperDuo bead	

FIGURE 1

FIGURE 2

FIGURE 3

FIGURE 4

Necklace

1 On a comfortable length of thread, pick up a Tila bead, a 15º seed bead, an 11º seed bead, an 8º seed bead, an 11º, and a 15º, and sew through the open hole of the Tila **(figure 1, a–b)**. Retrace the thread path **(b–c)**, and tighten the beads.

2 Pick up a 15º, an 11º, and four 8ºs, and sew through the first 8º just added to form a loop **(figure 2)**. Snug up the beads.

3 Pick up an 11º, a 15º, a Tila, a 15º, an 11º, and four 8ºs, and sew through the first 8º just added to form a loop **(figure 3)**. Snug up the beads. Repeat this stitch for the desired length of the necklace, allowing 1–1½ in. (2.5–3.8 cm)

for the last Tila and clasp. End and add thread as needed.

4 For the last stitch, pick up an 11º, a 15º, a Tila, a 15º, an 11º, an 8º, an 11º, and a 15º, and sew through the open hole of the same Tila. Continue through the other hole of the same Tila, the next five beads, and the following hole of the same Tila to tighten the beads **(figure 4, a–b)**.

5 Pick up a 15º and a SuperDuo bead, and sew through the center 8º on the adjacent loop **(b–c)**. Pick up a SuperDuo and a 15º, and sew through the open hole of the next Tila **(c–d)**. Repeat these stitches for the remainder of the necklace.

6 After exiting the last Tila at the end of the necklace, sew through the next

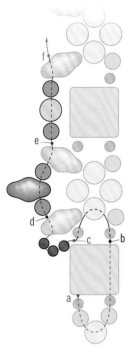

FIGURE 5

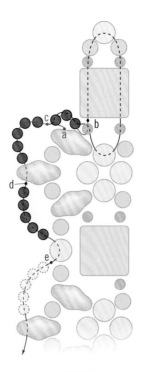

FIGURE 6

FIGURE 7

five beads and the other hole of the end Tila **(figure 5, a–b)**. Continue through the following 15º, 8º, and 15º as shown **(b–c)**.

7 Pick up three 15ºs, and sew through the open hole of the adjacent SuperDuo **(c–d)**. Pick up an 11º, a SuperDuo, and an 11º, and sew through the open hole of the following SuperDuo **(d–e)**. Pick up an 11º, an 8º, and an 11º, and sew through the open hole of the next SuperDuo **(e–f)**. Repeat these two stitches for the remainder of the necklace, ending and adding thread as needed. Use a tension that is not too tight, otherwise the necklace will curve too sharply.

8 Exiting the end SuperDuo, pick up three 15ºs, and sew through the 15º next to the end Tila **(figure 6, a–b)**. Continue through the adjacent hole of the end

Tila, the next five beads, the other hole of the same Tila, the existing 15º, 8º, and 15º, and the three 15ºs added at the start of this step **(b–c)**.

9 Pick up five 15ºs, and sew through the open hole of the next SuperDuo **(c–d)**. Pick up five 15ºs, and sew through the following 8º **(d–e)**. Repeat these two stitches for the remainder of the necklace, using a tension that allows the SuperDuos to lay flat, as too tight of a tension will make the beadwork curl. End and add thread as needed.

10 With the thread exiting the last outer SuperDuo, pick up five 15ºs, and sew

through the next four 15ºs, the adjacent hole of the end Tila, and the next three beads to exit the end 8º **(figure 7, a–b)**.

Clasp

1 Pick up four 15ºs and the clasp. Sew back through the last 15º just added, pick up three 15ºs, and continue through the 8º your thread exited at the start of the step **(b–c)**. Retrace the thread path a few times, and end the thread.

2 Add 12 in. (30 cm) of thread to the other end of the necklace, exiting the end 8º, and repeat step 1 to add the other half of the clasp. ⊙

did you know?

Tila beads were one of the first two-hole beads released and have been around for more than five years.

Stitch a winding path of
flower components joined
together with pearls,
crystals, and seed beads.

designed by **Julie Moore Tanksley**

BEAD WEAVING

Trail of roses
bracelet

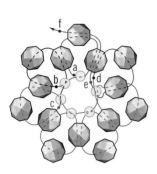

FIGURE 1

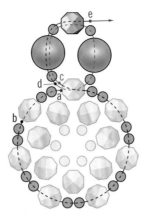

FIGURE 2

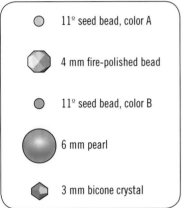

○ 11º seed bead, color A

⬡ 4 mm fire-polished bead

● 11º seed bead, color B

● 6 mm pearl

⬡ 3 mm bicone crystal

FIGURE 3

Difficulty rating

Materials
pink bracelet 8 in. (20 cm)
- **12** 6 mm glass pearls (dark green)
- **98** 4 mm fire-polished beads (opaque french rose)
- **18** 3 mm bicone crystals (Swarovski, olivine)
- **11º** seed beads
  - **1 g** color A (Toho PF557, galvanized starlight)
  - **5 g** color B (Miyuki 1981, nickel plated AB)
- **1** clasp
- Fireline, 6 lb. test
- beading needles, # 11 or #12

purple bracelet colors
- 6 mm pearls (Swarovski, Scarabaeus green)
- 4 mm fire-polished beads (orchid aqua polychrome)
- 3 mm bicone crystals (Swarovski, fuchsia)
- 11º seed beads
  - color A (Toho P470, permanent finish galvanized silver)
  - color B (Miyuki D4218, dusty orchid)

Base

1 On a comfortable length of thread, pick up six color A 11º seed beads, and tie the beads into a ring with a square knot, leaving a 6-in. (15 cm) tail. Sew through the next A.

2 Pick up three 4 mm fire-polished beads, and sew through the A your thread exited, going in the same direction. Continue through the next A in the ring **(figure 1, a-b)**.

3 Pick up two fire-polished beads, sew through the adjacent fire-polished bead, the A your thread exited at the start of this step, and the next A **(b-c)**. Repeat this stitch four times using a tight tension, but after you add the last stitch, do not sew through the next A **(c-d)**.

4 Sew through the adjacent fire-polished bead in the first stitch, pick up a fire-polished bead, and sew through the adjacent fire-polished bead in the last stitch added, the A your thread exited at the start of this step **(d-e)**, and the next two fire-polished beads in the first stitch **(e-f)**. You should have a total of seven fire-polished beads in the outer ring.

5 Pick up two color B 11º seed beads, and sew through the next fire-polished bead in the outer ring **(figure 2, a-b)**. Repeat this stitch six times to complete the round **(b-c)**.

6 Pick up a B, a 6 mm pearl, a B, a fire-polished bead, a B, a pearl, and a B, and sew through the fire-polished bead your thread exited at the start of this step **(c-d)**. Continue through the next B, pearl, B, and fire-polished bead using a tight tension **(d-e)**.

7 Pick up a fire-polished bead, an A, and a fire-polished bead, and sew through the fire-polished bead your thread exited at the start of this step **(figure 3, a-b)**. Continue through the next fire-polished bead and A **(b-c)**.

8 Pick up five As, and sew through the A your thread exited at the start of this step to form a ring. Continue through the next A **(c-d)**.

103

FIGURE 4

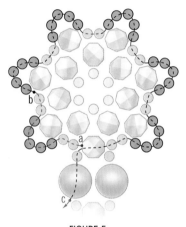

FIGURE 5

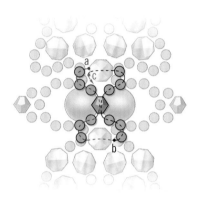

FIGURE 6

FIGURE 7

9 Repeat steps 3–5 to complete the next component. Your thread should be exiting the fire-polished bead at the point of the connection. Sew through the beadwork to exit the third fire-polished bead in the outer ring from the connection **(figure 4)**, and then repeat steps 6–8.

note Because there is an odd number of fire-polished beads in the outer ring of the flower component, the connections cannot be centered. The design will alternate between having three fire-polished beads between the connection on one side of the component and two on the other side to make a slight zigzag between the components.

10 Continue working components and connectors for the desired length bracelet, ending with step 5, and allow-

ing about 1¼ in. (3.2 cm) for the clasp. End and add thread as needed.

Embellishment
1 With the working thread exiting the fire-polished bead at the tip of the last connection, sew through the next two Bs. Pick up five Bs, skip the next fire-polished bead in the outer ring, and continue through the following two Bs **(figure 5, a–b)**. Repeat this stitch five times to add picots all around the component, and sew through the next fire-polished bead, B, and pearl **(b–c)**.
2 Pick up seven Bs, and sew through the same pearl, going in the same direction to form a loop around the pearl **(figure 6, a–b)**. Continue through the next four Bs in the loop **(b–c)**. Pick up a B, a 3 mm bicone crystal, and a B, and sew through the B your thread is exiting **(c–d)**. Continue through the next three Bs in the loop and the pearl

(d–e). Retrace the thread path of the beads added in this step (not shown in the figure for clarity).
3 Sew through the next B, fire-polished bead, B, and pearl **(e–f)**. Repeat step 2 to add the embellishment to this pearl **(f–g)**, and continue through the next B and fire-polished bead **(g–h)**.
4 Pick up three Bs, a bicone, and three Bs, and sew through the corresponding fire-polished bead in the next compo-nent **(figure 7, a–b)**. Pick up three Bs, sew back through the bicone just added, pick up three Bs, and continue through the fire-polished bead your thread exited at the start of this step **(b–c)**.
5 Sew through the next B, pearl, B, fire-polished bead, and two Bs **(figure 8, a–b)**. (The top embellishment added in the previous step is not shown in the figure for clarity.)
6 Work as in step 1 to add two or three picots, depending on how many fire-

polished beads you have on this side of the flower component in the outer ring **(b–c)**. Sew through the following fire-polished bead, B, and pearl **(c–d)**.

note The other edge of each flower component will be embellished after this side of the base is complete.

7 Repeat steps 2–6 for the remainder of this edge of the base, ending and adding thread as needed.

8 When you reach the end component, work as in step 6 to add six picots **(figure 9, a–b)**, and continue through the next fire-polished bead, B, pearl, B, fire-polished bead, and two Bs **(b–c)**.

(The top embellishment added in the previous step is not shown in the figure for clarity.)

9 Add picots to this side of the base as before, and then sew through the next fire-polished bead, B, pearl, B, fire-polished bead, and two Bs. Repeat these stitches for the remainder of the base, and end the working thread and tail.

Clasp

Add 18 in. (46 cm) of thread to the beadwork, exiting the center bead in one of the two picots on the end on the bracelet, with the needle pointing toward the other edge **(figure 10, point a)**. Pick up four Bs and the loop of the clasp, and sew back through the last B added **(a–b)**. Pick up three Bs, and sew through the next six Bs as shown **(b–c)**. Retrace the thread path of the connection several times, and end the thread. Repeat this step on the other end of the bracelet. ●

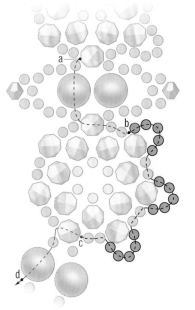

FIGURE 8

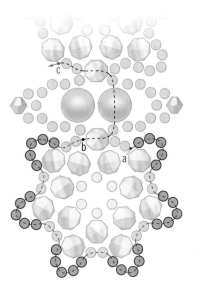

FIGURE 9

FIGURE 10

BEAD WEAVING
Step in time
earrings

Create scalloped earrings that resemble the light, graceful, and elegant designs of the Edwardian Era.

designed by **Sue Sloan**

Component

1 On 1 yd. (.9 m) of thread, pick up two 4 mm fire-polished beads, an 11º seed bead, a SuperDuo bead, an 11º, two 4 mms, an 11º, two 4 mms, an 11º, a SuperDuo, an 11º, two 4 mms, and an 11º, and sew through the beads again to form a ring (not shown in illustration for clarity). Leaving a 6-in. (15 cm) tail, tie a square knot, and sew through the next two 4 mms, 11º, SuperDuo, 11º, two 4 mms, and 11º **(figure 1, a–b)**.

2 Pick up six 11ºs, a SuperDuo, and three 11ºs, and sew through the open hole of the following SuperDuo **(b–c)**. Pick up three 11ºs, a SuperDuo, and six 11ºs, skip the next three beads, and sew through the following 11º. Retrace the thread path, and sew through the two 4 mms, 11º, SuperDuo, 11º, two 4 mms, and five 11ºs **(c–d)**.

3 Pick up three 11ºs, and sew through the open hole of the next SuperDuo **(figure 2, a–b)**. Pick up three 11ºs, a SuperDuo, five 11ºs, a SuperDuo, and

three 11ºs, and sew through the open hole of the following SuperDuo **(b–c)**.

4 Pick up three 11ºs, skip the next two 11ºs, and sew through the following five 11ºs **(c–d)**. Sew through the beadwork as shown **(d–e)**.

5 Pick up three 11ºs, and sew through the open hole of the next SuperDuo **(e–f)**. Pick up three 11ºs, a SuperDuo, and three 11ºs, and sew through the open hole of the following SuperDuo. Pick up three 11ºs, skip the next 11º, and sew through the following two 11ºs **(f–g)**.

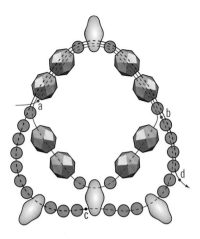

FIGURE 1

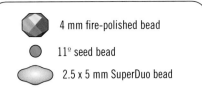

🔶 4 mm fire-polished bead

🔴 11º seed bead

🔷 2.5 x 5 mm SuperDuo bead

FIGURE 2

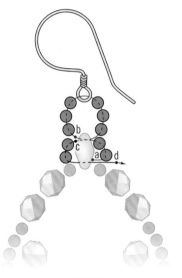

FIGURE 3

Assembly

1 With the working thread, sew through the beadwork to exit the inner hole of the SuperDuo at the top of the component. Pick up two 11ºs, and sew through the open hole of the same SuperDuo **(figure 3, a–b)**.

2 Pick up three 11ºs, the loop of an ear wire, and three 11ºs, and sew through the outer hole of the SuperDuo your thread exited at the start of this step **(b–c)**. Retrace the thread path of the top loop to reinforce the connection. Pick up two 11ºs, and sew through the inner hole of the same SuperDuo **(c–d)**. To cinch up the beads, sew through the 11ºs on each side of the top SuperDuo. End the threads.

3 Make a second earring. ●

make a swap

If desired, use a single 8–9 mm bead in place of each pair of 4 mms. Teardrop-shaped crystals add a bit of sparkle whereas glass or gemstones add earthy appeal.

Difficulty rating

  ⬡ ⬡ ⬡

Materials

blue earrings 1⅜ in. (3.5 cm)
- **16** 4 mm fire-polished beads (blue metallic suede)
- **14** 2.5 x 5 mm SuperDuo beads (light gray)
- **1 g** 11º seed beads (Toho 1207, marbled opaque turquoise blue)
- **1** pair of earring findings
- Fireline, 6 lb. test
- beading needles, #11 or #12

green earrings colors
- 4 mm fire-polished beads (light green metallic suede)
- 2.5 x 5 mm SuperDuo Beads (metallic violet rainbow)
- 11º seed beads (Miyuki D4204, old gold Duracoat)

crystal earrings colors
- **8** 9 x 6 mm teardrop crystals (Swarovski, crystal AB)
- 2.5 x 5 mm SuperDuo Beads (metallic Aztec matte gold)
- 11º seed beads (Toho 221, bronze)

CHEVRON CHAIN

Lotus
flower
necklace

Stitch a quick and stylish
pendant with Czech glass
and seed beads.

designed by **Julia Gerlach**

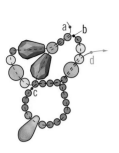

FIGURE 1

FIGURE 2

FIGURE 3

FIGURE 4

 7 x 5 mm teardrop bead

 4 mm glass bead, color A

 4 mm glass bead, color B

 3 mm glass bead

 2 mm glass bead

8º seed bead

11º seed bead

 3.8 x 7.8 mm pewter drop

Difficulty rating

Materials
necklace 24 in. (61 cm) with
2 x 1-in. (5 x 2.5 cm) pendant
- **8** 7 x 5 mm teardrop beads (blue zircon)
- **3** 3.8 x 7.8 mm pewter drops (antique brass)
- 4 mm Czech glass round beads
  - **7** color A (alabaster pastel lime)
  - **1** color B (shiny pumpkin)
- **4** 3 mm Czech glass round beads (shiny pea green)
- **10** 2 mm Czech glass round beads (shiny turquoise blue)
- **17** 8º seed beads (silver-lined light peridot opal)
- **59** 11º seed beads (antique bronze)
- **2** 4 mm 22-gauge jump rings (antique brass)
- **24 in. (61 cm)** 2 mm oval cable chain (antique brass)
- beading needles, #12
- Fireline, 8 lb. test
- **2** pairs of bentnose, flatnose, and/or chainnose pliers

1 Attach a stop bead to 1 yd. (.9 m) of thread, leaving a 6-in. (15 cm) tail.
2 Pick up a 2 mm round bead, an 11º seed bead, a 3 mm round bead, a 7 x 5 mm teardrop bead (narrow end first), an 11º, an 8º seed bead, a color A 4 mm round bead, an 8º, an 11º, and a teardrop (wide end first). Sew back through the first three beads picked up in this step **(figure 1, a–b)**.
3 Pick up an 11º, two 8ºs, an A 4 mm, and four 11ºs, and sew through the 11º below the previous teardrop **(b–c)**.
4 Pick up three 11ºs, a 2 mm, a pewter drop, a 2 mm, and seven 11ºs, and sew back through the 11º closest to the A 4 mm as well as the A 4 mm and the following 8º **(c–d)**.

5 Pick up an 8º, an 11º, a 2 mm, an 11º, a 3 mm, and a teardrop (narrow end first). Sew through the fifth 11º below the previous A 4 mm **(figure 2, a–b)**.
6 Pick up an 8º, an A 4 mm, an 8º, an 11º, and a teardrop (wide end first), and sew back through the 3 mm, 11º and 2 mm added in the previous step **(b–c)**.
7 Repeat steps 3–6 twice **(c–d)**.
8 Sew through the next 11º, two 8ºs, and two 11ºs at the top of the beadwork **(figure 3, a–b)**. Pick up an 11º, and sew through the two 11ºs your thread just exited, and continue through the next two 8ºs and two 11ºs **(b–c)**.
9 Pick up an 11º, and sew though the two 11ºs your thread just exited, and

continue through the next two 8ºs, 11º, and 2 mm **(c–d)**.
10 Sew through the beadwork to exit the last 11º added, with the needle pointing toward the other 11º added at the top of the piece **(figure 4, a–b)**. Pick up a color B 4 mm round bead, and sew through the other top 11º **(b–c)**. Remove the stop bead, snugging up the beadwork if necessary, and end the threads.
11 Open a 4 mm jump ring, and slide it through an edge 11º at the top of the pendant. Attach an end link of chain, and close the jump ring. Repeat on the other side of the pendant with the remaining jump ring and the other end of the chain. ●

Inspired by the iconic origami fortune teller (a.k.a. "cootie catcher" beloved by kids everywhere, this textured bracelet works up easily with two-hole triangles and seed beads.

BEAD WEAVING

Triangle treasure bracelet

designed by **Marie New**

Base

How to pick up the triangle beads: With the point of the triangle with no hole facing away from you, pick up the bead through the left hole (LH) or the right hole (RH), per the instructions.

1 On a comfortable length of thread, pick up a repeating pattern of an 8º seed bead and a triangle bead (RH) four times. Tie the working thread and tail together with a square knot to form a ring, leaving a 6-in. (15 cm) tail. Retrace the thread path, and continue through the next 8º **(figure 1)**. Make sure the triangles point up and the open hole is on the outside of the ring.

2 Pick up an 11º seed bead and a 15º seed bead, and sew through the open hole of the next triangle **(figure 2, a–b)**. Pick up a 15º and an 11º, and sew through the following 8º **(b–c)**. Repeat these stitches three times **(c–d)**, and continue through the next eight beads as shown **(d–e)**.

3 Pick up a 15º, an 11º, an 8º, an 11º, and a 15º, and sew through the adjacent five beads to form a loop. Continue through the first 15º, 11º, and 8º added in this step **(figure 3, a–b)**.

4 Pick up a repeating pattern of a triangle (RH) and an 8º three times, pick up a triangle (RH), and sew through the 8º your thread exited at the start of this step **(b–c)**. Continue through the next 11º, 15º, and triangle (LH) **(c–d)**.

5 Pick up a 15º and an 11º, and sew through the next 8º. Pick up an 11º and a 15º, and sew through the open hole of the following triangle **(figure 4, a–b)**. Repeat these stitches twice **(b–c)**, and sew through the next 17 beads as shown **(c–d)**.

6 Repeat steps 3–5 for the desired length, allowing ⅜ in. (1 cm) for the clasp, but in the last unit, sew through only 11 beads instead of 17 beads **(figure 5, point a)**. End and add thread as needed.

7 To work the first unit of the second row, repeat steps 3–5, but at the end of step 5, sew through the next 11 beads instead of 17 beads (a–b).

8 For the next unit, work as in step 3–5, but end by sewing through 11 beads instead of 17. With your thread exiting the 15º as shown in **figure 6, point a**, sew through the corresponding five beads in the first row **(a–b)** and the following 11 beads in the new unit **(b–c)**.

9 Work as in step 8 for the remainder of the base, ending and adding thread as needed. End the working thread and tail.

Edging and clasp

1 Add a comfortable length of thread to the base, exiting the end 15º on the top edge, with the needle pointing toward the other end **(figure 7, point a)**.

2 Pick up two 15ºs, an 11º, and two 15ºs, skip the adjacent 11º, 8º, and 11º,

and sew through the next 15º and the adjacent hole of the following triangle **(a–b)**.

3 Pick up an 11º, and sew through the adjacent hole of the next triangle and the following 15º **(b–c)**.

4 Repeat steps 2–3 along this edge of the base, ending with step 2 **(figure 8, point a)**. Sew through the next 15º **(a–b)**.

5 Pick up five 15ºs and the end loop of the clasp, skip the next 11º, and sew through the following 8º, 11º, and 15º **(b–c)**. Pick up five 15ºs and the center loop of the clasp, and sew through the next triangle, two 15ºs, and triangle **(c–d)**.

6 Pick up five 15ºs, sew through the center loop of the clasp again, and continue through the next 15º, 11º, and 8º **(d–e)**. Pick up five 15ºs, and sew through the remaining loop of the clasp and the next 15º, triangle, and 15º **(e–f)**. Sew through the beadwork, and retrace the thread path of the clasp connection.

7 Repeat steps 2–3 along the other edge of the base, ending with step 2, and ending and adding thread as needed. Repeat steps 5–6 to attach the other half of the clasp. End the thread. ●

Difficulty rating

Materials
cream bracelet 7¼ in. (18.4 cm)
- 120 6 mm CzechMates two-hole triangle beads (opaque luster Picasso)
- 4 g 8º seed beads (Toho 329, gold lustered African sunset)
- 3 g 11º seed beads (Toho 508, higher metallic iris olivine)
- 2 g 15º seed beads (Toho 2102, sapphire opal silver-lined)
- 1 3-strand tube clasp
- Fireline, 6 lb. test, or Toho One-G thread
- beading needles, #11 or #12

topaz/gold bracelet colors
- 6 mm CzechMates two-hole triangle beads (luster rose gold)
- 8º seed beads (Toho 995, gold-lined rainbow aqua)
- 11º seed beads (Toho 221, bronze)
- 15º seed beads (Toho 952, aqua-lined yellow)

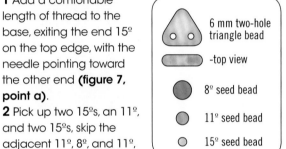

6 mm two-hole triangle bead	
-top view	
8º seed bead	
11º seed bead	
15º seed bead	

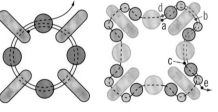

FIGURE 1   FIGURE 2

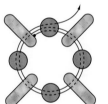

FIGURE 3

FIGURE 4

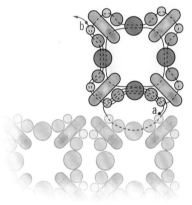

FIGURE 5

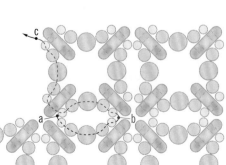

FIGURE 6

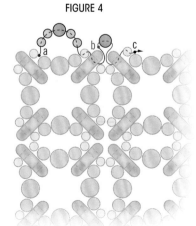

FIGURE 7

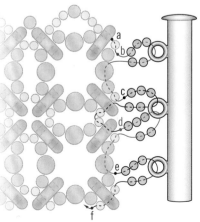

FIGURE 8

Pre-mixed bead blends are great, but it can be hard to know what to do with them. Start with a pair of earrings and then see where the beads take you!

designed by **Julia Gerlach**

BEAD WEAVING

Beaded
diamonds

Bead mixes vary — some contain several shades of the same size bead whereas others, like the one I used, contain beads of several different colors and styles. This bead mix contains three colors of 11º seed beads, four colors of 8º seed beads, one color of 6º seed beads, and two colors of 6 mm bugle beads. For these earrings, you'll need one color each of 11ºs (seafoam) and 8ºs (gold) and both colors of bugle beads (I used the shiny one as color A and the matte one as color B). You won't need all the beads in all three packages of the mix, but you'll probably need all three

packs to make sure you have enough of each individual bead. It's better to have too many than fall short.

Earring dangle

1 On 2 yd. (1.8 m) of thread, pick up four 8º seed beads. Leaving a 6-in. (15 cm) tail, tie the beads into a ring with a square knot, and sew through the first 8º again.
2 Pick up an 11º seed bead, and sew through the next 8º. Repeat this stitch three times, exiting the first 8º **(figure 1)**.
3 Pick up a color A bugle bead, an 11º, an A, an 8º, an A, an 11º, and an A, and sew through the 8º your thread exited at the start of this step **(figure 2, a–b)**. Retrace the

thread path through the bugles, skipping the seed beads, and sew through the first bugle again **(b–c)**. Pull tight so the seed beads pop out at the corners, forming a diamond shape.
4 Pick up an A, and sew through the first bugle again **(figure 3)**. Pull tight so the bugles are side by side. Note: figures 3–8 show the bugles spread apart so you can see thread paths, but in reality, they should be tight together. Pick up a color B bugle, and sew through the adjacent A **(figure 4)**. Sew back through the B and the first A again, and then sew through the adjacent A and the next 8º **(figure 5)**.

5 Pick up an A, an 11º, an A, an 8º, an A, and an 11º, and sew through the adjacent A and 8º **(figure 6, a–b)**. Retrace the thread path through the bugles, skipping the seed beads, and sew through the first bugle again **(b–c)**. Pull tight.
6 Repeat steps 4–5 twice. Sew through the adjacent A in the first diamond and the A your thread just exited **(figure 7)**. Add a B as before, and sew through the beadwork to exit an 8º at the tip of a diamond **(figure 8, a–b)**.
7 Sew through all the tip 8ºs **(b–c)**, and pull them into a tight ring.

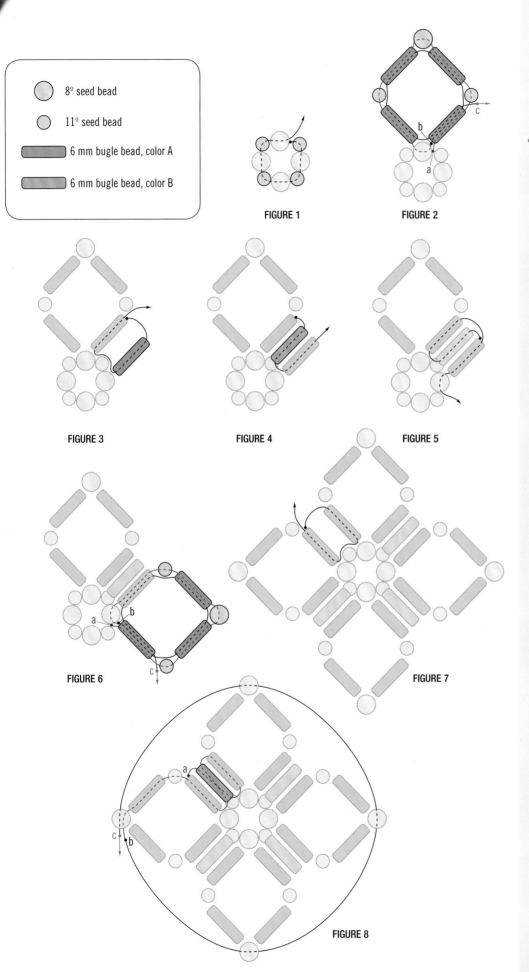

Legend:
- 8º seed bead
- 11º seed bead
- 6 mm bugle bead, color A
- 6 mm bugle bead, color B

FIGURE 1

FIGURE 2

FIGURE 3

FIGURE 4

FIGURE 5

FIGURE 6

FIGURE 7

FIGURE 8

Difficulty rating

Materials
earrings 1½ in. (3.8 cm)
- **3** 8 g packages of Toho bead mix (mint/forest and gold)
- **1** pair of earring findings
- **2** 2-in. (5 cm) head pins, 22–26 gauge
- beading needles, #11
- Fireline, 6 lb. test
- chainnose pliers
- roundnose pliers
- wire cutters

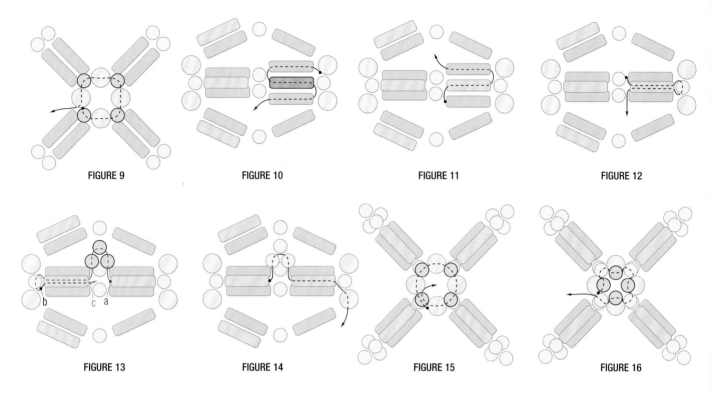

FIGURE 9   FIGURE 10   FIGURE 11   FIGURE 12

FIGURE 13   FIGURE 14   FIGURE 15   FIGURE 16

8 Pick up an 11º, and sew through the next 8º. Repeat this stitch three times, exiting the first 8º **(figure 9)**.

9 Sew through the adjacent A, pick up a B, and sew through the next A **(figure 10)**.

10 Sew back through the B and the adjacent A **(figure 11)**.

11 Sew through the B and the adjacent end 11º, and sew back through the B **(figure 12)**.

12 Pick up three 11ºs, sew through the opposite B and the adjacent end 11º **(figure 13, a–b)**, and then sew back through the same B **(b–c)**. Sew back through the third and first 11ºs added in this step, and continue through the opposite B and the next 8º in the ring **(figure 14)**.

13 Repeat steps 9–12 three times.

14 Sewing through the end 8ºs, work a round of tubular peyote stitch using 11ºs, and step up through the first 11º added in this step **(figure 15)**.

15 Sewing through the beads added in the previous round, work another round of peyote using 11ºs **(figure 16)**. Retrace the thread path through the new beads added in this round.

16 Sew through the beadwork to exit an 8º on the other end of the beadwork, and repeat steps 14–15. End the threads.

17 Repeat steps 1–16 to make a second diamond.

Assembly

1 On a head pin, string an 11º and one end hole of a diamond. String two bugles on the head pin, and then guide the head pin through the other end hole of the diamond. String an 11º, and make a wrapped loop (Basics).

2 Open the loop of an ear wire, attach the dangle, and close the loop.

3 Repeat steps 1–2 to complete the second earring. ◐

what else?

After you're done with the earrings, make more projects with the leftover beads. Make another pair of earrings with different bead colors, or see what else you can come up with. I made this pendant with my leftovers (plus a few extras from my stash). You can get the instructions for this pendant at www.BeadAndButton.com/freeprojects.

CRYSTALLIZED
square
bracelet

A sturdy right-angle weave base is adorned with QuadraTiles and seed beads, and capped off with crystals for over-the-top endless sparkle.

designed by **Maria Teresa Moran**

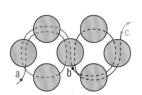

FIGURE 1

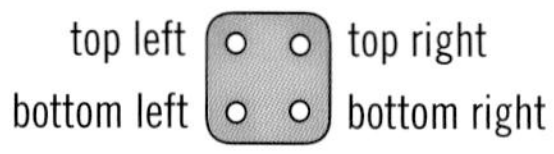

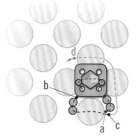

top left | top right
bottom left | bottom right

FIGURE 2

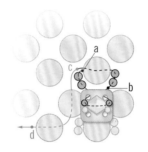

FIGURE 3

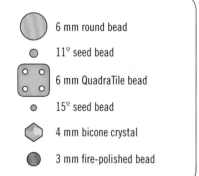

- ⬤ 6 mm round bead
- ● 11º seed bead
- 🔲 6 mm QuadraTile bead
- ● 15º seed bead
- ⬡ 4 mm bicone crystal
- ⬤ 3 mm fire-polished bead

FIGURE 4

Base

1 On a comfortable length of doubled 6 lb. Fireline, pick up four 6 mm beads, and sew through the beads again to form a ring, leaving 6-in. (15 cm) tail. Continue through the first three 6 mms added **(figure 1, a–b)**.

note If you prefer to work with a single thread, retrace the thread path of each round for the entire base.

2 Working in right-angle weave (RAW), pick up three 6 mms, and sew through the 6 mm your thread exited at the start of this step. Continue through the first two 6 mms just added **(b–c)**, and tighten. Continue working in RAW using a tight tension for the desired length of the bracelet, less ⅝ in. (1.6 cm) for the clasp, ending with an even number of stitches. This 7¼ in. (18.4 cm) bracelet is 18 stitches long.

3 Continue working in RAW using 6 mms to add two more rows. End and add thread as needed, and end the working thread and tail.

Top embellishment

With the QuadraTile in the position shown **(figure 2)**, the holes will be referred to as top left (TL), top right (TR), bottom left (BL), and bottom right (BR).

1 Attach a comfortable length of 10 lb. Fireline (single thread) to the base, exiting an end 6 mm along the bottom edge with the needle pointing toward the end of the base **(figure 3, point a)**.

2 Pick up two 11º seed beads, a QuadraTile (BR), a 15º seed bead, a 4 mm bicone crystal, and a 15º, and sew down through the QuadraTile (BL) **(a–b)**, snugging the beadwork to the 6 mms. Pick up two 11ºs, and sew through the 6 mm your thread exited at the start of this step **(b–c)**. Continue through the next two 6 mms as shown **(c–d)**.

3 Pick up two 11ºs, and sew up through the QuadraTile (TL). Pick up a 15º, sew through the crystal, pick up a 15º, and sew down through the QuadraTile (TR) **(figure 4, a–b)**. Pick up two 11ºs, and sew through the 6 mm your thread exited at the start of this step **(b–c)**. Continue through the next two 6 mms as shown **(c–d)**.

4 Work the same embellishment as in steps 2–3 but sew through left holes instead of right holes, and vice versa **(figure 5, a–b)**. Once the embellishment is complete, continue through the next three 6 mms in this RAW unit and the following three 6 mms in the next RAW unit as shown **(b–c)**.

5 Work as in steps 2–4 for the remainder of the base. End and add thread as needed, and end the working thread.

Base embellishment and clasp

1 Attach a comfortable length of 6 lb. Fireline (single thread) to an end edge 6 mm with the needle pointing toward the other end of the base **(figure 6, point a)**. Pick up a 3 mm fire-polished bead, and sew through the next edge 6 mm **(a–b)**. Repeat this stitch for the remainder of this edge **(b–c)**. Pick up a 3 mm, sew through the end 6 mm in this row, pick up a 3 mm, and sew through the next 6 mm in the next row **(c–d)**. Repeat these stitches for the remainder of the base, making sure to add a 3 mm at each corner and between the end 6 mms. End and add thread as needed.

2 With the thread exiting the top end 6 mm **(figure 7, point a)**, pick up four 15ºs, and sew through the end loop of the clasp. Continue back through the last 15º added, pick up three 15ºs, and sew through the 6 mm your thread exited at the start of this step. Continue through the next two beads **(a–b)**. Repeat these stitches twice to attach the remaining loops of the clasp, but continue through only one bead instead of two after attaching the last loop **(b–c)**. Retrace the thread path of the clasp connections, and end the thread.

3 Attach 18 in. (46 cm) of 6 lb. Fireline (single thread) to the other end of the base, and repeat step 2 for this end. ●

design option

If desired, substitute rose montées for the bicone crystals and/or QuadraLentils for the QuadraTiles.

Materials

pink bracelet 7¼ in. x 1¼ in. (18.4 mm x 3.2 mm)

- **129** 6 mm round beads (druk, luster opaque gold/satin)
- **54** 6 mm CzechMates four-hole QuadraTile beads (opaque ultra green luster)
- **54** 4 mm bicone crystals (Swarovski, sand opal AB2X)
- **76** 3 mm fire-polished beads (saturated pink)
- **5 g** 11º seed beads (Toho PF552, light dusty rose)
- **2 g** 15º seed beads (Toho PF552, light dusty rose)
- **1** 3-strand tube clasp
- Fireline, 10 lb. and 6 lb. test
- beading needles, #11 or #12

green bracelet colors

- 6 mm round beads (druk, Picasso opaque olive)
- 6 mm CzechMates four-hole QuadraTile beads (metallic dark blue suede)
- 4 mm bicone crystals (Swarovski, turquoise AB2X)
- 3 mm fire-polished beads (bronze)
- 11º seed beads (Miyuki 2031, matte metallic dark olive)
- 15º seed beads (Toho 221, bronze)

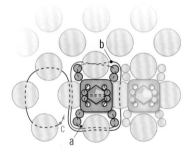

FIGURE 5

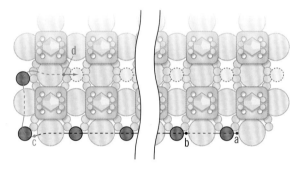

FIGURE 6

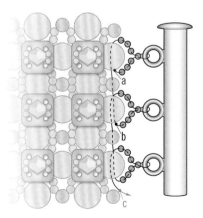

FIGURE 7

Creating organic shapes in CRAW

Learn the tricks to making flourishes and branches in cubic right-angle weave (CRAW), and then use your new-found skills to make a statement necklace.

designed by **Alla Maslennikova**

2-needle CRAW

1 Attach a needle to each end of a comfortable length of monofilament ("thread" from now on), and center a color D 15º seed bead.

2 With one needle, pick up a color A 15º seed bead and a D **(figure 1, a–b)**. With the other needle, pick up an A, and cross through the D picked up with the other needle **(aa–bb)**. Repeat this stitch twice, but pick up two As on the first needle instead of an A and a D **(b–c and bb–cc)**.

3 Complete the first cube: With each needle, pick up an A, and cross through the D at the other end of the strip **(figure 2)**. With one needle, sew through the adjacent A, sewing toward the next D. Continue through the four As on this side of the cube, and then sew through the adjacent D **(figure 3)**. Repeat with the other needle to cinch up the opposite side of the cube **(figure 4)**. The thread ends should be exiting opposite sides of the same D. Note: The D beads signify the front surface of the rope.

4 With one needle, pick up an A and a D. With the other needle, pick up an A, and cross through the D picked up with the other needle **(figure 5, a–b and aa–bb)**. Repeat this stitch, but pick up two As with the first needle **(b–c and bb–cc)**.

5 Complete the cube: With each needle, pick up an A, and sew through the corresponding A on the bottom layer **(figure 6)**. With each needle, sew through the adjacent four side beads of the new cube, and exit the new D **(figures 7 and 8)**.

6 Repeat steps 4–5 for the desired length.

Curves

1 Place the strip of beadwork vertically on your work surface, exiting a bead on the side you want the beadwork to curve toward. With each needle, sew through the next two vertical beads on this side, and cross through the next horizontal bead **(figure 9, a–b and aa–bb)**. Repeat for the length of the curve, sewing through an extra vertical bead at the end if needed **(b–c and bb–cc)**.

2 Working back toward the other end, retrace the thread path, and pull the threads tight to create the curve **(photo a)**.

Branches

1 To begin a branch, work a cube but pick up two Ds instead of one in the first stitch (for a total of three beads), and cross the second needle through both Ds **(figure 10, a–b and aa–bb)**. In the second stitch, pick up three As on one needle. Pick up an A on the second needle, and cross it through the last two As picked up with the first needle **(b–c and bb–cc)**. Finish the cube with a single A on each needle **(figure 11)**, and then cinch up each side as before. This will create a cube with two beads on one side on both the top and bottom surface.

2 Work a second cube as in step 1, sewing through the pairs of beads on the top and bottom surface of the previous cube **(photo b)**.

3 Sew through the beadwork so your needles exit opposite sides of a D. Begin to create the split that will become two separate ropes by stitching a cube off of this D. Sew

don't lose your needles

To prevent your needles from falling off the monofilament, thread the line on the needle, and then tie an overhand knot at the end of the short tail that passed through the needle's eye. The knot will be able to pass through the beads but won't slip through the eye of the needle.

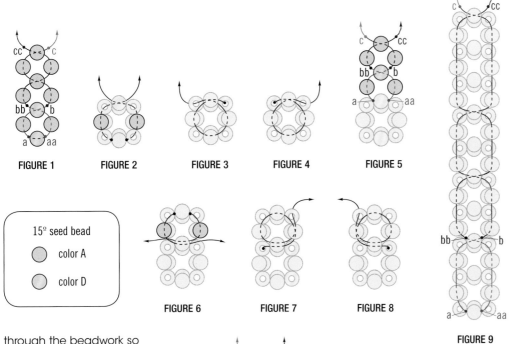

FIGURE 1　　FIGURE 2　　FIGURE 3　　FIGURE 4　　FIGURE 5

15º seed bead

⬤ color A

⬤ color D

FIGURE 6　　FIGURE 7　　FIGURE 8

FIGURE 9

through the beadwork so your needles exit opposite sides of the other D in the previous cube, and stitch an adjacent cube **(photo c)**. This cube will share three adjacent side beads with the other cube in this row.
4 To complete the split, work in CRAW off of each cube. Do not share side beads between cubes **(photo d)**.

Joins

To join two strips, align them where you want the join to be. Exit an edge bead on one strip, sew through the corresponding edge bead on the other strip, and sew through the edge bead on the first strip again. Repeat, sewing through an adjacent edge bead in the second strip **(photo e)**. Retrace the thread path through the join a couple of times.

Accent beads

Exit an edge bead where you want to add an accent bead between two strips. On both needles, pick up an accent bead, and sew through the corresponding edge bead on the other strip **(photo f)**. Retrace the thread path.

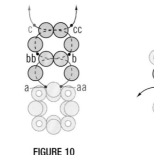

FIGURE 10　　FIGURE 11

Difficulty rating

Materials

necklace 20 in. (51 cm)
- cabochons
  - **1** 40 x 25 mm long oval or rectangle, kyanite
  - **1** 18 x 13 mm oval or rectangle, kyanite
  - **2** 18 x 13 mm ovals, paua shell
  - **4** 10 x 8 mm ovals, mother-of-pearl
- round white pearls
  - **4** 7 mm
  - **4** 6 mm
  - **6** 4–5 mm
  - **9** 3.5–4 mm
  - **4** 3 mm
  - **4** 2 mm
- 15º seed beads
  - **5 g** color A (Toho 773, steel blue-lined crystal)
  - **15 g** color B (Miyuki 1105, silvery gray-lined crystal)
  - **3 g** color C (Miyuki 1521, light beige-lined crystal)
  - **3 g** color D (Miyuki 1522, golden beige-lined crystal)
- **1** hook clasp
- chain
  - **2 in. (5 cm)** 3 mm link cable chain (small link)
  - **1 in. (2.5 cm)** 6 mm link cable chain (medium link)
- **4 in. (10 cm)** 22-gauge wire
- **1** 2-in. (5 cm) head pin, 22-gauge
- **3** 3 mm jump rings
- **2** 5 mm oval jump rings
- leather or Ultrasuede
- beading foundation or felt
- transparent monofilament line, 2 lb. test
- Fireline, 6 lb. test
- beading needles, #11
- **2** pairs of chainnose, bentnose, or flatnose pliers
- roundnose pliers
- wire cutters

g

h

i

Winter's embrace necklace

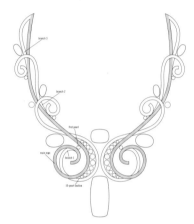

The template shown here (above) is based on Alla's original sketch (top) of her "Winter's embrace necklace" (pictured on p. 118). For a full-size necklace template, go to www.BeadAndButton.com/template.

Getting started

Begin by creating a life-size drawing of your necklace. Made with 15ºs, each CRAW rope measures approximately 4.5 mm in width. To make the necklace as shown, go to www. BeadAndButton.com/template to print a full-size version of Alla's "Winter's embrace" necklace.

Cabochons

1 Cut a piece of beading foundation and a piece of leather that is slightly larger (no more than 1 mm

at each side) than each cabochon.

2 Thread a needle with a comfortable length of Fireline, and make an overhand knot at the end. Stack the corresponding foundation and leather for a cabochon, and working near the edge, sew through the two layers from the foundation side. Sew through the layers again in the same direction to form a loop over the edge but before you pull tight, sew through the loop so the working thread is exiting at the edge **(figure 12, a–b)**.

3 Pick up two color A 15º seed beads, and sew through the layers about 2 mm away, from the foundation side. Align the beads on the edge of the foundation and leather, and sew through the loop **(b–c)**. Repeat this stitch around the cab, and sew through the first A added in the round **(photo g)**.

4 Working off the beads added in the previous step, work a round of tubular

FIGURE 12

peyote with As **(photo h)**.

5 Continue in peyote, working one or two rounds in colors B, C, and D 15º seed beads (darkest to lightest) to complete the bezel **(photo i)**. If possible, select slightly wider beads for the bottom rounds and narrower beads for the top rounds so you won't have to work any decreases to make the bezel fit the cab perfectly. Do not end the thread.

6 Work as in steps 2–5 for the five remaining cabs.

Left neck strap

Work this neck strap beginning with the central spiral of the main rope (near the focal cab). All directionals in this section are based on the beadwork being positioned with the D 15ºs facing up and the working thread at the top of the strip.

1 Using color A and D 15ºs as in "2-needle CRAW," stitch a strip of nine CRAW cubes. Create a curve to the left as in "Curves." Work another CRAW cube. This is the beginning of the main rope, which is colored yellow on the template.

2 Working over four rows, create a split as in "Branches" **(photo j)**.

3 Continue working the main rope: Work four cubes, select-

ing larger 15ºs on the right side and smaller 15ºs on the left side to make a slight lean. Tighten the last two cubes as in "Curves" **(photo k)**. Work 20–25 more cubes. End and add thread as needed.

4 Center a new thread in the end D of the branch 1 rope. Work 20–25 cubes. Cross the main rope over branch 1 where indicated on the template, and attach the ropes as in "Joins."

5 Continue the main rope until you reach the point where the first pearl should be attached. Using a 3.5–4 mm pearl, work a join between this part of the main rope and the initial spiral **(photo l)**.

6 Continue branch 1 until you get to the point where the first pearl in the 10-pearl section should be added. Join branch 1 to the main rope through the smallest pearl **(photo m)**. Working two or three cubes at a time, continue branch 1, joining it to the main rope through the pearls. Use five pearls in gradually larger sizes and then five pearls in gradually smaller sizes. Check the shapes against the pattern frequently as you work.

7 After the pearl section is complete, cross the main rope over branch 1, and work

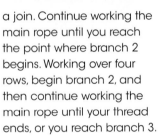

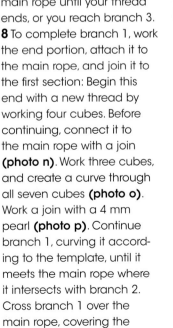

a join. Continue working the main rope until you reach the point where branch 2 begins. Working over four rows, begin branch 2, and then continue working the main rope until your thread ends, or you reach branch 3.

8 To complete branch 1, work the end portion, attach it to the main rope, and join it to the first section: Begin this end with a new thread by working four cubes. Before continuing, connect it to the main rope with a join **(photo n)**. Work three cubes, and create a curve through all seven cubes **(photo o)**. Work a join with a 4 mm pearl **(photo p)**. Continue branch 1, curving it according to the template, until it meets the main rope where it intersects with branch 2. Cross branch 1 over the main rope, covering the branch 2 split, and join

(photo q). Continue working branch 1 until it meets the starting end, and work a final cube to attach the ends.

9 Using the Fireline remaining on an 18 x 13 mm cab, sew the cab in place between branch 1 and the beginning spiral of the main rope **(photo r)**. There is no set thread path — simply align the cab and sew through the appropriate beads in the bezel and the ropes. Note that where the cab meets the branch, the branch will be sitting higher than the cab, so you will want to attach an upper bead on the

cab with a lower bead on the branch. End the Fireline.

10 Continue working the main rope until you reach the end of it. Exit a side bead of the last cube, and make a loop: Pick up five As, and sew through the bead at the end of the rope again. Continue through the first three As picked up. Make a second loop: Pick up five As, and sew through the middle A in the previous loop again. Retrace the thread path, and then exit a side A on the front surface of the last cube in the main rope. Work a cube off of the bead, and then exit

the end side bead. Pick up two As, and sew through the connector A between the two loops. Pick up two As, and sew through the end side bead on the last cube you stitched (see **photo s** for the completed double loop).

11 Working off the last cube you stitched, begin working on branch 3 for about 23 cubes, or until the beadwork reaches the portion of branch 3 you already started. Work one more cube to attach the branch segments.

12 Work as in step 8 to complete branch 2 **(photo t)**.

13 Working as in step 9, refer to the template to attach a 12 x 8 mm cab at the points where branches 1 and 2 and branches 2 and 3 overlap.

Right neck strap and assembly

1 Repeat all the steps of "Left neck strap," but work all the curves in the opposite directions so this neck strap is a mirror image of the first one. Sew the two neck straps together in the center with a couple of joining stitches.

2 Using the Fireline attached to the remaining cabs, attach them to the neck straps as in step 10 of "Left neck strap." If needed, use a pearl on each side of the upper cab **(photo u)**.

3 Cut a 2-in. (5 cm) piece of 22-gauge wire, and make a plain loop: Make a right-angle bend about ⅜ in. (1 cm) from one end. Grasp the tip of the wire with round-nose pliers, and rotate the wire to make a loop. String a 4 mm pearl, and make

another plain loop. Repeat to make another pearl unit.

4 On a head pin, string a 4 mm pearl, and make a plain loop.

5 Cut two 1-in. (2.5 cm) pieces of small-link chain and one 1-in. (2.5 cm) piece of medium-link chain.

6 Open a loop of a pearl unit, and attach it to one end of a small-link chain. Repeat with the other pearl unit and small-link chain.

7 Open a 3 mm jump ring, and use it to attach the other

loop of a pearl unit to the hook clasp. Using another 3 mm jump ring, attach the other pearl unit to the medium-link chain. Use the final 3 mm jump ring to attach the pearl dangle to the end of the medium-link chain **(photo v)**.

8 Open an oval jump ring, and attach one chain to the end loop on a neck strap **(photo w)**. Repeat with the other chain and the remaining neck strap. ◉

Bead single crochet

Go beyond the basics with bead single crochet. After learning the technique, use it to make a lovely diamond-pattern bracelet with a stylish ombré gradient.

designed by
Candice Sexton

Bead single crochet creates beautiful ropes for necklaces and bracelets. The beads sit at an angle, which visually differentiates this technique from the slightly more common bead slip stitch technique.

Bead single crochet techniques

Bead stringing

• Using a Big-Eye needle, string all the beads according to the pattern. The last bead strung will be the first bead you crochet with. Use a ruler or a sticky note to track your progress, and frequently double-check your work to avoid making stringing errors.

• If desired, string paper markers between rows to track your progress.

• Do not trim the cord from the spool.

Chain stitch

1 Make a loop in the cord, crossing the ball end over the tail. Insert the hook in the loop, yarn over the hook **(figure 1)**, and pull through the loop **(figure 2)**. This is a slip knot.

2 Catch the working thread with the hook (from now on known as a "yarn over") **(figure 3)**, and pull the cord through the loop. Repeat for the desired number of chain stitches **(figure 4)**.

Join a chain into a ring

Begin with a beadless chain equal to the number of stitches in each round of your pattern. With the loop from the last stitch on the hook, insert the hook under the two threads that form a "V" in the first stitch **(photo a)**. Yarn over, and pull through the stitch and the loop on the hook **(photo b)**.

Single crochet: tubular

Insert the hook under the two threads that form a "V" in the first stitch. Yarn over **(photo c)**, and pull through the stitch **(photo d)**. You will have two loops on your hook. Make a second yarn over **(photo e)**, and pull the cord through both loops, leaving one loop on the hook **(photo f)**. Repeat

FIGURE 1   FIGURE 2   FIGURE 3   FIGURE 4

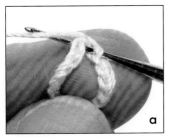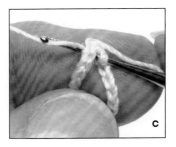

a   b   c   d

Difficulty rating

Materials

**peach/teal bracelet
8¾ in. (22.2 cm)**

- 11º seed beads
  - **4 g** color A (Toho 779, peach coral)
  - **15 g** color B (Toho 557, gold)
  - **4 g** color C (580A, gilt-lined light peach opal)
  - **4 g** color D (256A, transparent champagne AB)
  - **4 g** color E (551, gilt-lined white opal)
  - **4 g** color F (571A, gilt-lined margarita opal)
  - **4 g** color G (571, gilt-lined light mint opal)
  - **4 g** color H (572B, gilt-lined light teal opal)
  - **4 g** color I (390, green color-lined seafoam green)
- **1** magnetic barrel clasp (to fit 10 mm cord)
- crochet cord (Lizbeth #40–80, cream)
- steel crochet hook, 0.75–1.25 mm
- tapestry needle
- Big-Eye beading needle
- **8 in. (20 cm)** ³⁄₁₆-in. (5 mm) cotton bolo cord
- 2-part epoxy or E6000 adhesive
- bits of paper (optional)
- safety pin or locking stitch marker

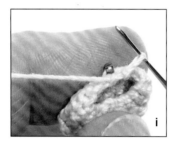

this stitch to create a tube of unbeaded crochet to the desired length.

Bead single crochet

Insert the hook under the two threads that form a "V" in the next stitch. Slide a bead up to the hook, yarn over **(photo g)**, and pull through the first stitch. Make a second yarn over **(photo h)**, and pull through both loops **(photo i)**. The bead will sit on the outside of the tube. Repeat this process around

the ring, making sure you complete the correct number of stitches for the round. After the first round is complete, it will be easier to keep track of your stitches because you will always insert your hook under the threads that are "behind" the next bead in the previous round **(photo j)**. As you work, frequently double-check to make sure you add a new bead to each bead in the previous round.

Ombré diamonds bracelet

Bead crochet rope

1 Thread a Big Eye needle onto the end of the crochet cord. Following the **pattern** from top to bottom and reading each row from right to left, string all the beads for the project. String a paper

11º seed beads

- ■ color A
- ■ color B
- ■ color C
- □ color D
- ⊡ color E
- □ color F
- ▨ color G
- ■ color H
- ■ color I

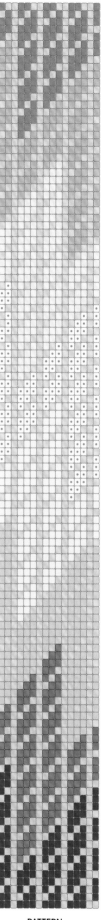

PATTERN

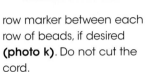

row marker between each row of beads, if desired **(photo k)**. Do not cut the cord.

2 Make a slip knot about 6 in. (15 cm) from the end of the cord, and insert your crochet hook into the loop of the slip knot. Work 16 chain stitches without beads **(photo l)**.

3 Join the chain into a ring.

4 Work in single crochet (without any beads) until you have a short tube that is about 3/8 in. (1 cm) long. This unbeaded tube will slide into the barrel clasp later, so test the fit now before moving on. Make sure you have 16 stitches in each round.

5 Slide the first 16 beads up to within about 6 in. (15 cm) of the hook. Work 16 stitches in bead single crochet, sliding one bead up to the hook

before the first yarn-over of each stitch **(photo m)**.

note
If you are getting near the end of the first beaded round and have more beads left than there are stitches in the previous round, don't worry. Just work an extra beaded stitch in one or more stitches in the previous round to make sure you end up with a total of 16 beads in the first round.

6 Working with the next 16 beads, continue in bead single crochet, sliding one bead into position before the first yarn-over of each stitch.

7 Repeat step 6 until the bead crochet rope is the desired bracelet length (less the length of the clasp) or

you've used all the strung beads. There are about 12 rounds per inch of completed beadwork. To take a break, insert a safety pin or locking stitch marker into the loop before setting your work down. This will ensure that your work doesn't accidentally come undone.

8 When the beaded portion is the desired length, work about 3/8 in. (1 cm) of unbeaded single crochet. Leaving a 6-in. (15 cm) tail, trim the cord, and pull it through the last loop.

Finishing

1 Gently slide the bead crochet tube onto a length of 3/16 in. (5 mm) braided cord **(photo n)**, being careful to avoid snagging your work. Align the cord so the end sits just inside the end of the tube.

2 Thread a tapestry needle on one tail, and sew through the unbeaded portion of the tube and the core **(photo o)**. Sew back and forth a few times to secure the cord in the tube, and trim the tail.

3 Fill the well of a clasp component about halfway with adhesive, and slide the unbeaded end of the tube into the well **(photo p)**. Allow to dry.

4 Repeat steps 1–3 at the other end of the tube. ●

stringing mistakes

Extra bead
If, once you're working, you find that you've strung an extra bead, the easiest solution is to simply crush the errant bead. To avoid cutting the cord, place the bead in the round hole of a pair of crimping pliers, and squeeze. Another option is to break the bead from within: Place the bead on your work surface, and insert a pin that is thicker than the bead hole is large. Force the pin into the hole until the bead breaks.

Missing bead
If you discover that you missed a bead, the best option is to skip that spot and go back later to add the missing bead. To do that, when you get to the spot where the missed bead was supposed to go, simply work a beadless stitch. After you are done with the piece. Anchor a short length of beading thread in the crochet tube, and exit at the point where the missing bead belongs. Sew the bead in place, angling it the same way as all the others.

Kumihimo on the double

Use a marudai, bead spinner, and a few clever techniques and bead choices to amp up your kumihimo designs.

designed by
Adrienne Gaskell

The beaded kongoh gumi Z-spiral braid, which I call 2-drop kongoh (because you drop one bead per cord each time you move a pair of cords), can be done on a kumihimo disk but I prefer the marudai in part because I find it goes at least twice as fast as using the disk.

Of course, if you prefer, this project can also be made using a disk. Instructions for the disk are available at www.BeadAndButton.com/basics.

This bracelet, which I call "Two-to-tango," consists of two 2-drop kongoh braids connected together in the center using two-hole lentil beads, SuperDuos, and 6º seed beads. For efficiency, I'll teach you to string the beads for both braids on the same cords. You'll braid the first braid, work a section of unbeaded braid, and then braid the second braid. Later, you'll fold the braid in half, and fit it into the clasp.

Setup

1 Cut four cords to 8 ft. (2.4 m) each. Line up the ends, center the cords in a 10 mm or larger split ring, and tie an overhand knot to secure the cords to the ring **(photo a)**. This creates the eight cords for your braid.
2 Feed the ring through the center hole of the marudai, slide a chopstick through the split ring, and tape the chopstick to the underside of the mirror (the "face" of the marudai) **(photo b)**. Arrange the cords around the mirror, placing two at the top (north), two at the bottom (south), and two on each side (east and west).
3 String each cord with the beads listed as follows. Refer to "Bead loading chart" to determine how many beads to string for your desired bracelet length.

Bead loading chart
Allows for a 1-in. (2.5 cm) clasp; braids are shorter than finished bracelet length.

Bracelet length	CORDS 1, 2, 4, 5, 6, 8 Total inches of 11º's on each warp	CORDS 3 AND 7 # of lentils on each warp
6½ in. (16.5 cm)	7 in. (18 cm)	26
7 in. (18 cm)	7 in. (18 cm)	28
7½ in. (19.1 cm)	8 in. (20 cm)	30
8 in (20 cm)	8 in. (20 cm)	32
8½ in. (21.6 cm)	9 in. (23 cm)	34
9 in. (23 cm)	9 in. (23 cm)	36

a

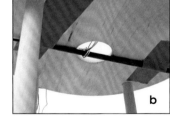

b

c

d

Materials
dark blue bracelet
7 x 1 in. (18 x 2.5 cm)
- **56** 6 mm CzechMates two-hole lentil beads (silver)
- **28** 2.5 x 5 mm SuperDuo Beads (purple)
- **56** 3 mm magatama teardrops (Toho 711, nickel-plated silver)
- **6 g** 6º seed beads (Toho 88, metallic cosmos)
- **8 g** 11º seed beads (Toho 88, metallic cosmos)
- **1** 1-in. (2.5 cm) magnetic clasp (www.adriennegaskell.com)
- **1** 10 mm (or larger) split ring
- S-Lon nylon cord (Tex 135, purple)
- S-Lon nylon Micro cord (Tex 70, black)
- Big-Eye beading needle
- marudai
- **8** 70-gram tama
- counterweights equaling about 150 g
- bead spinner with curved bead-spinner needle
- pliers or hemostat
- cord burner
- toothpicks
- two-part epoxy
- vise

Information for the orange and turquoise bracelet is listed at www. BeadAndButton.com/resources

Cords 1, 2, 4, 5, 6, and 8:
String 7–9 in. (18–23 cm) of 11ºs. To load them super-fast, use a bead spinner! (See "Spinning is fun," p. 130.)
Cord 3: String a repeating pattern of a 3 mm magatama, an 11º, a 6 mm two-hole lentil, and an 11º until you have strung the number of lentils indicated in the "Bead loading chart." End the pattern with a lentil.
Cord 7: String a repeating pattern of a 6 mm two-hole lentil, an 11º, a 3 mm magatama, and an 11º until you

have strung the number of lentils indicated in the "Bead loading chart." End the pattern with a magatama.
4 After you string each cord, tie a tama loop at the end of the cord, and attach a tama:
• About 3 in. (7.6 cm) from the end of the cord, make a fold. With the folded end, make a loop. Pass the folded end through the loop, and pull tight **(photo c)**. This loop should be pretty small, but the size isn't critical.
• Next, pass the working cord through the loop, making a large, loose loop **(photo d)**. Insert the tama or into the new loop, and pull snug.

• Begin wrapping the cord onto the tama, winding about half of the beads onto the tama as you go. Push the remaining beads up onto the mirror. Stop winding when you have about 6 in. (15 cm) of cord between the tama and the bottom edge of the mirror. Make a slipping hitch: With the working cord coming from the bottom of the tama, grasp the middle of the cord with your dominant hand palm down **(photo e)**. Flip your hand over, wrapping the cord around your fingers to form a loop **(photo f)**. Slip the loop over the tama **(photo g)**, and tighten the

e

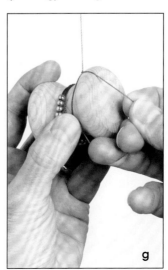

f

g

cord. **Photo h** shows the finished slipping hitch. Push the beads off the mirror down to the tama.

Braiding

1 Remove the chopstick from the split ring below the mirror, and attach your counterweight to the split ring.
2 Work a 2-drop kongoh braid with no beads for ½ in. (1.3 cm):

Movement 1: Lift cords 2 and 6 simultaneously. Hold the cords, not the tama; the tama should hang freely. The

11° seed beads

repeating pattern starting with 3 mm magatama

repeating pattern starting with 6 mm lentil

cords hang over your fingers about 1 in. (2.5 cm) from the mirror. Working in a clockwise direction, place cord 2 to the right of cord 5 and cord 6 to the left of cord 1 **(figure 1)**. Using both hands simultaneously, adjust the top and bottom pairs to look like **figure 2**.

Movement 2: Lift cords 4 (right hand) and 8 (left hand) simultaneously. Working in a clockwise direction, place cord 8 above cord 3 and cord 4 below cord 7 **(figure 3)**. Using both hands simultaneously, adjust the east and west pairs to look like **figure 4**.
Repeat the two movements until the unbeaded braid is ½ in. (1.3 cm) and all the cords are back in their original positions.

Note: The cords switch positions as you braid, but the active cords are always the ones in positions 2 and 6 and 4 and 8. It takes a total of four pairs of movements for the cords to return to their original positions. It may help to label tamas 3 and 7 so you can easily tell them apart (putting a sticker on one end of each tama is a great way to do this!).

3 Continue working as in step 2, but now add beads using my "Drop, skip, jump" method: Lift cords 2 and 6. With your thumbs, isolate the top bead on each cord. While lifting the cords about 1 in. (2.5 cm) above the

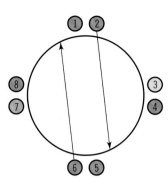

FIGURE 1

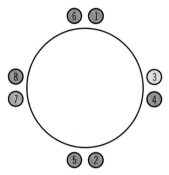

FIGURE 2

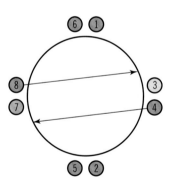

FIGURE 3

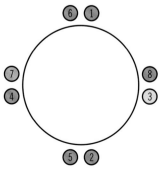

FIGURE 4

 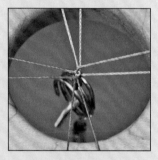

the point of the braid

It is helpful to understand what the braid is supposed to look like as you're working it. The two sets of photos here show the point of the braid both without beads (above) and with beads (below). In both sets, the photo on the left shows what the braid looks like after movement 1 and the photo on the right shows the braid after movement 2. Look closely and you will see that in each case the cords that were just moved cross over the adjacent perpendicular cords. As you are braiding, if you ever get confused about where you are in the sequence, look at the point of the braid to see which cords are on top. Those will be the last ones you worked with and you'll know that you need to move the other set next.

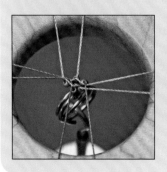 

DROP

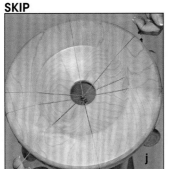

SKIP

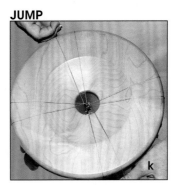

JUMP

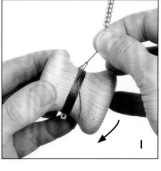

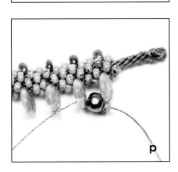

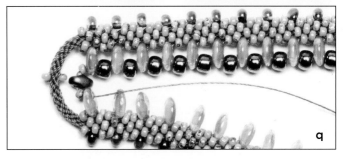

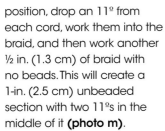

mirror and keeping tension on the cords, let the beads drop toward the point of the braid **(photo i)**. Lower the cords down to touch the mirror, and "skip" the cords until the beads drop under the horizontal cords into their new positions **(photo j)**. Watch as the beads slip under the previously braided cords all by themselves! Lift the cords slightly, and "jump" the cords into their new positions **(photo k)**. Continue to add beads on each move and keep braiding until you've used half the lentils that were strung on cords 3 and 7.

As you braid, your cords will get shorter and you'll need to adjust them as the tama get too close to the mirror. To do so, lift the tama slightly to release the tension on the cord, and rotate the tama toward you a bit **(photo l)**. The slipping hitch will release the cord, giving you more cord to work with. To release more beads onto the working cord, remove the slipping hitch from the tama. Slide more beads toward the mirror, and make a new slipping hitch. After working the last lentil into the braid, work three more pairs of movements, each time dropping one 11º on each cord (adding a total of six more 11ºs).

4 Braid ½ in. (1.3 cm) with just the cords. When cords 3 and 7 are next in the active

position, drop an 11º from each cord, work them into the braid, and then work another ½ in. (1.3 cm) of braid with no beads. This will create a 1-in. (2.5 cm) unbeaded section with two 11ºs in the middle of it **(photo m)**.

5 Work as in step 3 to braid the second braid. End this braid with a ½-in. (1.3 cm) section without beads.

6 Using pliers or a hemostat, grasp the unbeaded end of the braid just under the point of the braid. While securely holding the pliers or hemostat, use your other hand to remove the counterweight. Lift the braid from the marudai, and rest the braid and the tama on your work surface. Still holding the braid with the hemostat or pliers, use a cord burner to burn off the excess cord **(photo n)**.

Keep burning the cords until the end of the braid is sealed.

7 Fold the unbeaded section, and check to see if it fits into the clasp opening **(photo o)**. If the 11ºs in the middle of the unbeaded section are in the way, break them with pliers and remove them. If the unbraided section doesn't fit into the clasp well, burn the braids apart, melting and sealing the ends as before.

8 Remove the split ring from the beginning of the braid. Melt and seal the remaining end of the first braid, burning off the bulky starting knot.

Join

1 On 7 ft. (2 m) of Micro cord, attach a stop bead, leaving a 6-in. (15 cm) tail. Thread a Big-Eye needle

on the other end.

2 Pick up a 6º seed bead, and on one braid, sew through the open hole of the second lentil from one end, working toward the other end **(photo p)**. Repeat this stitch to add a 6º between each pair of lentils along the entire braid.

3 Pick up an 11º, a SuperDuo, and an 11º, and sew through the open hole of the end lentil on the other braid **(photo q)**. Working as in step 2, add a 6º between each pair of lentils on this braid.

4 Pick up an 11º a SuperDuo, and an 11º, and sew through the end lentil on the first braid. Retrace the thread path through all the lentils and 6ºs in each braid as well as the 11ºs and SuperDuos at each end. Sew through the first lentil

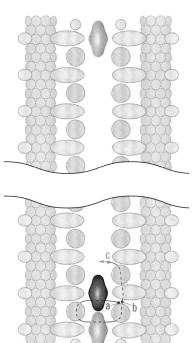

FIGURE 5

of the first braid, and adjust the tension as needed to remove most of the slack. Do not pull too tight or you will inadvertently shorten your bracelet. This is especially important if you're using Czech 6ºs, which are sometimes quite a bit smaller than Japanese seed beads. Remove the stop bead, and tie the working thread and tail with a square knot. Sew through the next 6º, and gently pull the knot into the 6º. Use a cord burner to trim the tail.

5 With the cord exiting the first 6º on braid 1, pick up a SuperDuo, and sew through the corresponding 6º on braid 2, the open hole of the previous SuperDuo, and the 6º your thread just exited **(figure 5, a–b)**. Retrace the thread path through the connection (not shown for clarity), and then sew through the next lentil and 6º **(b–c)**. Repeat these stitches for the length of the bracelet. After exiting the last 6º, sew through the open hole of the SuperDuo at this end of the bracelet, the end 6º on the other braid, and the last SuperDuo added. Retrace the thread path through the last stitch, make a few half-hitch knots in the beadwork, and burn off the extra cord.

Clasp

1 Check that the unbeaded ends of the braids fit into the appropriate openings of the clasp so that the beads butt up against the clasp. If any of the ends are too long, use the cord burner to trim.

2 Place half the clasp in a vise so that the opening points up.

3 Following the manufacturer's instructions, dispense equal amounts of two-part epoxy onto a piece of plastic or aluminum foil, and mix thoroughly. Use a toothpick to fill the opening of the clasp about halfway with a small amount of epoxy. Spread additional epoxy on one end of each braid.

sticky situation
Apply the epoxy all the way up to the beads but not on or amongst them.

4 Insert the unbeaded portion of the braids into the opening. Hold in place while pushing the braids down into the clasp for several minutes. Set aside for one hour before gluing the other ends of the braids into the other half of the clasp.

5 Allow the epoxy to cure for 24 hours before wearing the bracelet. ●

Spinning beads is a huge time-saver! One caveat — you can't use a spinner on cords that require the beads be strung in a specific pattern or orientation because the beads load randomly.

During testing for this project, it took only 45 minutes total to string the beads onto all eight cords — and most of that time was spent stringing the two patterned cords (cords 3 and 7).

To quickly load your six cords with 11ºs, pour your beads into the bowl of the bead spinner, filling the bowl to about one-third capacity. Thread your cord into the eye of the bead-spinner needle.

If your cord won't fit through the eye of the needle (or if the cord and the needle are too thick to pass through your beads), make a leader:
• Cut a 6-in. (15 cm) piece of 4–6-lb. Fireline, and thread it through the eye of the needle. Tie the ends together with an overhand knot.
• Now, thread your cord into the loop of Fireline.

Rotate the bowl by turning the spindle in whichever direction is most comfortable for you. As the bowl spins, dip the tip of the needle into the beads, pointing it in the opposite direction the bowl is spinning, and watch as the beads load onto the needle. You should be able to get 3–4 in. (7.6–10 cm) of beads loaded onto your needle in 30 seconds or so. Adjust the needle position as needed.

Spinning is fun!

BEAD WEAVING

Seed *of* life
earrings

Made up of seven interlocking circles, the seed of life pattern is often used to symbolize the building blocks of life. This fun beaded version is super easy to make — perfect for spring!

designed by **Svetlana Chernitsky**

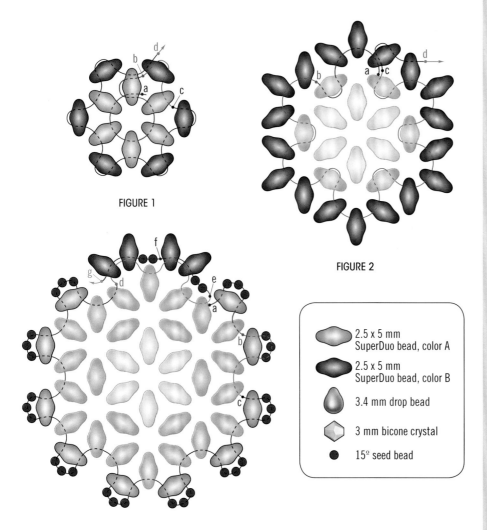

FIGURE 1

FIGURE 2

FIGURE 3

Difficulty rating

Materials
gold/dark purple earrings
1³⁄₈ in. (3.5 cm)
- 2.5 x 5 mm SuperDuo beads
  - **32** color A (metallic Aztec gold matte)
  - **60** color B (luster metallic amethyst)
- **4** 3.4 mm drop beads (Miyuki, metallic dark bronze)
- **2** 3 mm bicone crystals (Swarovski, smoky quartz)
- **1 g** 15º seed beads (Toho 332, gold luster raspberry)
- **1** pair of earring findings
- Fireline, 6 lb. test
- beading needles, #11 or #12

gold/indigo colors
- 2.5 x 5 mm Twin seed beads (in place of SuperDuos)
  - color A (Preciosa, jet plum pearl)
  - color B (Preciosa, silky light gold)
- 3.4 mm drop beads (Miyuki, metallic dark bronze)
- 3 mm bicone crystals (Swarovski, smoky quartz)
- 15º seed bead (Toho 459, gold luster dark topaz)

2.5 x 5 mm SuperDuo bead, color A

2.5 x 5 mm SuperDuo bead, color B

3.4 mm drop bead

3 mm bicone crystal

15º seed bead

Earrings
1 On 1½ yd. (1.4 m) of thread, pick up six color A SuperDuo beads, tie a square knot, and sew through the first A again to form a ring, leaving a 9-in. (23 cm) tail. Sew through the open hole of the same A **(figure 1, a–b)**.

2 Pick up a color B SuperDuo bead, sew through the open hole of the same B, and continue through the open hole of the next A **(b–c)**. Repeat this stitch five times to complete the round, and step up through the first B added **(c–d)**.

3 Work in a counterclockwise direction: Pick up three Bs, sew down through the next B added in the previous round, and continue up through the other hole of the same B **(figure 2, a–b)**. Repeat this stitch five times to complete the round **(b–c)**. To step up, sew through the inner hole of the next B, and continue through the open hole of the same B and the open hole of the following B **(c–d)**.

tension tips
If your stitching tension is a little loose, your earrings could end up a little floppy. To avoid this, stitch with tight tension or retrace your thread path through each round.

4 Work in a clockwise direction: Pick up an A and three 15º seed beads, sew through the open hole of the same A, and continue through the open hole of the next B in the previous round **(figure 3, a–b)**. Pick up an A and

did you know?
Preciosa Ornela originally introduced the two-hole Twin seed bead in late 2011 to early 2012, but the size and thickness of these beads were somewhat inconsistent. In response, in late 2012 Preciosa released a new version called the pressed Twin bead, which offers a more consistent and uniform size. Both types of beads are still available, so read descriptions closely.

pretty pendant

Make a pendant to match your earrings! Either make it exactly the same as the earring or simplify it by working step 4 all the way around and adding a hanging loop.

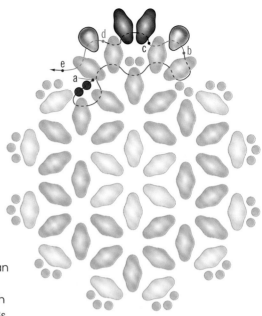

FIGURE 4

three 15ºs, sew through the open hole of the same A, and continue through the open hole of the following two Bs **(b–c)**. Repeat these two stitches to add a total of 10 bead sets, stopping two stitches before the round is completed **(c–d)**.

5 Pick up two Bs, sew through the open hole of the next B in the previous round, pick up two Bs, and sew through the outer holes of the following two Bs **(d–e)**.

6 Work in a counterclockwise direction: Pick up two 15ºs, and sew through the inner holes of the next two Bs in the previous round **(e–f)**. Repeat this stitch once **(f–g)**.

7 Pick up two 15ºs, and sew clockwise through the beadwork as shown **(figure 4, a–b)**.

8 Pick up a drop bead, and sew through the open hole of the next B **(b–c)**. Pick up two Bs, and sew through the open hole of the following B **(c–d)**. Pick up a drop, and sew through the open hole of the next B **(d–e)**. Sew through the beadwork as shown **(figure 5, a–b)**.

9 Pick up two 15ºs and the loop of an ear wire, and sew through the open hole of the next B **(b–c)**. Sew through the other hole of the two adjacent Bs **(c–d)**. Retrace the thread path, and end the working thread.

10 To embellish the center, thread a needle on the tail. If necessary, sew through the open space between the beads to position the tail on the front side of the beadwork. Pick up a 3 mm bicone crystal, skip the next two As in the inner ring, and sew through the inner hole of the following A. Sew back through the crystal, the inner hole of the opposite A, and the inner hole of the following A **(e–f)**. The crystal will sit slightly elevated in the center. End the tail.

11 Repeat steps 1–10 to make a second earring. ●

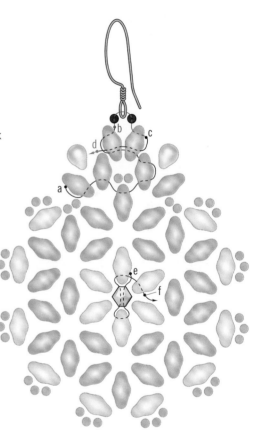

FIGURE 5

interchangeable

Svetlana says: You can use Twin seed beads in place of SuperDuos. I recommend using original Twin seed beads for color A and pressed Twin beads for color B. If you do this, you'll also need to adapt steps 6–7 by picking up one 15º instead of two.

NETTING

Hexagonal
lace cuff

Use Twin beads, seed beads, and farfalle beads
to create simple hexagons and connect them
for a dramatic cuff-style bracelet.

designed by **Kerrie Slade**

Whether you make this bracelet
with three rows or two (see p. 137),
you'll love stitching these lacy
star-shaped components.

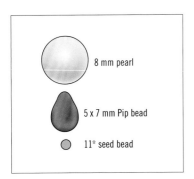

8 mm pearl

5 x 7 mm Pip bead

11° seed bead

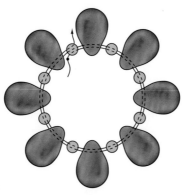

FIGURE 1

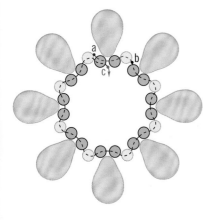

FIGURE 2

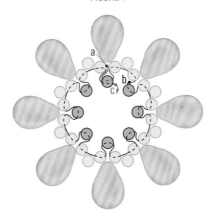

FIGURE 3

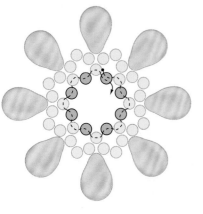

FIGURE 4

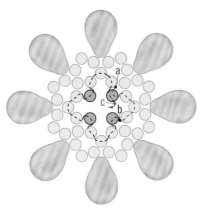

FIGURE 5

Difficulty rating

◆ ⬡ ⬡ ⬡ ⬡

Materials
bracelet 7 in. (18 cm)

- **5** 8 mm glass pearls (white)
- **40** 5 x 7 mm Pip beads*
  (#23980_29400, green/purple iris)
- **5 g** 11° seed beads
  (Czech 18565, metallic aqua terra)
- **3 in.** (7.6 cm) cable chain
  (2 x 3 mm links)
- **10** 4 mm jump rings, 22-gauge
- **2** 6 mm jump rings, 18-gauge
- lobster claw clasp
- Fireline 6 lb. test
- beading needle, #12
- **2** pairs of chainnose, flatnose, and/or
  bentnose pliers

Flowers

1 Work the back of the flower in rounds:
Round 2: On 33 in. (85 cm) of thread,
pick up an 11° seed bead and a Pip
bead eight times. Sew through all the
beads again to form a ring, leaving
a 6-in. (15 cm) tail. Step up by sewing
through the first 11° again **(figure 1)**.
Round 2: Pick up two 11°s, and sew
through the next 11° in the previous
round **(figure 2, a–b)**. Repeat this stitch
seven times to complete the round, and
step up through the first 11° added in
this round **(b–c)**. Keep a firm tension,
and make sure that all the new 11°s

are on the same side of the Pips.
Round 3: Pick up an 11°, and sew
through the next two 11°s in the
previous round **(figure 3, a–b)**. Repeat
this stitch seven times to complete the
round, and step up through the first
bead added in this round **(b–c)**.
Round 4: Pick up an 11°, and sew
through the next 11° in the previous
round. Repeat this stitch seven times
to complete the round, and step up
through the first 11° added in this round
(figure 4).
Round 5: Work a decrease round: Pick
up an 11°, and sew through the next

139

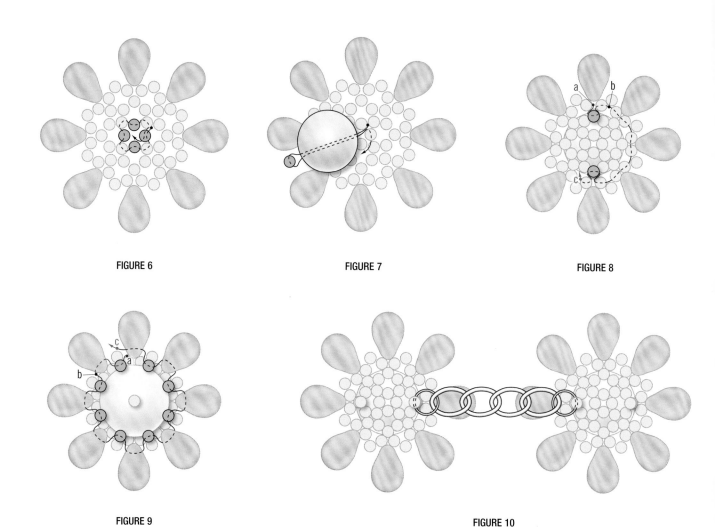

FIGURE 6

FIGURE 7

FIGURE 8

FIGURE 9

FIGURE 10

11º in the previous round and the next two adjacent 11ºs **(figure 5, a–b)**. Repeat this stitch three times to complete the round, and step up through the first 11º added in this round **(b–c)**.
Round 6: Pick up an 11º, and sew through the next 11º in the previous round. Repeat this stitch three times to complete the round, and step up through the first 11º added in this round **(figure 6)**.
2 Retrace the thread path through all eight 11ºs added in the last two rounds. Pull your thread firmly as you work. Exit an 11º in the last round **(round 6)**.
3 Sew through the center opening to the front of your work and pick up an 8 mm pearl and an 11º. Sew back through the pearl, and continue through the next 11º in round 6 **(figure 7)**. To secure the pearl firmly in the center of your Pip flower, retrace the thread path through the pearl and 11º and the

beads in round 6 until you have sewn through all four 11ºs added in round 6.
4 Sew through to the back of the flower, and exit in the middle of a pair of beads added in round 2. Pick up an 11º, and sew through the other bead in the pair **(figure 8, a–b)**. Sew through the beadwork to exit the middle of the opposite pair of 11ºs, and repeat the stitch **(b–c)**. Retrace the thread path to reinforce the newly added beads. These are the beads to which you will attach the chains.
5 Sew through the beadwork to exit a Pip on the front of the flower. Pick up an 11º, and sew through the next Pip **(figure 9, a–b)**. Repeat this stitch seven times to complete the round, keeping a firm tension **(b–c)**. End the working thread and tail (Basics).
6 Repeat steps 1–5 to create a total of five flowers.

Assemble the bracelet

1 Cut the chain into four ½-in. (1.3 cm) pieces and two ¼-in. (6 mm) pieces.
2 Open a 4 mm jump ring (Basics). On any flower, pass the open ring through an 11º added in step 4 of "Flowers" and an end link of a ½-in. (1.3 cm) chain. Close the jump ring. Open another 4 mm ring, and pass it through the other end link and an 11º added in step 4 of another flower **(figure 10)**.
3 Repeat step 2 to attach the remaining flowers.
4 Use a 4 mm jump ring to connect a ¼-in. (6 mm) piece of chain to an end flower. Open a 6 mm jump ring, and attach it to a lobster claw clasp and the end of the chain. Repeat this step to add the final chain section at the other end of the bracelet but omit the lobster claw clasp. The 6 mm ring will serve as the catch for the clasp. ●

THREE-DROP PEYOTE STITCH

Santa baby
bracelet

Wrap this old-school St. Nick
around your wrist and
fasten it with a festive
snowball clasp.

designed by **Josie Fabre**

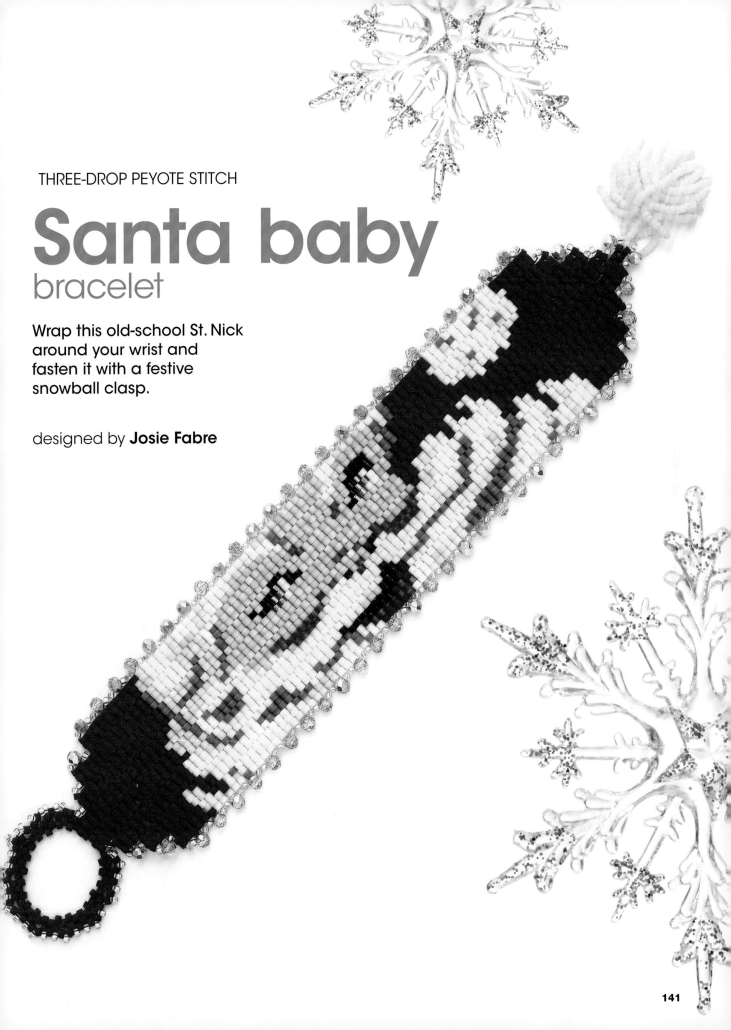

Difficulty rating

Materials

bracelet 7 in. (18 cm)

- 11º cylinder beads (Miyuki)
  - **4 g** color A (DB0753, opaque matte red)
  - **3 g** color B (DB351, opaque matte white)
  - **1 g** color C (DB1589, matte ghost gray)
  - **1 g** color D (DB0357, matte pale gray)
  - **2 g** color E (DB1512, opaque matte peaches-and-cream)
  - **1 g** color F (DB0654, opaque dark red)
  - **1 g** color G (DB1262, matte transparent dark cranberry)
  - **1 g** color H (DB0044, silver-lined aqua)
  - **1 g** color J (DB0868, opaque pink Champagne)
- 15º seed beads
  - **2 g** color K (Toho 21, silver-lined crystal)
  - **2 g** color L (Toho 41, opaque white)
- 60–65 3 mm crystal rondelles (silver and clear)
- nylon beading thread, size D or Fireline 4 lb. or 6 lb. test
- beading needles, #12

Bracelet band

1 On a comfortable length of thread, attach a stop bead, leaving an 18-in. (46 cm) tail. Starting at the upper-right corner of the **pattern** for the body of the bracelet, pick up 24 color A 11º cylinder beads for rows 1 and 2. (The tapered ends are shown separated from the body so you can see where the decrease rows begin.)

2 Following the **pattern**, work the body of the bracelet in even-count three-drop peyote stitch using the appropriate-color cylinders. End and add thread as needed, and end the working thread and tail when you complete the band.

3 Follow the **pattern** to taper this end of the band: Sew under the adjacent edge thread bridge, and sew back through the last six beads your thread exited. Work four rows with three stitches per row, five rows with two stitches per row, and five rows with one stitch per row. Sew through the beadwork to exit the last stitch added, and work four single-bead stitches. If you have at least 1 yd. (.9 m) of thread remaining, set it aside. If your thread is shorter than 1 yd. (.9 m), end it, and add a new one, exiting where the old one ended.

tip While working the taper, you may find it helpful to sew through to the other edge of the band before starting the next set of decrease rows. This will allow you to work even-count turns instead of odd-count turns for most of the taper.

4 With the remaining tail, taper the starting end of the band, working seven rows with three stitches per row, three rows with two stitches per row, and four rows with one stitch per row. End the thread.

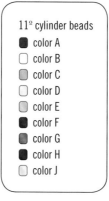

11º cylinder beads
- ■ color A
- □ color B
- ▨ color C
- □ color D
- ▨ color E
- ■ color F
- ▨ color G
- ■ color H
- ▨ color J

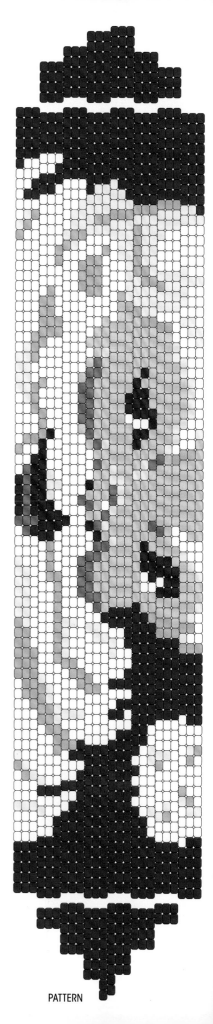

PATTERN

Daisies on the double bracelet

Stitch two dainty daisy chains and join them with a row of Pellet beads for an easy bracelet with everyday style.

designed by **Julia Gerlach**

Difficulty rating

Materials

bracelet 7¼ in. (18.4 cm)

- **24** 3 x 4 mm faceted rondelles (teal AB)
- **22** 4 mm crystal pearls (Swarovski, platinum)
- **22** 4 x 6 mm Pellet beads (crystal full chrome)
- **3 g** 15º seed beads (Miyuki 4201, galvanized silver)
- **1** 14 x 9 mm filigree 2-strand box clasp
- **4** 4 mm jump rings (if needed)
- beading needles, #12
- Fireline 6 lb. test
- **2** pairs of chainnose, flatnose, and/or bentnose pliers (optional)

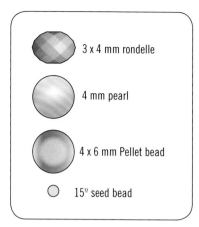

3 x 4 mm rondelle

4 mm pearl

4 x 6 mm Pellet bead

15º seed bead

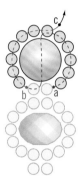

FIGURE 4

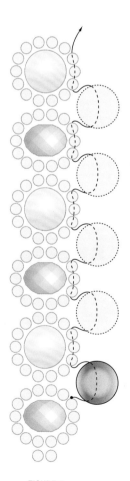

FIGURE 5

FIGURE 1

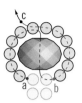 

FIGURE 2   **FIGURE 3**

Daisy chains

1 On 2 yd. (1.8 m) of thread and leaving an 8-in. (20 cm) tail, pick up four 15º seed beads, and sew through them all again to create two parallel pairs **(figure 1)**.

2 Pick up six 15ºs and a 3 x 4 mm rondelle, and sew through the 15º next to the one your thread exited at the start of this step **(figure 2, a–b)**.

3 Pick up six 15ºs, and sew through the last 15º picked up before the rondelle in the previous step **(b–c)**.

4 Pick up two 15ºs, sew through the last two 15ºs your thread exited in the previous step, and then sew through the two new 15ºs **(figure 3)**.

5 Pick up six 15ºs and a 4 mm pearl, and sew through the 15º next to the one your thread exited at the start of this step **(figure 4, a–b)**.

6 Pick up six 15ºs, and sew through the last 15º picked up before the pearl in the previous step **(b–c)**.

7 Repeat steps 4–6 for the desired length, alternating between a rondelle and a pearl in the center of each stitch. End the chain with a pair of 15ºs, as in step 4. Do not end the thread.

8 Repeat steps 1–7 to make a second daisy chain.

Assembly

1 Add a new 18-in. (46 cm) thread at one end of a daisy chain, and exit the fourth 15º from the end pair of 15ºs. Pick up a Pellet bead, and sew through the middle three 15ºs on this edge of the next pearl **(figure 5)**. Repeat this stitch for the length of the chain. End the working thread and tail.

2 Add a new thread at one end of the other daisy chain, and work as in step 1,

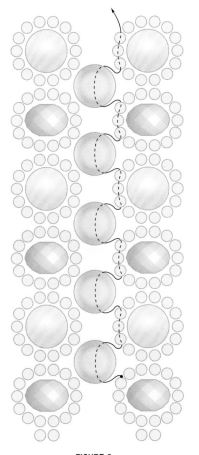

FIGURE 6

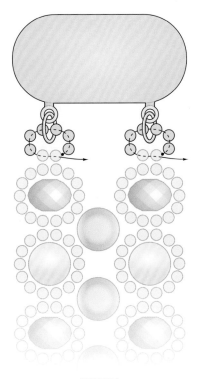

FIGURE 7

but sew through the Pellet beads attached to the other chain instead of adding new ones **(figure 6)**. End the thread.

3 With a thread remaining at one end of a chain, pick up six 15°s and a jump ring attached to the clasp. Sew through the end pair of 15°s again **(figure 7)**. Retrace the thread path a few times, and end the thread.

note The clasp I used came with jump rings, but they were too small to accommodate the 15°s so I removed them and replaced them with larger (4 mm) jump rings.

4 Repeat step 3 to attach each end of both chains to the clasp. ●

A Pellet bead looks like a compressed hourglass, with the hole passing through the narrow "waist" in the center of the bead.

Multi-Stitch
Projects

PEYOTE STITCH / SQUARE STITCH

Garden path
bracelet

Create a stylized garden, artfully adorned with rows of frolicking seed beads swaying on a square-stitch base and a cultivated bezel setting as the centerpiece.

designed by **Cary Bruner**

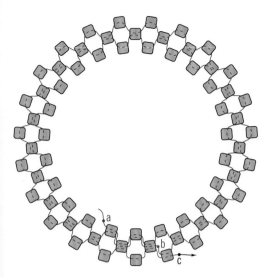

FIGURE 1

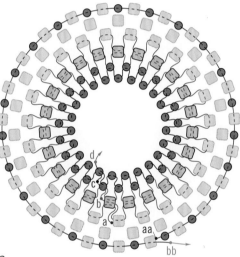

FIGURE 2

a

Difficulty rating

□ 11º cylinder
bead, color A

□ 11º cylinder
bead, color B

● 8º seed bead

• 15º seed bead

● 11º seed bead

⬡ 3 mm bicone
crystal

Materials
green bracelet 7 x 1⅜ in. (18 x 3.5 cm)
- **1** 18 mm rivoli (purple haze)
- bicone crystals (Swarovski)
  - **23** 4 mm (purple haze)
  - **55** 3 mm (light rose)
- **14 g** 8º seed beads (Miyuki 318Q,
  opaque olive luster gold)
- **1 g** 11º seed beads (Miyuki 318J, light
  olivine luster gold)
- 11º cylinder beads (Miyuki)
  - **1 g** color A (DB133, opaque
  rainbow luster olive)
  - **1 g** 11º color B (DB105, transparent
  gold luster dark red)
- **2 g** 15º seed beads (Miyuki F460I, olive
  bronze matte metallic iris)
- **1** 34 mm slide-end tube clasp
- chainnose pliers
- beading needles, #11 or #12
- Fireline, 6 lb. test
- cardboard or thread bobbin (optional)

*Information for the gray bracelet is
listed at www.BeadAndButton.com/resources.*

Bezel

1 On 3 yd. (2.7 m) of thread, pick
up 46 color A 11º cylinder beads,
leaving a 1-yd. (.9 m) tail. Sew
through the first four As picked up,
going in the same direction, and
pull the thread tight to form a ring.
These beads will shift to form the
first two rounds as the next round
is added **(figure 1, a-b)**. If desired,
wrap the tail thread around a thread
bobbin or piece of cardboard.
2 Work in rounds of tubular peyote
stitch as follows, stepping up at the
end of each round. To keep the tension
even, you will alternate the threads
you stitch with.
Round 3: Using the working thread,
work a round using As **(b-c)**.
Round 4: Unwind the tail and using
the tail, work a round using color B 11º
cylinder beads on the inside of the
ring **(figure 2, a-b)**.
Round 5: Using the tail, work a round
using 15º seed beads **(b-c)**. Place the
rivoli into the bezel so the front faces the
15ºs just added (not shown in the figure
for clarity).
Round 6: Using the thread on the back
of the bezel, work a round using 15ºs,
but do not step up at the end of the
round **(aa-bb)**. Pull the thread tight
to secure the rivoli.
Round 7: Using the thread on the front
of the bezel, work a round using 15ºs
(c-d). Retrace the thread path to cinch
up the beads, and end the tail.

Round 8: With the thread on the back
of the bezel, use a tight tension to work
a round with Bs, and step up at the
end of the round **(photo a)**. Since you
skipped the step-up after round 6, the
new Bs will sit adjacent to the 15ºs.

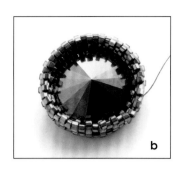
b

c

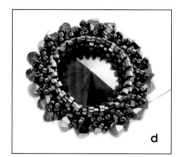
d

e

Rounds 9-10: Work two more rounds using As, stepping up at the end of each round **(photo b)**.

3 Continuing with the bezel positioned face-down, sew through the beadwork to exit the closest B in round 8 (the round of Bs that is closest to the back of the bezel). Pick up two 15ºs, an 11º seed bead, a 4 mm crystal, an 11º, and two 15ºs, and working in the reverse direction, sew through the previous B in the round, with the needle pointing back toward the B your thread is exiting **(photo c)**. The thread should exit above the loop.

4 Work as in step 3 to add a total of 23 loops around the outside of the bezel **(photo d)**. Each new loop will overlap part of the previous loop. End and add thread as needed.

5 Sew under the last and first loop added in order to position the thread on the front surface of the bezel. Sew through the beadwork to exit the nearest B in the round of Bs closest to the front of the rivoli **(photo e)**.

6 Pick up two 15ºs, a 3 mm bicone crystal, and two 15ºs, and working as before (going in the reverse direction), sew through the previous B in the same round with the needle pointing back toward the B your thread is exiting **(figure 3)**. Pull the thread tight. The thread should be exit above the loop.

7 Work as in step 6 to add a total of 23 loops around the bezel. Each new loop will overlap part of the previous loop. Sew through the beadwork to exit an "up" A in the last round on the back of the bezel, and set the bezel aside for later.

Base

1 On a comfortable length of thread, string a stop bead, leaving a 6-in. (15 cm) tail. Pick up 14 8º seed beads **(figure 4, a-b)**.

2 To start the next row, pick up two 8ºs, sew through the adjacent two 8ºs in the previous row, and continue through the two 8ºs just added **(b-c)**.

3 Pick up two 8ºs, sew through the adjacent two 8ºs in the previous row,

and continue through the next two 8ºs in the same row. Sew through the adjacent four 8ºs in the new row **(figure 5)**. Repeat this stitch five times to complete the row.

4 Work as in steps 1-3 for the desired bracelet length (less the length of the clasp). End and add thread as needed. To make a 6¼-in. (15.9 cm) base, work a total of 57 rows. Remove the stop bead, and end the working thread and tail.

Clasp

1 Gently slide an end row of the base within the slide-end tube clasp.

2 Center the beadwork within the clasp, and check the fit. If the base's width isn't wide enough to fill the tube, place a loose 8º inside the tube on each end.

3 Use a pair of chainnose pliers to fold the open end of the clasp flat.

Edge embellishment

1 Add a comfortable length of thread to one end row of the base (not counting the row inside the clasp), with the needle exiting an edge 8º facing away from the beadwork **(figure 6, point a)**.

2 Sew under the nearest edge thread bridge, pick up four 15ºs, skip a row, and sew under the next edge thread bridge in the same direction to form a loop **(figure 6)**. Repeat this stitch for the remainder of the edge. End and add thread as needed.

FIGURE 3

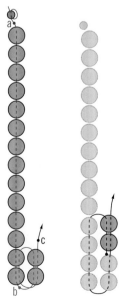
FIGURE 4   FIGURE 5

FIGURE 6

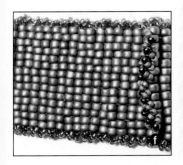

make a matching pendant!

Make a second bezel setting, and add a bail: With the working thread, sew through the beadwork to exit a B on the back of the bezel, pick up 20 11ºs, and sew through the corresponding B on the front of the bezel. Retrace the thread path to reinforce the connection, and end the thread.

3 Sew through the end row of 8ºs to reach the opposite edge, and work as in step 2 to add loops on this edge.

Top embellishment

1 To get into position to add the top embellishment, sew through the next 13 8ºs in the second-to-last end row **(figure 7, a–b)**.

2 Place the base horizontally on your bead mat. Pick up two 15ºs, an 11º, and two 15ºs, and sew through the adjacent 8º in the same row, with the needle pointing toward the 8º your thread just exited, to create a loop that is leaning toward the clasp **(b–c)**. The loop should be positioned on the right side, and the thread should be exiting on the left side of the 8º. Repeat this stitch four times, sewing over the previous loop as each new loop is added. This will position each new loop to slightly overlap the previous loop.

3 Pick up two 15ºs, a 3 mm crystal, and two 15ºs, and work as in step 2, except position the loop to face away from the clasp. The loop should be leaning

toward the left, and the thread should be exiting on the right side of the loop **(figure 8)**.

4 To complete the row, work as in step 2 to add five additional loops, except continue to position the loops and thread in the same direction as the loop with the crystal just added **(figure 9, a–b)**. This set of five loops should be leaning to the left, away from the clasp, and the thread should be exiting to the right of each loop. This will cause each embellishment row to form a slight arch **(photo f)**.

5 Sew under the last loop added, and continue through the beadwork as shown to get into position to add the next row of embellishment **(c–d)**.

6 Work as in steps 2–5 to complete a total of 10 top embellishment rows. End and add thread as needed. Set the working thread aside.

7 With the base still positioned horizontally, add a comfortable length of thread to the opposite end of the base, with the thread exiting the end bead of the second-to-last row. Work as in steps 2–5

to add a total of 10 top embellishment rows to this end of the base. Set this working thread aside.

Assembly

1 Place the bezel on the top of the base, centered within the top embellishment rows. With the working thread from the bezel, sew through an adjacent 8º on the base, and continue through the nearest "up" A cylinder in the last round of the bezel. Repeat this stitch around the outside of the bezel to secure it to the base. End the bezel's working thread.

2 With the working thread from either top embellishment row, work as before to add additional rows of embellishment until the embellishment reaches the edge of the bezel. For the row closest to the bezel, you may want to omit the center loop with the crystal. End this working thread.

3 Work as in step 2 to add top embellishment rows to the opposite side of the base. ●

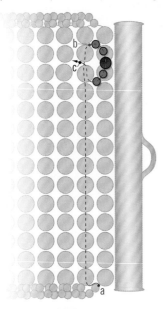

FIGURE 7

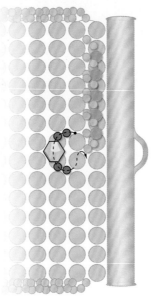

FIGURE 8

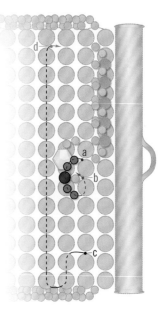

FIGURE 9

Surfin' around
the waves

You'll love this pendant, which uses a lovely
stitching pattern and adds a rivoli in the center.

designed by **Jimmie Boatright**

Pendant

1 On a comfortable length of thread, attach a stop bead, leaving an 8-in. (20 cm) tail.

2 Pick up two color A 11º cylinder beads, two color B 11º cylinder beads, two color C 11º cylinder beads, two color D 11º seed beads, two color E 11º seed beads, two color F 11º hex-cut seed beads, two color G 8º seed beads, and two color H 8º hex-cut seed beads **(figure 1, a–b)**. These beads will form the first two rows as the third row is added. Do not tie any knots in these rows because you will be removing them when you join the ends together.

3 Work in flat even-count peyote stitch as follows, picking up one bead per stitch and referring to **figure 1**:

Row 3: H, G, F, E, D, C, B, A **(b–c)**.
Row 4: A, A, B, C, D, E, F, G **(c–d)**.
Row 5: G, F, E, D, C, B, A, A **(d–e)**.
Row 6: A, A, A, B, C, D, E, F **(e–f)**.
Row 7: F, E, D, C, B, A, A, A **(f–g)**.
Row 8: A, A, A, A, B, C, D, E **(g–h)**.
Row 9: F, E, D, C, B, A, A, A **(h–i)**.
Row 10: A, A, A, B, C, D, E, F **(i–j)**.
Row 11: G, F, E, D, C, B, A, A **(j–k)**.

Row 12: A, A, B, C, D, E, F, G **(k–l)**.
Row 13: H, G, F, E, D, C, B, A **(l–m)**.
Row 14: A, B, C, D, E, F, G, H **(m–n)**.
Row 15: Color I 6º seed bead, H, G, F, E, D, C, B **(n–o)**.
Row 16: B, C, D, E, F, G, H, I **(o–p)**. Work an increase turn: Pick up an I and an A, and sew back through the I just picked up **(p–q)**. This creates a point.
Row 17: I, H, G, F, E, D, C, B **(q–r)**.
Row 18: A, B, C, D, E, F, G, H **(r–s)**.
Row 19: H, G, F, E, D, C, B, A **(s–t)**.
Row 20: A, A, B, C, D, E, F, G **(t–u)**.
Row 21: G, F, E, D, C, B, A, A **(u–v)**.
Row 22: A, A, A, B, C, D, E, F **(v–w)**.
Row 23: F, E, D, C, B, A, A, A **(w–x)**.
Row 24: A, A, A, A, B, C, D, E **(x–y)**.

4 Repeat rows 9–24 to create a total of nine "bumps" (the protruding curves) and "dips" (the concave areas between the bumps), ending with row 18 on the last repeat. End and add thread as needed.

5 Remove the stop bead, and take out the first two rows of the beadwork. Zip the two ends of the beadwork together, and end the threads.

Difficulty rating

Materials
pendant 2¾ in (7 cm)

- 1 12 mm rivoli (Swarovski, purple haze)
- 4 g 6º seed beads, color I (Toho 222, dark bronze)
- 3 g 8º hex-cut seed beads, color H (Toho SB2631, silver-lined matte amber AB; www.fusionbeads.com)
- 3 g 8º seed beads, color G (Miyuki 454, metallic dark plum iris)
- 3 g 11º hex-cut seed beads, color F (Miyuki 188, metallic purple gold iris)
- 3 g 11º seed beads
  - color D (Miyuki 4218, Duracoat galvanized dusty orchid)
  - color E (Toho 704, matte Andromeda)
- 11º cylinder beads
  - 4 g color A (Miyuki DB0611, dyed silver-lined wine)
  - 3 g color B (Miyuki DB1843, Duracoat galvanized dark mauve)
  - 3 g color C (Miyuki DB1831, Duracoat galvanized silver)
- 1 g 15º seed beads (Miyuki 4201, Duracoat galvanized silver)
- Fireline, 6 lb. test
- beading needles, #11 or #12
- thread bobbin or a piece of cardboard

note Lay out your beads in order on your work surface, and label them A–I. This will help you pick up the correct beads for each stitch, alternating between ascending and descending order.

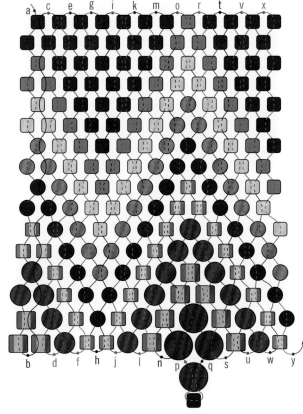

FIGURE 1

■		11º cylinder bead, color A
■		11º cylinder bead, color B
■		11º cylinder bead, color C
●		11º seed bead, color D
●		11º seed bead, color E
▣		11º hex-cut seed bead, color F
●		8º seed bead, color G
▣		8º hex-cut seed bead, color H
●		6º seed bead, color I
○		15º seed bead

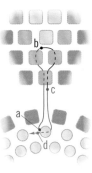

FIGURE 2

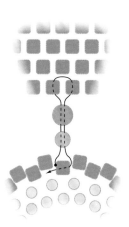

FIGURE 3

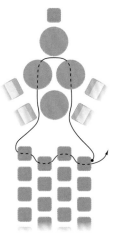

FIGURE 4

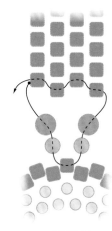

FIGURE 5

Bezel

1 On 4 ft. (1.2 m) of thread, pick up 30 As, and sew through the first three beads again to form a ring, leaving a 3-ft. (.9 m) tail. These beads will shift to form rounds 1 and 2 as the next round is added. Wrap the tail on a thread bobbin or a piece of cardboard.

2 Work rounds of tubular peyote stitch for the back of the bezel as follows, and step up at the end of each round.

Round 3: Work a round using As.

Rounds 4–5: Work both rounds using 15º seed beads.

3 Flip the beadwork over, and place the rivoli face up into the beadwork. Unwind the tail, and stitching off the As in round 1, work two rounds of 15ºs for the front of the bezel, using a tight tension. End the working thread, but not the tail. With the tail, sew through the beadwork to exit the first round of 15ºs added on the front of the bezel.

Center attachment

You will be connecting the inside-edge cylinder beads of each bump to the front of the bezel and the dips to the back of the bezel.

1 With the working thread of the bezel, sew through the edge B on the top of a bump and the next diagonal B **(figure 2, a–b)**. Turn, sew back through the adjacent B, and continue back through the first B **(b–c)**. Sew through the 15º your thread exited on the bezel, going in the same direction as before

a

(c–d), and continue through the bezel to exit the next 15º in the same round that is nearest to the following bump.

2 Work as in step 1 to attach the remaining eight bumps around the bezel, sewing through one or two 15ºs in the same round so the bumps are equally spaced around the bezel. Then sew through the bezel to the back of the pendant, exiting the last round of As nearest the 15ºs.

3 With the back of the pendant facing up, pick up a D and a G, and sew through the nearest edge A near the center of the adjacent dip. Turn, and sew back through the adjacent edge A and the G and D just added, and continue through the A your thread exited at the start of the step, going in the same direction as before **(figure 3)**. Repeat this stitch to attach the remaining eight dips around the bezel, sewing through the beadwork to the nearest A in the same round of the bezel that is nearest the next dip, and end the thread.

b

Bail

1 On 30 in. (76 cm) of thread, attach a stop bead, leaving a 10-in. (25 cm) tail. Pick up four As, and work in flat even-count peyote stitch for 28 rows to form a strip. With the working thread exiting the right side of the strip, sew through a right-hand 6º on the back of the pendant, with your needle pointing toward the outside edge of the pendant. Turn, and sew back through the adjacent 6º, with your needle pointing toward the center of the pendant. Continue through the last two rows of the strip as shown **(figure 4 and photo a)**. Retrace the thread path, and end the working thread.

2 Remove the stop bead from the tail. Sew through the nearest G and D that attach the corresponding dip to the bezel, the adjacent A in the bezel, the D and G that attach the next dip to the bezel, and the last two rows of the strip as shown **(figure 5 and photo b)**. Retrace the thread path through this connection, and end the tail. **◦**

All aglow
bracelet

Attach sparkling cup chain to a base of right-angle weave, and adorn it with crystals and Rizo beads for a radiant shine.

designed by **Ora Shai**

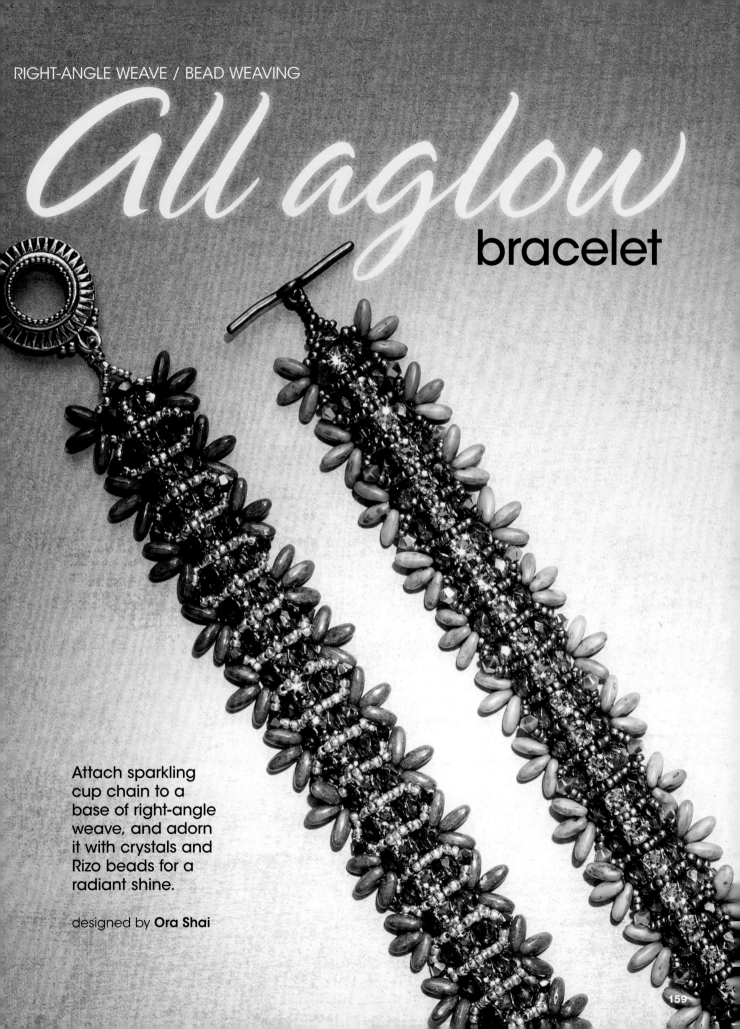

Difficulty rating

Materials

silver/purple bracelet 8 in. (20 cm)

- **78** 2.5 x 5 mm Rizo beads (luster opaque amethyst)
- **76** 4 mm fire-polished beads (transparent amethyst luster)
- **24** 3 mm bicone crystals (Swarovski, crystal rose gold)
- **2 g** 11º seed beads (Toho PF558, permanent galvanized aluminum)
- **2 g** 15º seed beads (Toho PF558, permanent galvanized aluminum)
- **5½ in. (14 cm)** 4 mm catch-free cup chain (blush rose)
- **1** toggle clasp
- Fireline, 6 lb. test
- beading needles, #12

Information for the alternate colorway is listed at www.BeadAndButton.com/ resources.

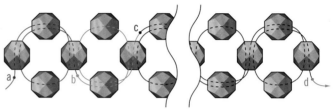

FIGURE 1

 4 mm fire-polished bead

 15º seed bead

 11º seed bead

 2.5 x 5 mm Rizo bead

 3 mm bicone crystal

 4 mm cup chain

Base

1 On a comfortable length of thread, pick up four 4 mm fire-polished beads. Sew through the beads again to form them into a ring, leaving a 6-in. (15 cm) tail. Continue through the first three 4 mms so your working thread is exiting opposite the tail, and snug up the beads **(figure 1, a–b)**.

2 Working in right-angle weave (RAW), pick up three 4 mms, and sew through the 4 mm your thread exited at the start of this step. Continue through the first two 4 mms just added **(b–c)**, and tighten. Continue working in RAW using a tight tension for the desired length of bracelet, less 1⅛ in. (2.9 cm) for the clasp, and ending with an odd number of stitches **(c–d)**. End and add thread as needed. This 8-in. (20 cm) bracelet is 25 stitches long.

3 Pick up three 15º seed beads, an 11º seed bead, eight 15ºs, and the loop of the toggle ring, and sew through the 11º just added **(figure 2, a–b)**. Pick up three 15ºs, and sew through the 4 mm your thread exited at the start of this step, going in the same direction **(b–c)**. Retrace the thread path to reinforce the connection (not shown in the figure for clarity).

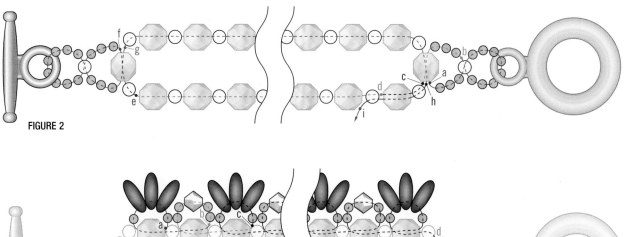

FIGURE 2

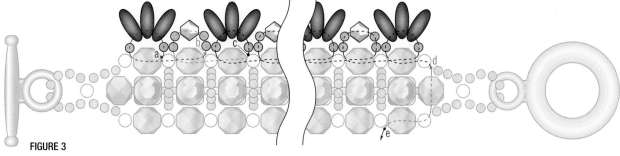

FIGURE 3

4 Pick up an 11º, and sew through the next 4 mm on the bottom edge **(c-d)**. Repeat this stitch for the remainder of the bottom edge **(d-e)**, keeping an even tension. Pick up an 11º, and sew through the end 4 mm **(e-f)**.

5 Work as in step 3 to add the toggle bar to this end of the base **(f-g)**.

6 Repeat step 4 to add 11ºs to the top edge of the base **(g-h)**.

7 Sew through the next 11º, 4 mm, and 11º on the bottom edge **(h-i)**.

8 Center the cup chain on top of the base, and align the end cup with the end 4 mm on the base. Pick up six 15ºs, cross over the space between the two end cups, and sew through the corresponding 11º on the top edge, with the needle facing the toggle ring **(photo)**. Sew back through the six 15ºs just added, and continue through the 11º your thread exited at the start of this step. Pull the thread tight, and sew through the next 4 mm and 11º.

9 Work as in step 8 for the remainder of the base. Sew through the end 4 mm, and continue through the next 11º and 4 mm on the top edge of the base **(figure 3, point a)**.

Edge embellishment

1 Pick up a 15º, three Rizo beads, and a 15º. Sew through the 4 mm your thread is exiting, going in the same direction, and continue through the next 11º and 4 mm **(figure 3, a-b)**.

2 Pick up two 15ºs, a 3 mm bicone crystal, and two 15ºs. Sew through the 4 mm your thread is exiting, going in the same direction, and continue through the next 11º and 4 mm **(b-c)**.

3 Work as in steps 1-2 for the length of the base, except on the last stitch continue through just the end 11º **(c-d)**. Sew through the end 4 mm, and the next 11º and 4 mm on the bottom edge of the base **(d-e)**.

4 Work as in steps 1-3 to embellish the bottom edge of the base. If your Rizo beads hang too loosely, sew through the outer edge embellishment beads again to cinch up the beads. End the working thread and tail. ●

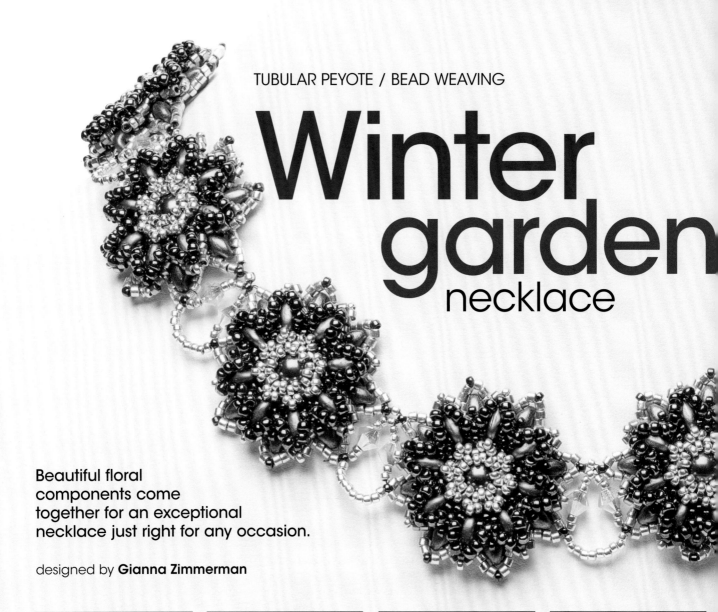

TUBULAR PEYOTE / BEAD WEAVING

Winter garden
necklace

Beautiful floral
components come
together for an exceptional
necklace just right for any occasion.

designed by **Gianna Zimmerman**

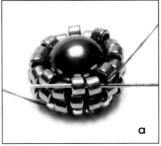

a

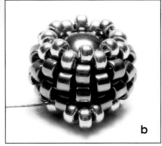

b

c

d

Components
Front layer
Use a medium tension
throughout the project.
A tight tension will make it
difficult to sew through the
beads, and the SuperDuos
may not lay flat.
1 On 4 ft. (1.2 m) of thread,
pick up 16 color A 11º cylinder beads, and sew through

the beads again to form a
ring, leaving an 8-in. (20 cm)
tail. These beads will shift to
form rounds 1 and 2 as the
next round is added.
2 Work rounds of tubular
peyote stitch as follows, and
step up at the end of each
round:
Rounds 3–4: Work two
rounds using As **(figure 1,**

a–b and b–c).
Rounds 5–6: Work two rounds
using color B 15º seed beads
(c–d and d–e). Sew back
through the beadwork to exit
the last round of As added.
Set the working thread aside.
3 With your tail thread, sew
under the nearest thread
bridge, pick up a 6 mm
pearl, and place it inside the

bezel. Sew under a thread
bridge on the opposite side
of the bezel, and continue
through the beadwork to exit
an A in round 1 **(photo a).**
4 Work in tubular peyote
stitch to work two rounds
using Bs, and end the tail.
5 With the working thread,
pick up three Bs, and sew
through the next A in this

162

FIGURE 1

FIGURE 2

Difficulty rating

Materials

necklace 17½ in. (44.5 cm) plus extender chain

- **13** 6 mm pearls (Swarovski, Tahitian)
- **24** 4 mm bicone crystals (Swarovski, crysolite opal AB2X)
- 2.5 x 5 mm SuperDuo beads
  - **8 g** color D (crystal bronze copper)
  - **8 g** color E (metallic suede light green)
- **8 g** 11º seed beads (Japanese 467, midnight metallic)
- 11º Miyuki Delica cylinder beads
  - **9 g** color A (DB0040, copper plated)
  - **7 g** color F (DB1831, Duracoat galvanized silver)
- 15º seed beads
  - **9 g** color B (Miyuki 4201, Duracoat galvanized silver)
  - **4 g** color C (Toho 222, dark bronze)
- **1** lobster claw clasp
- 2-in. (5 cm) extender chain
- **2** 6 mm jump rings
- Fireline, 6 lb. test
- beading needles, #11 or #12
- **2** pairs of chainnose, flatnose, and/or bentnose pliers

Legend:

◼ 11º cylinder bead, color A

○ 15º seed bead, color B

● 15º seed bead, color C

⬭ 2.5 x 5 mm SuperDuo, color D

⬯ 11º seed bead

⬭ 2.5 x 5 mm SuperDuo, color E

◻ 11º cylinder bead, color F

⬡ 4 mm bicone crystal

same round **(photo b)**. Repeat this stitch seven times to complete the round, making sure the beads form picots, and sew through the following A in round 2 **(photo c)**.

6 Pick up three color C 15º seed beads, and sew through the next A in this same round **(photo d)**. Repeat this stitch

seven times to complete the round, making sure the beads form picots, and sew through the first two Cs added in this round **(figure 2, point a)**. The Bezel is not shown in the remaining figures for clarity.

7 Pick up a C, a color D SuperDuo bead, and a C, and sew through the center C of the next picot **(a–b)**.

Repeat this stitch seven times to complete the round, and sew through the first C, D, and C added **(b–c)**.

8 Pick up an 11º seed bead, and sew through the next C, D, and C **(c–d)**. Repeat this stitch seven times to complete the round, and continue through the first 11º added **(d–e)**.

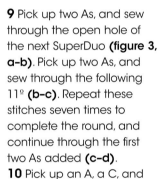

9 Pick up two As, and sew through the open hole of the next SuperDuo **(figure 3, a–b)**. Pick up two As, and sew through the following 11º **(b–c)**. Repeat these stitches seven times to complete the round, and continue through the first two As added **(c–d)**.
10 Pick up an A, a C, and an A, and sew through the next two As. Skip the following 11º, and continue through the next two As **(d–e)**. Repeat these stitches seven times to complete the round, and continue through the first A added in this round **(e–f)**.
11 Pick up an A, a B, and an A, and sew through the next two As **(figure 4, a–b)**. Pick up a C, skip the following A, 11º, and A, and continue through the next two As **(b–c)**.

FIGURE 3

Repeat these stitches seven times to complete the round, and continue through the next C **(c–d)**.
12 On the front side of this layer, pick up three 11ºs, and sew through the next 11º **(figure 5, a–b)**. Pick up three 11ºs, and sew through the next C added in step 10 **(b–c)**. Repeat these stitches seven times to complete the round **(c–d)**, and end the thread.

Back layer
1 Flip the beadwork over to the back side, and add 1 yd. (.9 m) of thread to the beadwork, exiting the second round of As in the bezel **(photo e)**. Pick up three Bs, and sew through the next A in this round **(photo f)**. Repeat this stitch seven times to complete the round, making sure the beads form picots, and sew through the first two Bs added in this step **(figure 6, point a)**.
2 Pick up three Bs, a color E SuperDuo, and three Bs, and sew through the center B of the next picot **(figure 6, a–b)**. Repeat this stitch seven times to complete the round, and sew through the first three Bs and SuperDuo added **(b–c)**.
3 Sew through the second A from the center in the top layer and the adjacent D,

FIGURE 4

(photo g). You may have to move the E out of the way a little to see the beads below clearly. Continue through the corresponding A on the other side of the D **(photo h)**. Sew through the inner hole of the next E **(photo i)**. Repeat these stitches seven times to complete the round, and continue through the following two Bs in the back layer **(figure 7, point a)**.
4 Pick up a C, skip the next three Bs, and sew through the following two Bs, E, and two Bs **(a–b)**. Repeat this stitch seven times to complete the round, and sew through the first C added in this round **(b–c)**.
5 Pick up three color F 11º cylinder beads, and sew through the open hole of the next E **(c–d)**. Pick up three Fs, and sew through the

new look
You can omit the 11ºs added in step 12 of "Front layer", or use 2 mm round crystals or 2 mm fire-polished beads in place of the 11ºs.

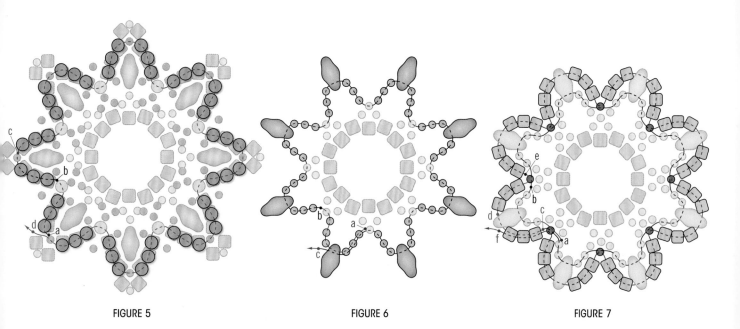

FIGURE 5

FIGURE 6

FIGURE 7

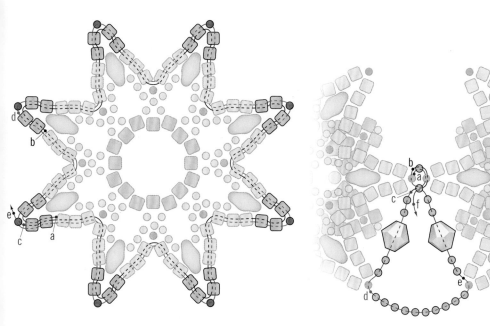

FIGURE 8

FIGURE 9

following C added in the previous round **(d–e)**. Repeat these stitches seven times to complete the round, and sew through the first three Fs added in this round **(e–f)**.

6 Pick up four Fs, sew down through the next three Fs, skip the next C, and sew up through the following three Fs **(figure 8, a–b)**. Repeat this stitch seven times to complete the round, and sew through the first two Fs added in this round **(b–c)**.

7 Pick up a C, sew down through the next five Fs, skip

the C, and sew up through the following five Fs **(c–d)**. Repeat this stitch seven times to complete the round, and sew through the first C added in this round **(d–e)**.

8 Make a total of 13 components. Do not end the thread on two of the components, but end it for the others

Joining

1 With the working thread from a component, pick up five Bs, and sew through the C your thread is exiting to form a clasp loop. Retrace

the thread path several times, and end the thread. Repeat this step on the other component with the working thread. These will be the end components that the clasp will be attached to.

2 Add 1 ft. (30 cm) of thread to the back layer of an end component, exiting a C on the third tip clockwise from the clasp loop, with the needle pointing up **(figure 9, point a)**.

3 Pick up a B, and sew down through a tip C on a new component. Pick up a B and sew up through the C your

thread exited at the start of the step **(a–b)**. Retrace the thread path (not shown in the figure for clarity), and continue through the next three beads **(b–c)**.

4 Pick up two Bs, a 4 mm bicone crystal, and two Bs, and sew through the next tip C on the end component **(c–d)**. Pick up 10 Bs, and sew through the corresponding tip C on the new component **(d–e)**. Pick up two Bs, a crystal, and two Bs, and sew through the B your thread exited at the start of this step **(e–f)**. Retrace the thread path, and end the thread.

5 To attach the remaining components, work as in steps 2–4 making sure to skip two tip Cs, going in a clockwise direction, between connections. The last component added should be an end component, making sure there are two skipped tip Cs between the connection and the clasp loop.

6 Open a jump ring, and attach half of the clasp to the clasp loop on an end component. Close the jump ring. Attach the extension chain to the other end of the necklace in the same way. ●

BEAD WEAVING / PEYOTE STITCH

Crescent
sunburst set

**Take advantage
of the versatility
of crescent beads
to create a pendant
and earring set
bursting with
dagger beads in
a symmetrical form.**

designed by
Kathy Simonds

Pendant

**How to pick up crescent
beads:** With the tips of the
crescent facing up or down
as indicated, pick up the
bead through the left hole
(LH) or the right hole
(RH), per the instructions **(figure 1)**.

1 On 2 yd. (1.8 m) of thread,
pick up a 6 mm druk bead,
leaving a 6-in. (15 cm) tail.
2 In a repeating pattern, pick
up a color A crescent bead
(LH, tips facing up) and an

11º seed bead three times,
and then pick up another
A (LH, tips facing up). Tie
the working thread and
tail together with a square
knot (not shown in the figure
for clarity) to form the beads
into a loop around one side
of the druk bead **(figure 2,
a–b)**. Sew through the druk
bead, going in the same
direction as before **(b–c)**.
3 Repeat step 2, except pick
up the As with the LH and
the tips facing down **(c–d)**

to form a loop on the other
side of the druk bead.
4 Sew through the next seven
beads in the ring as shown
(figure 3, a–b). Pick up an
11º, and sew through the
following seven beads
in the ring **(b–c)**. Pick up
an 11º, and sew through
the next A **(c–d)**. Retrace
the thread path through
all the beads in the ring,
and exit the last 11º added
(d–e). If needed, reposition
the crescents so they

Difficulty rating

 ◯ ◯

Materials

mauve pendant 2 in. (5 cm)
- **16** 5 x 16 mm CzechMates two-hole dagger beads (rose gold)
- **2 x 10 mm** CzechMates two-hole crescent beads
  - **8** color A (rose gold)
  - **8** color B (matte metallic flax)
- **1** 6 mm round druk bead (suede gold topaz)
- **8** 2 mm fire-polished beads (jet bronze)
- **1 g** 11º seed beads (Toho 221, bronze)
- Fireline, 6 lb. test
- beading needles, #11 or #12

mauve earrings 1½ in. (3.8 cm)
- **8** 5 x 16 mm CzechMates two-hole dagger beads (rose gold)
- 10 mm CzechMates two-hole crescent beads
  - **16** color A (rose gold)
  - **6** color B (matte metallic flax)
- round druk beads
  - **2** 6 mm (suede gold topaz)
  - **10** 4 mm (suede gold tanzanite)
- **6** 2 mm fire-polished beads (jet bronze)
- **1 g** 11º seed beads (Toho 221, bronze)
- **1** pair of earring findings

Information for the alternate colorways is listed at www. BeadAndButton.com/resources.

tips facing up   tips facing down

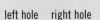

left hole   right hole   left hole   right hole

FIGURE 1

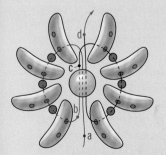

FIGURE 2   FIGURE 3

🔵 6 mm druk bead

5 x 10 mm two-hole crescent bead, color A
- top view

● 11º seed bead

5 x 10 mm two-hole crescent bead, color B
- top view

5 x 16 mm two-hole dagger bead

2 mm fire-polished bead

4 mm druk bead

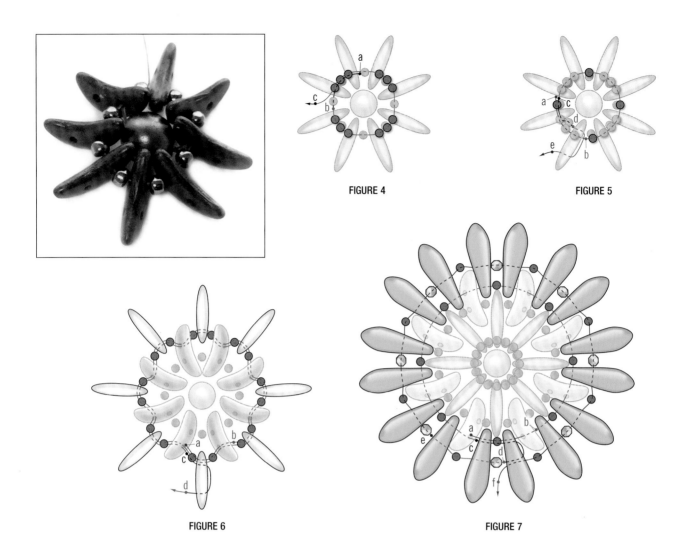

FIGURE 4

FIGURE 5

FIGURE 6

FIGURE 7

overlap the edge of the druk bead **(photo)**.

5 Turn the beadwork over so the tips of the crescents are facing down — this will now become the back. Working on the front, pick up three 11ºs, skip the next A, 11º, and A, and sew through the following 11º **(figure 4, a–b)**. Repeat this stitch three times to complete the round, and continue through the first three 11ºs added in this step **(b–c)**.

6 Pick up an 11º, and sew through the next three 11ºs **(figure 5, a–b)**. Repeat this stitch three times to create a ring of 11ºs around the druk bead **(b–c)**. Retrace the

thread path of the ring using a tight tension (not shown in the figure for clarity). Sew through the next two 11ºs in the ring, and the following 11º added in step 2 (under the top ring of 11ºs) **(c–d)**. Sew through the next A, and continue through the open hole of the same A **(d–e)**.

7 Turn the pendant over so the back surface is facing up. Pick up an 11º, a color B crescent (LH, tips facing down), and an 11º, and sew through the open hole of the next A **(figure 6, a–b)**. Repeat this stitch seven times to complete the round, and retrace the thread path using a tight tension to form

the beadwork into a slight dome shape **(b–c)**. Sew through the next 11º and B, and continue through the open hole of the same B **(c–d)**.

8 Turn the pendant over so that the front surface is facing up. Pick up a dagger bead, an 11º, and a dagger, and sew through the open hole of the next B **(figure 7, a–b)**. Repeat this stitch seven times to complete the round **(b–c)**, and retrace the thread path using a tight tension (not shown in the figure for clarity). Sew through the next dagger, 11º, and dagger, and continue through

the open hole of the same dagger **(c–d)**.

9 Pick up a 2 mm fire-polished bead, and sew through the open hole of the next dagger. Pick up an 11º, and sew through the open hole of the following dagger **(d–e)**. Repeat these two stitches seven times to complete the round **(e–f)**, and retrace the thread path using a tight tension.

Bail

1 Turn the pendant over so the back surface is facing up, and sew through the beadwork as needed to exit an 11º added in the second-to-last round

168

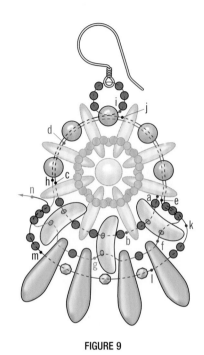

ACTUAL SIZE

FIGURE 8

FIGURE 9

(in step 8) **(figure 8, point a)**. Pick up four 11ºs, skip the next dagger, B, and dagger, and sew through the following 11º **(a-b)**.

2 Pick up an 11º, sew back through the four 11ºs just added, and continue back through the next 11º **(b-c)**. Pick up an 11º, and sew through the four 11ºs previously added **(c-d)**.

3 Using the four 11ºs just added as the initial row, work in flat even-count peyote using 11ºs for a total of 20 rows. Fold the strip over, and zip up the end row to the first row to form the bail, and end the thread.

Earrings

1 Work as in steps 1–6 of "Pendant."

2 Using the same orientation as the pendant, turn the beadwork over so the front surface is facing up. Pick up an 11º, a B (LH, tips facing up), and an 11º, and sew through the open hole of the next A **(figure 9, a–b)**. Repeat this stitch twice **(b-c)**. Pick up a 4 mm druk bead, and sew through the open hole of the next B **(c-d)**. Repeat this last stitch four times **(d-e)**.

3 Pick up three 11ºs, and sew through the open hole of the following B **(e-f)**. Pick up a dagger, an 11º, and a dagger, and sew through the open hole of the next B **(f-g)**. Repeat this last stitch once, pick up three 11ºs, and sew through the nearest hole of the following A **(g-h)**. Retrace the thread path of the outer ring of all the beads (not shown in the figure for clarity). Sew through the next five beads as shown to exit the center 4 mm druk bead **(h-i)**.

4 Pick up three 11ºs, the loop of an ear wire (making sure it faces the correct way), and three 11ºs, and sew through the druk bead, going in the same direction **(i-j)**. Retrace the thread path to reinforce the connection

(not shown in the figure for clarity).

5 Sew through the next five beads in the outer ring, and continue through the following set of three 11ºs **(j-k)**. Pick up two 11ºs, and sew through the open hole of the following dagger **(k-l)**. Pick up a 2 mm fire-polished bead, and sew through the open hole of the next dagger. Repeat this stitch twice **(l-m)**. Pick up two 11ºs, and sew through the next set of three 11ºs **(m-n)**. End the working thread and tail.

6 Repeat steps 1–5 to make a matching earring. ⦿

Reversible

Component base

1 On 3 yd. (2.7 m) of thread, pick up a 3 mm pearl, a 15º seed bead, a 3 mm bicone crystal, a 15º, a crystal, and a 15º. Sew through the beads again (not shown in figure for clarity) to form a ring, leaving a 10-in. (25 cm) tail. Continue through the beadwork to exit the first crystal added **(figure 1, a–b)**.

2 Pick up a 15º, a crystal, a 15º, a 3 mm pearl, and a 15º, and sew through the crystal your thread exited at the start of this step. Continue through the first 15º and crystal added **(b–c)**.

3 Pick up a 15º, a 3 mm pearl, a 15º, a crystal, and a 15º, and sew through the crystal your thread exited at the start of the step. Continue through the next four beads to exit the following crystal **(c–d)**.

4 Repeat steps 2–3 **(d–e)**.

5 Pick up a 15º, and sew through the next crystal added in step 1 **(e–f)**. Pick up a 15º, a 3 mm pearl, and a 15º, and sew through the crystal your thread exited at the start of this step **(f–g)**.

6 Sew through the next 15º **(figure 2,** a–b), and continue through the remaining 15ºs in the inner ring, using a tight tension **(b–c)**. Continue through the beadwork as shown to exit a 3 mm pearl **(c–d)**. This creates a circle unit.

7 Pick up two 15ºs, a 3 mm pearl, and a 15º, and sew through the pearl your thread just exited to form the start of a pearl strip **(figure 3, a–b)**. Continue through the next two 15ºs and pearl just added **(b–c)**.

8 Pick up a 15º, a 3 mm pearl, and two 15ºs, sew through the pearl your thread exited at the start of this step,

radiance

Double your options with this reversible necklace that goes from a little bling on one side to "wow" on the other.

designed by **Donna Sutton**

Difficulty rating

Materials
necklace 22 in. (56 cm)

- crystal pearls (Swarovski, iridescent green)
  - **8** 4 mm
  - **307** 3 mm
- **297** 3 mm bicone crystals (Swarovski, indicolite AB2X)
- seed beads (Miyuki 457L, metallic light bronze)
  - **15 g** 11º
  - **30 g** 15º
- **1** clasp
- Fireline, 6 lb. or 8 lb. test
- beading needles, #11 or #12

FIGURE 1

FIGURE 2

FIGURE 3

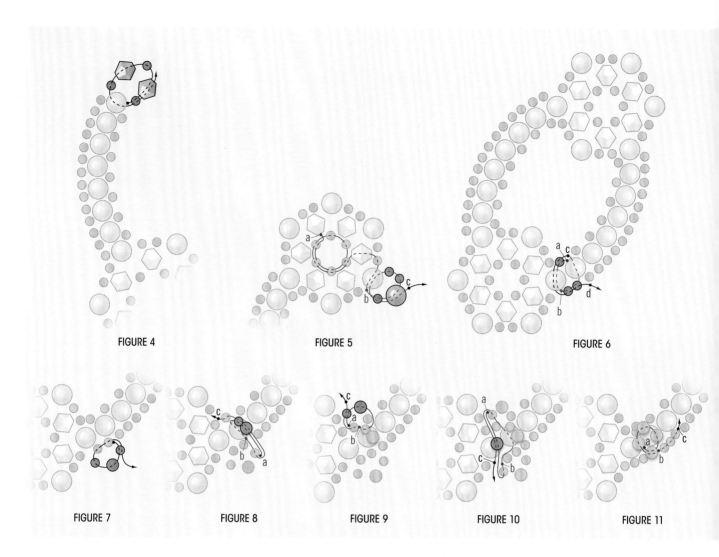

FIGURE 4

FIGURE 5

FIGURE 6

FIGURE 7

FIGURE 8

FIGURE 9

FIGURE 10

FIGURE 11

and continue through the next 15º and pearl just added **(c-d)**.

9 Repeat steps 7–8 twice and step 7 once more to add five more 3 mm pearls to the pearl strip.

10 Make another circle unit: Pick up a 15º, a crystal, a 15º, a crystal, and a 15º, and sew through the 3 mm pearl your thread exited at the start of this step. Continue through the next 15º and crystal **(figure 4)**. Repeat steps 2–3 twice, and then finish the circle unit as in step 5.

11 Sew through the inner ring of 15ºs and through the beadwork as shown to exit the second pearl past the connection of the circle unit, with the needle pointing toward the connection **(figure 5, a–b)**.

12 Repeat step 8 to form the start of another pearl strip **(b-c)**, then repeat steps 7–8 twice and step 7 once more to add five more new 3 mm pearls.

13 Pick up a 15º, and sew through the corresponding pearl in the first circle

unit **(figure 6, a-b)**. Make sure there is one pearl in the circle unit between the two pearl strips. Pick up two 15ºs, and sew through the pearl your thread exited at the start of this step **(b-c)**. Continue through the beadwork to exit the two 15ºs just added **(c-d)**.

CRAW embellishment

1 Pick up a 15º, an 11º seed bead, and a 15º, and sew through the two 15ºs your thread exited at the start of this step. Continue through the first 15º added **(figure 7)** to form the first side of this cubic right-angle weave (CRAW) unit.

2 Pick up an 11º and a 15º, and sew through the next pearl in the pearl strip with the needle pointing toward the outside edge of the strip **(figure 8, a-b)**. Continue up through the 15º your thread exited at the start of this step, the 11º and 15º just added, and the next 15º on the inside of the component **(b-c)**

to complete the second side of the CRAW unit.

3 Pick up a 15º and 11º, and sew down through the 15º added in the previous step **(figure 9, a-b)** and the 15º your thread exited at the start of this step, and continue up through the 15º just added **(b-c)** to form the third side of the CRAW unit.

4 Pick up an 11º, and sew down through the nearest 15º on the first side of the CRAW unit **(figure 10, a-b)**, through the 3 mm pearl, up through the 15º added on the third side, and through the 11º just added **(b-c)** to complete the last side of the CRAW unit. The 11ºs form the top of the CRAW unit.

5 Sew through the 11º on the first side, and continue through the remaining top 11ºs, exiting the 11º on the first side **(figure 11, a-b)**. Continue down through the next 15º and the following two 15ºs on the outer edge of the pearl strip **(b-c)**. For clarity, not all 15ºs on the

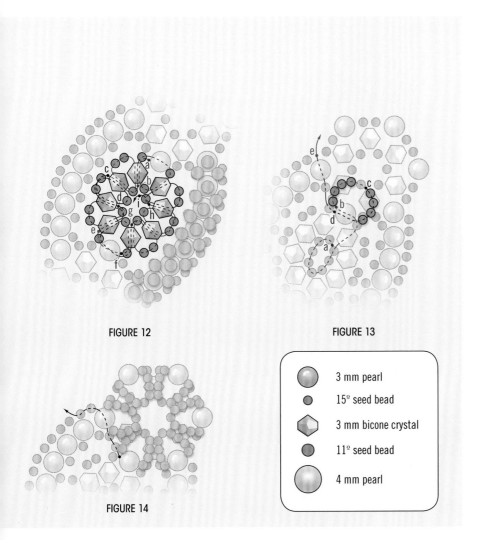

FIGURE 12

FIGURE 13

FIGURE 14

- ⬤ 3 mm pearl
- ● 15º seed bead
- ⬡ 3 mm bicone crystal
- ● 11º seed bead
- ⬤ 4 mm pearl

design options
Use the necklace components to make a matching pair of earrings or a bracelet.

CRAW unit are shown in the figure.

6 Repeat steps 1–3, and then work as in step 4, but sew through the next 11º from the previous CRAW unit instead of picking up a new one. Repeat step 5.

7 Work as in step 6 five more times to create a CRAW unit on each pearl in the pearl strip, but after sewing through the 11ºs in the last unit, sew through the beadwork to exit the center pearl between the two pearl strips **(figure 12, point a)**.

Crystal center

1 Pick up a 15º, a crystal, a 15º, a crystal, and a 15º, and sew through the pearl your thread exited at the start of this step. Continue through the next 15º and crystal **(a–b)**.

2 Pick up a 15º, a crystal, and two 15ºs, sew through the crystal your thread exited at the start of this step, and continue through the next 15º and crystal **(b–c)**.

3 Pick up two 15ºs, a crystal, and a

15º, and sew through the crystal your thread exited at the start of this step. Continue through the next two 15ºs and crystal **(c–d)**.

4 Repeat step 2 **(d–e)**.

5 Pick up a 15º, and sew through the nearest pearl **(e–f)**. Pick up a 15º, a crystal, and a 15º, and sew through the crystal your thread exited at the start of this step. Continue through the 15º, the pearl, the 15º, and the crystal just added **(f–g)**.

6 Repeat steps 2–3 **(g–h)**.

7 Pick up a 15º, and sew through the next crystal. Pick up two 15ºs, sew through the crystal your thread exited at the start of this step, and continue through the following 15º **(h–i)**.

8 Sew through the eight 15ºs in the center to form a ring, and continue through the next crystal, 15º, and center pearl **(figure 13, a–b)**.

Circle unit embellishment

1 Making sure you're working on the CRAW side of the component, pick up four 15ºs, skip the nearest crystal, and sew through the adjacent 15º in the inside ring of the circle unit **(b–c)**. Pick up four 15ºs, and sew through the pearl your thread exited at the start of this step **(c–d)**. Continue through the next two 15ºs and pearl on the outside edge of the circle unit **(d–e)**. Repeat these stitches five times for the remainder of the pearls in the circle unit.

2 Sew through the next two 15ºs on the outside edge of the circle unit, the following 3 mm pearl, and the two 15ºs on the outside edge of the pearl strip, **(figure 14)**.

3 Repeat steps 1–7 of "CRAW embellishment" for this pearl strip.

4 Repeat step 1 to embellish the other circle unit. End the working thread, but not the tail.

FIGURE 15

FIGURE 16

FIGURE 17

FIGURE 18

FIGURE 19

5 Repeat all the steps for "Component base," "CRAW embellishment," Crystal center," and "Circle unit embellishment" to make 12 components for a 22-in. (56 cm) necklace or 10 components for an 18-in. (46 cm) necklace.

Pendant

1 Make a circle unit as in steps 1–6 of "Component base," but substitute a 4 mm pearl for the 15º, 3 mm pearl, and 15º added in step 5. Exit the 3 mm pearl to the left of the 4 mm pearl at the end of step 6 **(figure 15, point a)**.

2 Make a pearl strip as in steps 7–8 of "Component base," but add only three 3 mm pearls **(a–b)**.

3 Pick up a 15º, a crystal, and two 15ºs, and sew through the pearl your thread exited at the start of this step. Continue through the 15º and crystal just added **(b–c)**.

4 Pick up a 15º, a crystal, a 15º, a crystal, and a 15º, and sew through the

crystal your thread exited at the start of this step. Continue through the four beads just added **(c–d)**.

5 Pick up a 15º, a 3 mm pearl, and two 15ºs, and sew through the crystal your thread exited at the start of this step. Continue through the 15º and pearl just added **(d–e)**.

6 Work as in steps 7–8 of "Component base" to complete another pearl strip with three 3 mm pearls **(e–f)**.

7 Connect the pearl strip to the circle unit: Pick up two 15ºs, and sew through the 3 mm pearl to the right of the 4 mm pearl as shown. Pick up a 15º, and sew through the pearl your thread exited at the start of this step **(f–g)**.

8 Sew back through the beadwork to exit the 15º to the right of the top crystal as shown **(figure 16, point a)**.

9 Work a pearl strip with four 3 mm pearls **(a–b)**.

10 Pick up two 15ºs, a crystal, and a 15º, and sew through the pearl

your thread exited at the start of this step. Continue through the two 15ºs and crystal **(b–c)**.

11 Pick up a 15º, a crystal, a 15º, 4 mm pearl, and a 15º, and sew through the crystal your thread exited at the start of this step. Continue through the next 15º, and crystal **(c–d)**.

12 Work a pearl strip with four 3 mm pearls **(d–e)**.

13 Pick up two 15ºs, and sew through the nearest 15º between the top two crystals. Pick up a 15º, and sew through the pearl and two 15ºs just added **(e–f)**.

14 Work as in steps 1–6 of "CRAW embellishment" to embellish this pearl strip and the remaining pearl strips in the pendant. End the working thread and tail.

174

Joining the components

1 With the tail from a component base (and the CRAW side of the base facing down), sew through the beadwork so the tail is exiting an end pearl in the circle unit **(figure 17, point a)**. Pick up a 15º, a crystal, and a 15º, and sew through the end pearl on a new component base (with the CRAW side facing down) on the end opposite the tail thread **(a–b)**. Pick up a 15º, a crystal, and a 15º, and sew through the pearl your thread exited at the start of this step **(b–c)**. Repeat these stitches once more between these two components to add another layer, and end this tail.

2 Repeat step 1 to connect four more components (for a total of six) to make one neck strap for a 22-in. (56 cm) necklace (or connect a total of five for an 18-in./46 cm necklace). Repeat these steps to make another neck strap.

Pendant connection

1 Add 18 in. (46 cm) of thread to the end component on a neck strap that doesn't have a tail thread, exiting the end pearl in the circle unit **(figure 18, point a)**.

2 Pick up a 15º, a 4 mm pearl, a 15º, a crystal, and a 15º, and sew through the 4 mm pearl at the top of the pendant, making sure the CRAW side of the pendant and neck strap is facing down **(a–b)**.

3 Pick up a 15º, a crystal, a 15º, a 4 mm pearl, and a 15º, and sew through the end pearl on the other neck strap (the end component without a tail thread), making sure the CRAW side is facing down **(b–c)**.

4 Pick up a 15º, a 4 mm pearl, a 15º, and a crystal, and sew back through the first 15º added in the previous step, the 4 mm pearl on the pendant, and the following 15º **(c–d)**. Pick up a crystal, a 15º, a 4 mm pearl, and a 15º, and sew through the end pearl **(d–e)**.

5 Repeat steps 2–3 to add another layer, and end the thread.

Clasp

1 With the tail from an end component on a neck strap, sew through the beadwork to exit an end pearl in the circle unit. Pick up four 15ºs, and sew through the loop of a clasp **(figure 19, a–b)**. Pick up four 15ºs, and sew back through the same side of the pearl to form a loop on this side of the pearl **(b–c)**. Repeat these stitches to add a loop of 15ºs on the other side of the pearl **(c–d)**. Retrace the thread path of the connection, and end the thread.

2 Work as in step 1 for the other half of the neck strap. •

BEAD EMBROIDERY / BRICK STITCH

Funky fringe earrings

Dagger beads add some fun and movement to these embroidered Lunasoft earrings.

designed by **Angie Mézes**

Embroidery

1 Apply a thin coat of E6000 to the back of a Lunasoft cabochon, and center the cab on the top half of a 1½-in. (3.8 cm) square of beading foundation. Allow the glue to dry.

2 Tie an overhand knot at the end of 2 ft. (61 cm) of thread. Sew up through the back of the foundation, exiting near the outer edge of the cab. Work in beaded backstitch around the cab: Pick up two color A 11º seed beads for each stitch, line them up next to the cab, and sew back through the foundation. Sew up between the two beads and through the second bead just added. End with an even number of beads, and sew through the first A in the round, the foundation, and back up through the foundation and next A. Sew through all the As once more, down through the foundation, and continue up through the foundation next to the round of As on the bottom edge of the cab near the center **(photo a)**.

3 Pick up a 6 mm pearl, and sew through the foundation slightly behind the hole of the pearl that the thread is exiting. Sew up through the foundation between the As and pearl, and continue through the pearl. Pick up a 15º seed bead, sew back through the pearl, down through the foundation, and back up through the foundation near where the pearl and As meet.

4 Picking up two As per stitch, work a round of beaded backstitch around the pearl **(photo b)**. Sew down through the beads and foundation. Make a half-hitch knot and end the thread. Carefully trim the foundation close to the beads, being careful not to cut any threads.

5 Glue the wrong side of the Ultrasuede to the back of the foundation. Allow the glue to dry, and trim the Ultrasuede close to the foundation.

6 Tie an overhand knot at the end of 2 ft. (61 cm) of thread, and trim the tail. Sew between the Ultrasuede and foundation, exiting the front of the foundation about 1 mm from the edge, hiding the knot between the two layers.

7 Work a brick stitch edging: Pick up two 11º cylinder beads, sew up through both foundation layers one bead's width away from where the thread is exiting, and continue back through the second bead added. For each subsequent stitch, pick up a cylinder, and sew up through both layers one bead's width

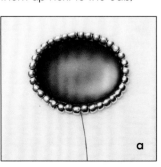

a

b

c

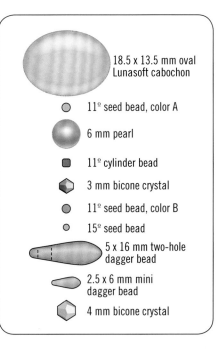

18.5 x 13.5 mm oval
Lunasoft cabochon

○ 11º seed bead, color A

● 6 mm pearl

▪ 11º cylinder bead

⬡ 3 mm bicone crystal

● 11º seed bead, color B

○ 15º seed bead

5 x 16 mm two-hole
dagger bead

2.5 x 6 mm mini
dagger bead

⬡ 4 mm bicone crystal

b
a e
c
d

FIGURE 1

Materials
earrings 1¼ x 2½ in (3.2 x 6.4 cm)
- **2** 18.5 x 13.5 mm oval Lunasoft cabochons (lavender)
- **2** 6 mm pearls (Swarovski, iridescent purple)
- **4** 4 mm bicone crystals (Swarovski, chrysolite opal AB2x)
- **14** 3 mm bicone crystals (Swarovski, fuchsia)
- **14** 5 x 16 mm CzechMate two-hole dagger beads (opaque luster green)
- **4** 2.5 x 6 mm mini dagger beads (metallic suede gold)
- 11º seed beads
  - **2 g** color A (Toho PF558, permanent finish galvanized aluminum)
  - **18** color B (Toho 221F, frosted bronze)
- **1 g** 11º Delica cylinder beads (Miyuki DB0455, galvanized dark plum)
- **1 g** 15º seed beads (Toho 84, metallic moss iris)
- **1** pair of earring findings
- Fireline, 6 lb. test
- beading needles, #11 or #12
- **2** 1½-in. (3.8 cm) squares of beading foundation
- **2** 1½-in. (3.8 cm) squares of Ultrasuede (tan)
- E6000 adhesive
- **2** pairs of chainnose, bentnose, and/or flatnose pliers
- scissors

away from where the thread is exiting, and continue through the new bead just added. Repeat this stitch around the perimeter **(photo c)**. When embellishing around the pearl, stitch 11 or 12 cylinder beads to this area. After adding the final bead, sew down through the first bead in the edging, through the foundation and Ultrasuede, and back through the first bead again. End the working thread in the edging beads.

Fringe

1 Thread a needle on each end of 1 yd. (.9 m) of thread, and count how many cylinder beads are around the outer ring of the pearl. You should have either 11 or 12 cylinders.

2 Add the first fringe strand as follows depending on how many cylinders are around the pearl:

If you have 11 cylinder beads: With one needle, sew through the fifth cylinder bead from the corner with the needle pointing toward the beadwork **(figure 1, a–b)**, and center the thread. Continue out through the next cylinder bead **(b–c)**. Pick up six As, a cylinder, a 3 mm bicone crystal, a cylinder, a color B 11º seed bead, three 15º seed beads, a dagger bead, and three 15ºs. Sew back through the B and the remaining nine beads in the fringe strand **(c–d)**. Continue through the cylinder your thread is exiting,

substitutions
You may substitute the two-hole dagger beads with one-hole dagger beads and the mini daggers with Rizo beads or other small drops.

and out through the following cylinder **(d-e)**.
If you have 12 cylinder beads: With one needle, sew through the fifth cylinder bead from the corner with the needle pointing toward the beadwork **(figure 2, a-b)**, and center the thread. Continue out through the next cylinder bead **(b-c)**. Pick up six As, a cylinder, a 3 mm bicone crystal, a cylinder, a color B 11º seed bead, three 15º seed beads, a dagger bead, and three 15ºs. Sew back through the B and the remaining nine beads in the fringe strand **(c-d)**. Continue through the cylinder adjacent to the one your thread is exiting, and out through the following cylinder **(d-e)**. This will center this fringe strand between the

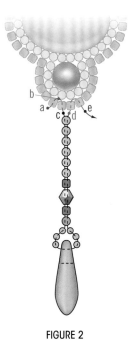

FIGURE 2

two cylinder beads.
3 With each thread, add three more identical fringes on each side of the center fringe, except decrease the number of As by one for each fringe **(figure 3, a-b and aa-bb)**.
4 On each thread, pick up an A, a B, two 15ºs, a mini dagger bead, and two 15ºs, and sew back through the B and A. Continue back through the cylinder your thread is exiting, and sew out through the adjacent cylinder **(b-c and bb-cc)**.
5 On each thread, pick up an A, a 4 mm bicone crystal, and a 15º, and sew back through the 4 mm and A. Continue through the cylinder your thread is exiting **(c-d and cc-dd)**, and end the threads.

Assembly
1 Identify the three top center cylinders in the edging. Add 12 in. (30 cm) of thread to the earring, exiting the right-hand cylinder of the center three. Pick up seven 15ºs, skip the center cylinder, and sew down through the next cylinder. Retrace the thread path, and end the threads.
2 Using chainnose pliers, open the loop of an earwire, and attach it to the center loop. Close the earwire.
3 Make a second earring. ●

FIGURE 3

NETTING / RIGHT-ANGLE WEAVE

Abbey rose pendant

Capture glittering chatons in a pendant inspired by what was once a window at Tintern Abbey in Wales, England.

designed by **Liz Thompson**

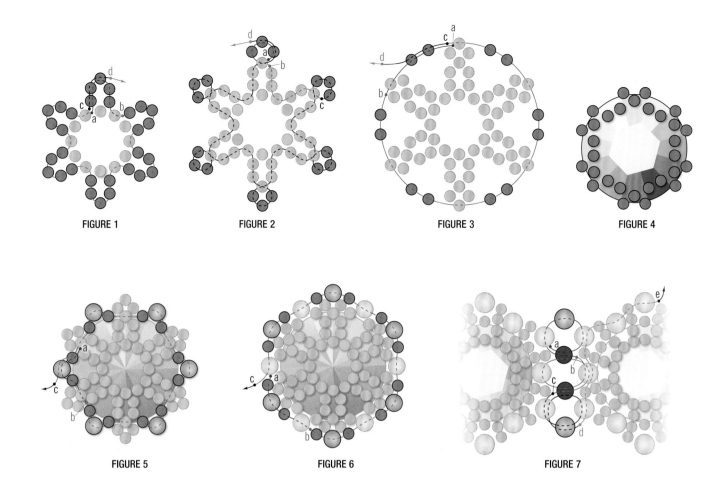

FIGURE 1

FIGURE 2

FIGURE 3

FIGURE 4

FIGURE 5

FIGURE 6

FIGURE 7

This pendant can be made with either SS40 or SS45 round rhinestone chatons. (The purple/bronze pendant features SS40, and the blue/ silver pendant uses SS45.) Tips are provided for adjusting bead counts based on your chaton size. The illustrations are shown using SS40 chatons.

Outer chatons

1 On 30 in. (76 cm) of thread, pick up 12 15º seed beads. Tie the beads into a ring with a square knot, leaving a 6-in. (15 cm) tail. Sew through the first 15º in the ring.
2 Pick up five 15ºs. Skip a 15º in the ring, and sew through the following 15º to form a loop **(figure 1, a-b)**. Repeat this stitch five times to complete the round, making a total of six loops **(b-c)**. Sew

through the first three 15ºs in the first loop to exit the center 15º **(c-d)**.
3 Pick up three 15ºs. Sew through the 15º your thread exited at the start of this step, sewing in the same direction, to form a picot **(figure 2, a-b)**. Sew through the following 15ºs as shown to exit the center 15º in the next loop **(b-c)**. Repeat these stitches five times to add a picot to each loop, and sew through the beadwork to exit the center 15º in the first picot **(c-d)**.
4 If you are using SS40 chatons, pick up two 15ºs, and sew through the center 15º in the next picot **(figure 3, a-b)**. (If you are using SS45 chatons, pick up three 15ºs between the picots.) Repeat this stitch five times to complete the round **(b-c)**, pulling gently on the thread to begin forming a cup shape, but do

not tighten. Sew through the first two 15ºs added in this step **(c-d)**.

note Make sure you are always sewing through the center 15º of each picot, as the picots may be tipped to one side.

5 Place a chaton face up in your beadwork, so that the point of the chaton exits the starting ring of 12 15ºs. Pull the thread tight to cinch the last round to the face of the chaton **(figure 4)**.

note If you are using SS45 chatons and have thread showing between the 15ºs in the last round, return to step 4, and try adding four 15ºs between the picots instead of three, or alternate three and four 15ºs between picots.

Retrace the thread path of the last round, tying a few half-hitch knots as you go. Turn your work over, and sew through the beadwork to exit the center 15º in one of the loops made in step 2 **(figure 5, point a)**.
6 Pick up a 15º, a 2 mm round bead, and a 15º, and sew through the center 15º in the next loop **(a-b)**. Repeat this stitch five times to complete the round, and sew through the first 15º and 2 mm added in this step **(b-c)**.
7 If using SS40 chatons, pick up a 15º, a 2 mm, and a 15º, and sew through the next 2 mm **(figure 6, a-b)**. Repeat this stitch five times to complete the round **(b-c)**, and retrace the thread path. Your bezeled chaton should now resemble a hexagon with six sides and a 2 mm at each

corner. End the working thread and tail.

If using SS45 chatons, work as above for a few stitches. If you have a lot of thread showing, try picking up two 15ºs, a 2 mm, and two 15ºs for each stitch.

8 Make a total of six outer chatons.

Center chaton

Work as in steps 1–6 of "Outer chatons," and end the working thread and tail. The center chaton will be slightly smaller than the others.

Connections

1 Add a comfortable length of thread to an outer chaton, exiting a corner 2 mm in a clockwise direction. Place another outer chaton next to this one, aligning the corner 2 mms.

2 Work a join with three right-angle weave (RAW) stitches:

• Pick up an 11º seed bead, and sew up through the corresponding corner 2 mm of the new outer chaton. Pick up a 2 mm, and sew down through the corner 2 mm of the first outer chaton. Continue through the first 11º added **(figure 7, a–b)**.

• Sew through the 2 mm between the corner 2 mms of the new outer chaton, pick up an 11º, and sew through the corresponding 2 mm of the first outer chaton. Continue through the 11º added in the previous stitch, the 2 mm of the new outer chaton, and the 11º just added **(b–c)**.

• Sew through the next corner 2 mm of the first outer chaton, pick up a 2 mm, and sew through the corresponding corner 2 mm of the new outer chaton. Continue through the 11º added in the previous stitch, the

corner 2 mm of the first outer chaton, and the 2 mm just added **(c–d)**. Sew clockwise through the beadwork to exit the next corner 2 mm of the new outer chaton **(d–e)**.

3 Work as in step 2 to join all six outer chatons into a ring, ending and adding thread as needed. Be sure to join the last chaton to the first. Exit a connecting 2 mm — that is, one of the 2 mms added in the connecting RAW stitches — on the inside of the ring.

4 Place the center chaton inside the ring so that its 2 mms fall between the connecting 2 mms. Pick up a 15º, sew through the next 2 mm of the center chaton, pick up a 15º, and sew through the following connecting 2 mm **(figure 8, a–b)**. Repeat these stitches five times around the center chaton **(b–c)**, and retrace

Difficulty rating:

Materials
purple/bronze pendant 2½ in. (6.4 cm)
- 7 SS40 (8.412–8.672 mm) round rhinestone chatons (Swarovski #1028, amethyst)
- 100–110 2 mm round beads (antiqued copper)
- 1 g 11º seed beads (Miyuki 462, metallic gold iris)
- 3 g 15º seed beads (Toho 459, gold lustered dark topaz)
- Fireline, 6 lb. test
- beading needles, #12 or #13

blue/silver pendant colors
- SS45 (9.852-10.187 mm) round rhinestone chatons
  - 6 (Swarovski #1088, light sapphire)
  - 1 (Swarovski #1088, crystal)
- 2 mm round beads (silver plated)
- 11º seed beads (Toho 711, nickel-plated silver)
- 15º seed beads (Toho 711, nickel-plated silver)

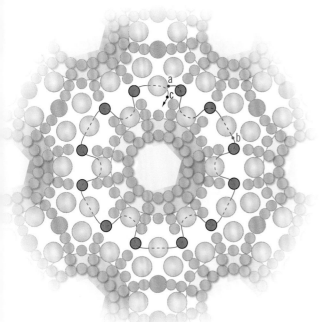

FIGURE 8

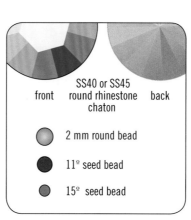

front   SS40 or SS45 round rhinestone chaton   back

2 mm round bead

11º seed bead

15º seed bead

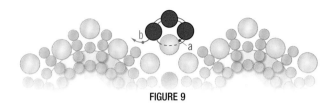

FIGURE 9

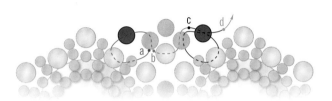

FIGURE 10

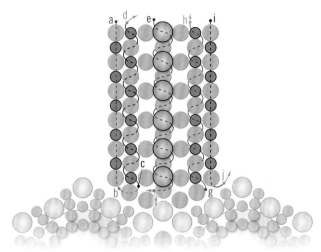

FIGURE 11

the thread path of the entire connection. Sew through the beadwork to exit a connecting 2 mm on the outside of the ring as shown **(figure 9, point a)**.

Bail

The instructions are for the bail shown on the purple/bronze pendant.

1 Using 11ºs, work a row of three right-angle weave (RAW) stitches as follows:

• Pick up three 11ºs and sew through the 2 mm to form a RAW stitch. Continue through the three 11ºs just added **(a-b)**.

• Work a modified RAW stitch: Sew through the nearest 15º and 2 mm. Pick up an 11º, and sew through the last 11º added in the previous stitch **(figure 10, a-b)**. Retrace the thread path of the stitch (not shown in illustration for clarity), and sew through the next 2 mm and 11º **(b-c)**.

• Pick up an 11º, and sew through the nearest 2 mm and 15º. Retrace the thread path of the stitch (not shown for clarity), and continue through the next 11º **(c-d)**.

2 Using 11ºs and working off the three RAW stitches completed in step 1, work a strip of RAW that is three stitches

wide and long enough to wrap around the necklace of your choice. End and add thread as needed. Fold the strip to the back of the pendant, and stitch the last row of RAW to the first row to form the bail.

3 Embellish the bail as follows, working from the back of the bail to the front for the first column of embellishment, from the front to the back for the second column, and so on:

• Exit the last 11º along the left edge of the bail. Pick up a 15º, and sew through the next edge 11º. Repeat this stitch for the entire edge

(figure 11, a-b).

• Sew through the adjacent 11º **(b-c)**. Pick up a 15º, and sew through the next 11º in the column. Repeat this stitch for the entire column **(c-d)**.

• Using 2 mms instead of 15ºs, embellish the center column as you did the previous column **(e-f)**.

• Using 15ºs, embellish the next column as you did the center column **(g-h)**.

• Using 15ºs, embellish the right edge as you did the left edge **(i-j)**. End the working thread. ●

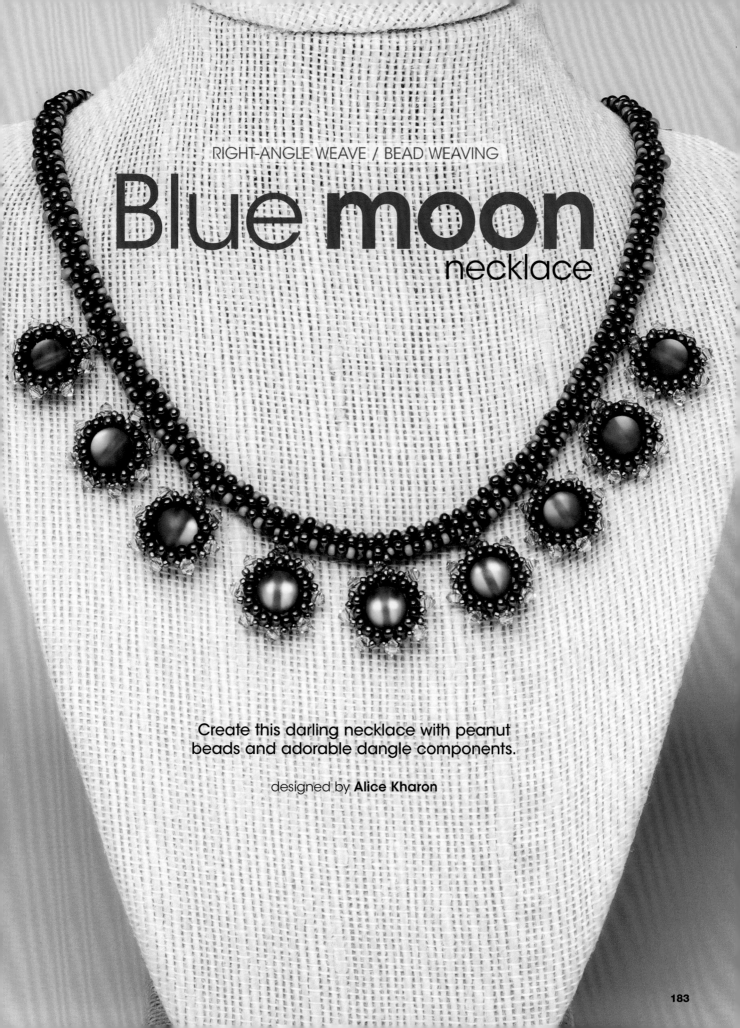

RIGHT-ANGLE WEAVE / BEAD WEAVING

Blue moon
necklace

Create this darling necklace with peanut
beads and adorable dangle components.

designed by **Alice Kharon**

Difficulty rating

Materials
necklace 16 in. (41 cm)
- **9** 8 mm round beads (synthetic moonstone, matte blue/gray)
- **14 g** 2 x 4 mm peanut beads (457A, copper metallic)
- **72** 3 mm bicone crystals (Swarovski, crystal silver shadow)
- **1 g** 8º seed beads (Miyuki 2028, matte sea foam luster)
- **2 g** 11º seed beads (Miyuki 2028, matte sea foam luster)
- **1 g** 15º seed beads, color A (Toho 221, bronze)
- **1 g** 15º seed beads, color B (Miyuki 2028, matte sea foam luster)
- Fireline, 6 lb. test
- beading needles, #11 or #12
- **1** toggle clasp

Neck strap
1 On a comfortable length of thread, pick up four peanut beads, and sew through them again to form a ring, leaving a 6-in. (15 cm) tail. Continue through the next three peanuts **(figure 1, a–b)**.
2 Working in right-angle weave (RAW), pick up three peanuts, sew through the peanut your thread exited at the beginning of this step, and continue through the first two peanuts just added **(b–c)**. Sew through the beads in this stitch again to cinch up the beads. Work an additional 34 RAW stitches, cinching up each stitch. End and add thread as needed.

Components
1 With the strip of beadwork horizontal, sew through the last stitch to exit the bottom peanut **(figure 2, a–b)**. This will put you in position to add a component.
2 Pick up a color A 15º seed bead, a 3 mm bicone crystal, and an A, and sew through the same peanut your thread exited at the start of this stitch and the next A and 3 mm just added **(b–c)**. Retrace the thread path to cinch up the beads.
3 Pick up an A, a peanut, and an A, sew through the 3 mm your thread exited at the start of this step, and continue through the following A and peanut just added **(figure 3)**.
4 Pick up seven peanuts and an 8 mm bead, and sew through the peanut your thread exited at the beginning of this step. Continue through the seven peanuts just added **(figure 4, a–b)**.
5 Pick up eight peanuts, and sew through the peanut at the top of the 8 mm to form a ring **(b–c)**. Sew through the ring of 16 peanuts, and continue through the next peanut **(c–d)**.
6 Pick up an A, a 3 mm, and an A, skip a peanut, and sew through the following peanut **(figure 5, a–b)**. Repeat this stitch six times for a total of eight crystals surrounding the ring of peanuts **(b–c)**. Sew through the next A and 3 mm at the top of the ring **(c–d)**.

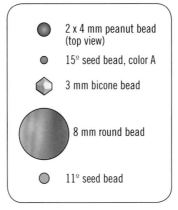

- 2 x 4 mm peanut bead (top view)
- 15º seed bead, color A
- 3 mm bicone bead
- 8 mm round bead
- 11º seed bead

FIGURE 1

FIGURE 2

FIGURE 3

7 Sew through the beadwork to exit the outer side bead of the last RAW stitch on the neck strap as shown **(d–e)**. Work five RAW stitches using peanuts.
8 Work as in steps 1–7 to make a strap with a total of nine components.
9 Work an additional 30 RAW stitches using peanuts to complete the neck strap.

Clasp

1 With the working thread, pick up nine As and the loop of the toggle ring, and sew back through the peanut to form a loop on this side of the peanut **(figure 6, a–b)**. Pull the thread tight.
2 Pick up nine As and the same toggle loop, and sew back through the peanut to form a loop on this side of the peanut **(b–c)**. Pull the thread tight.

Embellishment

1 With the working thread, pick up an 11º, and sew through the next top peanut in the neck strap **(c–d)**. Repeat this stitch for the length of the neck strap using an even tension. At the end

of the strap, pick up an 11º, and sew through the end bead of the first stitch.
2 Repeat steps 1–2 of "Clasp" to add the toggle bar.
3 To embellish the bottom row, pick up an 11º, and sew through the following bottom peanut in the neck strap. Repeat this stitch twice. Pick up an 8º, and sew through the next peanut. Pull the thread tight.
4 Repeat step 3 seven times.
5 Pick up an 11º, and sew through the following peanut. Repeat this stitch twice. The next peanut should have a component attached to it. Pick up a color B 15º seed bead, and sew through the next peanut. Repeat this stitch once.
6 Repeat step 5 eight times.
7 Repeat step 3 eight times, and then finish embellishing the neck strap by working three more stitches with 11ºs. End both the working thread and tail. ●

make it longer

To add length, work an additional even number of RAW stitches on each end of the necklace, and embellish with size 11º seed beads only. Eight stitches will add approximately 1¼ in. (3.2 cm) of length.

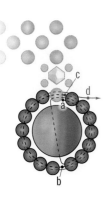

FIGURE 4

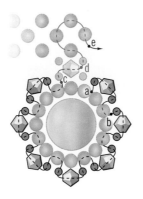

FIGURE 5

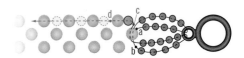

FIGURE 6

185

All buckled up
bracelet

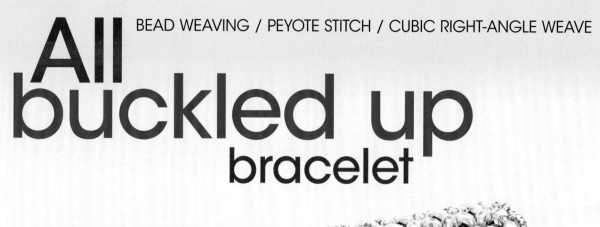

Craft an enticing bracelet featuring
SuperDuos and sparkling crystals
fastened with a clever beaded buckle.

designed by **Donna Sutton**

FIGURE 1

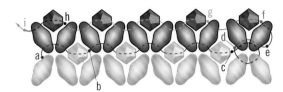

FIGURE 2

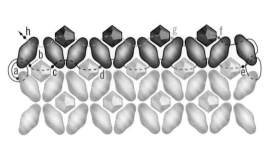

FIGURE 3

2.5 x 5 mm
SuperDuo bead

3 mm bicone crystal

8º seed bead

15º seed bead

Difficulty rating

Materials

blue bracelet 7½ x 1⁵/₁₆ in. (19.1 x 3.3 cm)
- **19 g** 2.5 x 5 mm SuperDuos (pastel petrol)
- **130** 3 mm bicone crystals (Swarovski, crystal metallic blue 2X)
- **10 g** 8º seed beads (Miyuki 454, metallic dark plum iris)
- **3 g** 11º seed beads (Miyuki 319P, berry breeze)
- **6 g** 15º seed beads (Miyuki 319P, berry breeze)
- **1 ¾ in.** (1.9 cm) hook-and-eye closure
- Fireline, 6 lb. test
- beading needles, #11 or #12

green/bronze bracelet colors
- SuperDuos (opaque green luster)
- 3 mm bicone crystals (Swarovski, crystal iridescent green)
- 8º seed beads (Miyuki F457P, matte bronze metallic)
- 11º seed beads (Miyuki F460, matte green gold iris)
- 15º seed beads (Toho 378A, bronze-lined aqua)

burgundy/green bracelet colors
- SuperDuos (red Picasso)
- 3 mm bicone crystals (Swarovski, light gray opal AB2X)
- 8º seed beads (Miyuki 460, metallic dark raspberry)
- 11º seed beads (Miyuki 356F, topaz sage-lined)
- 15º seed beads (Miyuki 374A, topaz aqua-lined)

Base

1 On a comfortable length of doubled thread, attach a stop bead leaving a 6-in. (15 cm) tail. Pick up 10 SuperDuo beads. Sew through the open holes of the last two SuperDuos just added **(figure 1, a–b)**.

2 Using an even tension, pick up a 3 mm bicone crystal, and sew through the open holes of the following two SuperDuos **(b–c)**. Repeat this stitch three times to form the first row **(c–d)**.

3 To start the next row, pick up two SuperDuos, and sew through the next crystal in the previous row **(figure 2, a–b)**. Repeat this stitch three times **(b–c)**. Pick up two SuperDuos, and make a turn: With the needle pointing toward the beadwork, sew through the closest holes of the two adjacent SuperDuos in the previous row **(c–d)**, continue through the two SuperDuos just added **(d–e)**, and sew through the open hole of the last SuperDuo added **(e–f)**.

4 Pick up a crystal, and sew through the open holes of the next two SuperDuos **(f–g)**. Repeat this stitch three times **(g–h)**. To complete the row, pick up a crystal,

and sew through the open hole of the following SuperDuo **(h–i)**.

5 To start the next row, make a starting turn: Pick up a SuperDuo, sew through the hole of the SuperDuo your thread exited at the start of this step, and continue through the inner hole of the SuperDuo just added **(figure 3, a–b)**.

6 Sew through the next crystal in the previous row **(b–c)**. Pick up two SuperDuos, and sew through the following crystal in the previous row **(c–d)**. Repeat this stitch three times **(d–e)**.

7 Make an ending turn: Pick up a SuperDuo, sew through the closest hole of the adjacent SuperDuo in the previous row, and continue through the inner hole of the SuperDuo just added. Sew through the open hole of the same SuperDuo, and the open hole of the next SuperDuo **(e–f)**.

8 Pick up a crystal, and sew through the open holes of the following two SuperDuos **(f–g)**. Repeat this stitch three times to complete the row **(g–h)**.

9 Work as in steps 3–8 for the desired bracelet length, less 1⅜ in. (3.5 cm) for the buckle clasp, ending after completing step 3.

Cubic RAW how-to

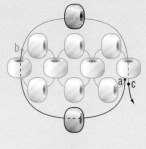

CRAW 1

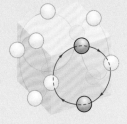

CRAW 2

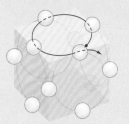

CRAW 3

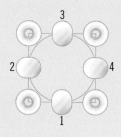

CRAW 4

Each cubic right-angle weave (or CRAW) unit has six surfaces — four sides, a top, and a bottom. Each surface is made up of four beads, but since the beads are shared, 12 beads are used to make the first unit, and only eight beads are used for each subsequent CRAW unit. For clarity, I used two colors of beads in the how-to photos.

Working the first CRAW unit

1 On the specified length of thread, pick up four beads. Tie the beads into a ring with a square knot (Basics), leaving the specified length tail, and continue through the first two beads in the ring. This ring of beads will count as the first stitch of the unit.
2 Work two right-angle weave stitches off of the bead your thread is exiting to create a flat strip of right-angle weave (Basics).

3 To join the first and last stitches: Pick up a bead, sew through the end bead in the first stitch **(CRAW 1, a–b)**, pick up a bead, and sew through the end bead in the last stitch **(b–c)**. **CRAW 2** shows a three-dimensional view of the resulting cube-shaped unit.
4 To stabilize the unit, sew through the four beads at the top of the unit **(CRAW 3)**. Sew through the beadwork to the bottom of the unit, and sew through the four remaining beads. This completes the first CRAW unit.

Working more CRAW units

1 Each new CRAW unit is worked off of the top four beads of the previous unit. These beads are identified in **CRAW 4**. Sew through the beadwork to exit one of these top beads.
2 *For the first stitch of the new unit:* Pick

up three beads, and sew through the top bead your thread exited at the start of this step. Continue through the three beads just picked up **(CRAW 5)**. Sew through the next top bead in the previous unit.
3 *For the second stitch of the new unit:* Pick up two beads, and sew through the side bead in the previous stitch, the top bead your thread exited at the start of this stitch **(CRAW 6)**, and the next top bead in the previous unit.
4 *For the third stitch of the new unit:* Repeat step 3 **(CRAW 7)**, and continue through the side bead in the first stitch of the new unit.
5 *For the fourth stitch of the new unit:* Pick up a bead, and sew through the side bead in the previous stitch and the top bead in the previous unit **(CRAW 8)**.

CRAW 5

CRAW 6

CRAW 7

CRAW 8

CRAW 9

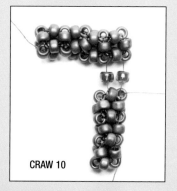

CRAW 10

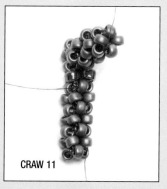

CRAW 11

CRAW 12

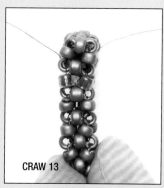

CRAW 13

6 To make the unit more stable, sew through the beadwork to exit a top bead in the new unit, and sew through all four top beads **(CRAW 9)**. This completes the new CRAW unit.

7 Repeat steps 2–6 for the desired number of CRAW units.

Working a joining unit

A joining unit is used to connect two completed CRAW units to each other. Units may be joined end to end or perpendicular to one another (as shown in the photos).

1 Sew through the beadwork to exit a top bead in one unit.

2 *For the first stitch of the joining unit:* Pick up a bead, sew through the corresponding bead in the other unit, pick up a bead, and sew through the bead your thread exited at the start of this step **(CRAW 10)**. Sew through the first bead added and the adjacent bead in the next side. If you are joining pieces at an angle, try to do the stitches on the inside of the angle first.

3 *For the second stitch of the joining unit:* Pick up a bead, and sew through the corresponding bead in the other unit, the previous joining bead, the bead your thread exited at the start of this stitch **(CRAW 11)**, and the bead just added. Sew through the adjacent bead in the next side.

4 *For the third stitch of the joining unit:* Pick up a bead, and sew through the corresponding bead in the other unit, the previous joining bead, the bead your thread exited at the start of this stitch **(CRAW 12)**. Sew through the adjacent bead in the next side.

5 *For the fourth stitch of the joining unit:* All beads are already in place. Simply sew through the four beads that remain unconnected **(CRAW 13)**.

Buckle clasp
Tabs

1 With the working thread, pick up an 8º seed bead, and sew through the open holes of the next two SuperDuos **(figure 4, a–b)**. Repeat this stitch three times **(b–c)**. Pick up an 8º, and sew through the open hole of the following SuperDuo **(c–d)** to complete the row. Sew through the other hole of the same SuperDuo, and continue through the last 8º added **(d–e)**.

2 Work in odd-count peyote stitch: Pick up two 8ºs, and sew through the following 8º **(e–f)**. Repeat this stitch three times to complete the row **(f–g)**.

3 Pick up an 8º, and sew through the next two 8ºs **(g–h)**. Repeat this stitch three times **(h–i)**.

4 To complete the row, make a figure-8 turn: Sew through the end 8º in the previous row **(i–j)**, pick up an 8º, and sew through the beadwork as shown **(j–k)**.

5 Work as in steps 2–4 to work a total of 20 rows, ending after step 2.

6 Make a decrease stitch: Sew around the nearest edge thread bridge, and continue back through the 8º your thread exited at the start of this step and the next two 8ºs in the end row **(figure 5, a–b)**. Pick up an 8º, and sew through the following two 8ºs **(b–c)**. Repeat this stitch twice **(c–d)**.

7 Make a decrease stitch: Sew around the nearest edge thread bridge, and continue back through the two 8ºs your thread is exiting at the start of this step and the next 8º in the last row added **(d–e)**. Pick up two 8ºs, and sew through the following 8º. Repeat this stitch once **(e–f)**.

8 Make a decrease stitch: Sew around the nearest thread bridge, and continue back through the 8º your thread exited at the start of this stitch and the next two 8ºs in the row just added **(f–g)**. Pick up an

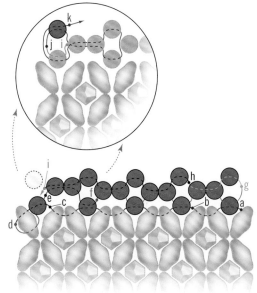

FIGURE 4

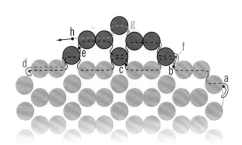

FIGURE 5

8º, and sew through the following two 8ºs **(g–h)**. End the working thread and tail.

9 Add 1 yd. (.9 m) of thread to the other end of the base, exiting the outer hole of an edge SuperDuo with the needle facing toward the beadwork. Work as in steps 1–5 to form an unfinished tab on this end of the base. End the tail, but not the working thread.

Buckle

1 On a comfortable length of thread, work a CRAW unit (see "Cubic RAW how-to," p. 188) using 11º seed beads and leaving a 6-in. (15 cm) tail.

2 Work five more CRAW units off the first one **(photo a)**. This completes the first leg of the buckle catch. Sew through the beadwork to exit a side bead in the last unit so that your thread is exiting perpendicular to the last unit.

3 Work 10 CRAW units in the new direction. This completes the second leg of the buckle catch **(photo b)**. Sew through the beadwork to exit a top bead in the last unit so that your thread is exiting perpendicular to the previous leg.

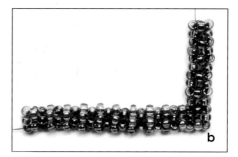

4 Repeat step 2 to complete the third leg of the buckle catch **(photo c)**.

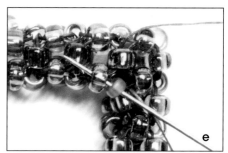

5 Work eight CRAW units, and then work a joining unit ("Cubic RAW how-to") to connect the fourth leg to the first **(photo d)**.

6 To stabilize the buckle catch, exit an edge 11º, and stitch in the ditch: Pick up a 15º seed bead, and sew through the next edge 11º in the adjacent CRAW unit **(photo e)**. Repeat this stitch around the inner and outer edges on all four sides of the buckle catch. End the threads.

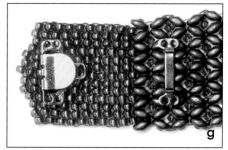

7 To attach the buckle catch to the base: Slide the catch onto the unfinished tab (the one that isn't tapered). Fold the tab over, and align the ends of the peyote rows. Using the working thread on the base, zip up the ends remembering to treat the pairs of "up" beads as a single bead **(photo f)**. Retrace the thread path, and end the thread.

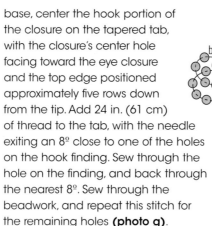
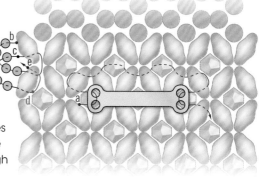

Clasp

1 Add 24 in. (61 cm) of thread to the base (the end opposite the catch), with the needle exiting at **figure 6, point a**.

2 With the eye portion of the closure centered on the base, sew up through the bottom hole of the closure and down through the adjacent hole. Continue through the beadwork as shown, and secure the other end of the eye closure as before. Sew through the beadwork to retrace the connection a few times, and end the thread.

3 Working on the same surface of the base, center the hook portion of the closure on the tapered tab, with the closure's center hole facing toward the eye closure and the top edge positioned approximately five rows down from the tip. Add 24 in. (61 cm) of thread to the tab, with the needle exiting an 8º close to one of the holes on the hook finding. Sew through the hole on the finding, and back through the nearest 8º. Sew through the beadwork, and repeat this stitch for the remaining holes **(photo g)**.

Edge embellishment

1 Place the bracelet vertically on your bead mat. Add a comfortable length of thread to the beadwork, and exit the top hole of an end SuperDuo on the edge **(figure 6, point b)**.

2 Pick up four 15º seed beads, sew through the top hole of the next edge SuperDuo, and continue through the bottom hole of the SuperDuo your thread exited at the start of this step **(b–c)**.

FIGURE 6

3 Pick up four 15ºs, cross over the loop just added, and continue through the bottom hole of the adjacent SuperDuo **(c–d)** and the top hole of the same SuperDuo **(d–e)**.

4 Work as in steps 2–3 for the remainder of this edge, sewing over two loops as each new loop is added. End and add thread as needed. Sew through the beadwork on the other end, and work as in steps 2–3 to add embellishment edging to the other side of the base. End the thread. ●

VENETIAN WINDOW
NECKLACE

Capture a gorgeous Czech glass button in a classic seed bead bezel to create a necklace of stunning beauty.

designed by **Graehound**

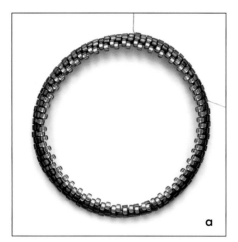

a

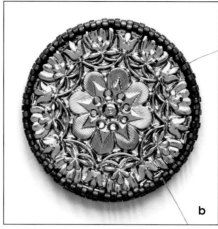

b

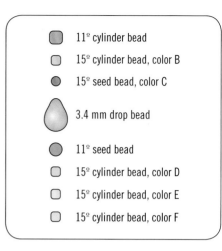

- 11º cylinder bead
- 15º cylinder bead, color B
- 15º seed bead, color C
- 3.4 mm drop bead
- 11º seed bead
- 15º cylinder bead, color D
- 15º cylinder bead, color E
- 15º cylinder bead, color F

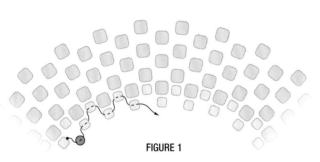

FIGURE 1

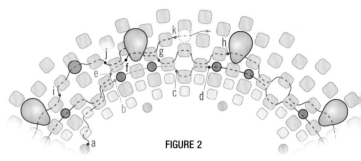

FIGURE 2

Pendant

Bezel

1 On a comfortable length of thread, pick up 90 size 11º cylinder beads, and sew through the first three beads again to form a ring, leaving a 6-in. (15 cm) tail. These beads will shift to form rounds 1 and 2 as the next round is added.
2 Work rounds of tubular peyote stitch as follows (45 stitches per round), stepping up at the end of each round and ending and adding thread as needed.
Rounds 3–6: Work four rounds using 11º cylinder beads.
Rounds 7–8: Work two rounds using color A 15º seed or cylinder beads (if desired, you can substitute one of the other 15º colors in the materials list). Sew through the beadwork to exit an 11º cylinder in round 1 **(photo a)**.
3 Place the button into the beadwork so the back of the button is against the 15ºs **(photo b)**.
4 Work two rounds using color B 15º cylinder beads. End the tail, but not the working thread.
5 Work a stitch using a color C 15º seed

bead, and then sew through the next four beads **(figure 1)**. Repeat this stitch 14 times to complete the round, and step up through the first C added.

Bezel embellishment

1 Sew through four beads as shown **(figure 2, a–b)**. Exiting in this location will keep the embellishment properly aligned with the Cs in the inner ring of the bezel.
2 Pick up a C, and sew through the next 11º cylinder in the same round. Repeat this stitch once **(b–c)**. This set of two beads will sit on top of the beadwork and will create a "frame" for the drop bead you'll add in the next round. Sew through the next two 11º cylinders without adding beads **(c–d)**. Repeat these two stitches 14 times to complete the round **(d–e)**. Sew through the next 11º cylinder in the adjacent round 3 (the one sitting behind the first C added in this round) **(e–f)**.
3 Pick up a 3.4 mm drop bead, and sew through the next 11º cylinder in the same round **(f–g)**. Sew through the next

four 11º cylinders of the bezel as shown **(g–h)**. The drop bead will sit one round back, centered behind the "frame" of Cs created in step 2. Repeat this stitch 14 times to complete the round, but after adding the last drop bead, end after sewing through only one 11º cylinder bead **(h–i)**.
4 Sew through the adjacent 11º cylinder in the next round. Pick up an 11º seed bead, and sew through the following 11º cylinder in the same round **(i–j)**. Sew through the next four 11º cylinders as shown **(j–k)**. Repeat this stitch 14 times to complete the round, and step up through the first 11º seed bead added. Set the pendant aside for now.

Bail

1 On a comfortable length of thread, pick up 30 Bs, and sew through the first three beads again to form a ring, leaving a 6-in. (15 cm) tail. These beads will shift to form rounds 1 and 2 as the next round is added.
2 Using a tight tension, work rounds of tubular peyote stitch (15 stitches

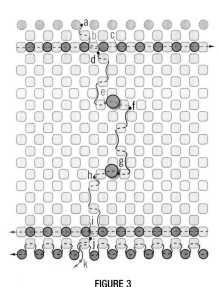

FIGURE 3

Difficulty rating

Materials

green pendant 1⅞ in. (4.8 cm)
- **1** 36 mm glass Czech button (www.ariadesignstudio.etsy.com)
- **15** 3.4 mm drop beads (Japanese, metallic dark gold)
- **1 g** 11º seed beads (Toho 1703, gilded marble turquoise)
- **3 g** 11º cylinder beads (Miyuki DB2004, metallic olive green iris)
- 15º seed beads (Miyuki)
  - **1 g** color A (F460G, matte green gold iris)
  - **1 g** color C (462, metallic gold iris)
- 15º cylinder beads (Miyuki)
  - **1 g** color B (DBS0380, matte metallic khaki iris)
  - **1 g** color D (DBS0029, metallic rainbow nickel-plated golden)
  - **1 g** color E (DBS1201, silver-lined marigold)
  - **1 g** color F (DBS0729, opaque turquoise green)
- Fireline, 6 lb. test
- beading needles, #12

necklace rope 15½ in. (38 cm)
- **10 g** 11º seed beads (Toho 1703, gilded marble turquoise)
- **1** lobster claw clasp
- **2** 4–6 mm jump rings
- **2** 6 mm bullet end caps
- C-Lon nylon cord (Tex 210)
- Big-Eye beading needle
- Kumihimo disk with **8** plastic bobbins and counterweight; or marudai with **8** tama and counterweight
- chopstick and painter's tape (if using a marudai)
- **1** 10 mm (or larger) split ring
- bead spinner (optional)
- E6000 adhesive
- two-part epoxy (optional)
- **2** pairs of chainnose, bentnose, and/or flatnose pliers

Information for the purple colorway is listed at www.BeadAndButton.com/resources.

---

per round) as follows, and step up at the end of each round.

Round 3: Work a round using Bs.

Round 4: Work a round using color D 15º cylinder beads.

Round 5: Work a round using color E 15º cylinder beads.

Round 6: Work a round using color F 15º cylinder beads.

Rounds 7-13: Work seven rounds using Es.

Round 14: Work a round using Fs.

Round 15: Work a round using Es.

Round 16: Work a round using Ds.

Rounds 17-19: Work three rounds using Bs.

Round 20: Work a round using Cs.

Bail embellishment

1 Working toward the opposite edge, sew through the next two rounds as shown to exit a B in round 18 **(figure 3, a–b)**.

2 Pick up a C, and sew through the following B in the same round **(b-c)**. This new C will sit on top of the beadwork.

Repeat this stitch 14 times to complete the round **(c-d)**.

3 Still working toward the opposite edge, sew through the beadwork as shown to exit an E in round 13 **(d-e)**.

4 Pick up an 11º seed bead, and sew through the next E in the same round **(e-f)**. Retrace the thread path of this stitch several times to reinforce the connection (not shown in the figure for clarity). This 11º seed bead will be an "anchor" for attaching the pendant.

5 Working toward the opposite edge, sew through the beadwork as shown to exit the corresponding E in round 7, directly below the 11º just added **(f-g)**. Work as in step 4 to add a second anchor bead **(g-h)**.

6 Still working toward the opposite edge, sew through the beadwork as shown to exit a B in round 2 **(h-i)**. Work as in step 2 to add embellishment Cs to this edge of the bail **(i-j)**.

7 Sew through the adjacent B in round 1, and work a round of tubular peyote using Cs **(j-k)**. End the working thread and tail.

c

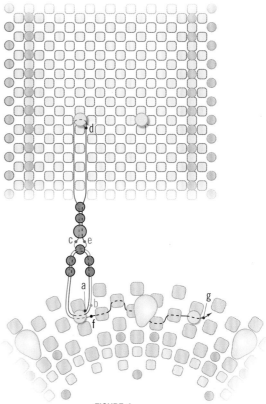

FIGURE 4

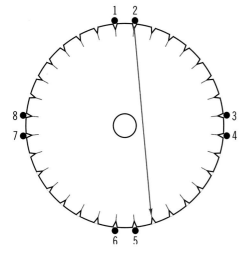

FIGURE 5

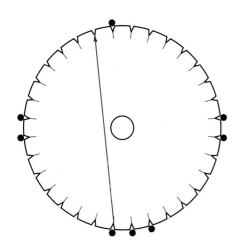

FIGURE 6

Pendant assembly

1 With the working thread on the pendant, pick up five Cs, and sew through the 11º seed bead your thread is exiting to form a loop **(figure 4, a–b)**. Retrace the thread path (not shown in the figure for clarity), and sew through the first three Cs added **(b–c)**.

2 Pick up an 11º seed bead and two Cs, sew through the anchor 11º seed bead on the left side of the bail **(c–d)**, and continue back through the two Cs and 11º seed bead just added **(d–e)**. Sew through the C your thread exited in the loop at the start of this step, the next two Cs, and the original 11º seed bead on the pendant, going in the same direction **(e–f)**. Retrace this thread path to reinforce the connection (not shown in the figure for clarity).

3 Sew through the beadwork as shown to exit the next 11º seed bead on the pendant **(f–g)**. Work as in steps 1–2 to connect the pendant to the anchor bead on the right side of the bail. End the threads.

Rope

This necklace is a beaded eight-cord kongoh gumi braid.

Setup

1 Cut four lengths of C-Lon nylon cord to 8 ft. (2.4 m) each. Line up the ends, center the cords in a 10 mm or larger split ring, and tie an overhand knot to secure the cords to the ring **(photo c)**. This creates the eight cords for your braid.

2 Feed the ring through the center hole of a kumihimo disk or marudai from front to back. If using a marudai, slide a chopstick through the split ring, and tape it to the underside of the mirror. Attach the counterweight. Arrange the cords around the disk or marudai, placing two at the top, two at the bottom, and two on each side.

3 Using a Big-Eye needle, string each cord with 12 in. (30 cm) of 11º seed beads. To string them super-fast, use a bead spinner. After stringing each cord, wind the end of the cord onto a bobbin or tama.

Braid

1 Position the kumihimo disk or marudai with the cords arranged as in **figure 5**.

2 Work a section of rope without beads. Using a disk: Pick up the top-right cord, and slide it into the slit to the right of the bottom two cords **(figure 5)**. Pick up the bottom-left cord, and slide it into the slit to the left of the top cord **(figure 6)**. Rotate the disk clockwise one-quarter turn. Repeat this step until you have about ½ in. (1.3 cm) of unbeaded rope. Using a marudai: Pick up cords 2 and 6 simultaneously. Working in a clockwise direction, place cord 2 to the right of cord 5 and cord 6 to the left of cord 1. Lift cords 4 (right hand) and 8 (left hand) simultaneously. Working in a clockwise direction, place cord 8 above cord 3 and cord 4 below cord 7.

3 Continue braiding with the same motions as in step 2, but add beads: Pick up a cord, slide the next bead up to the point of the rope, and tuck the bead under the cord that crosses over it. Complete the move by placing the cord into the appropriate position. As you work, make sure the beads don't pop out from under the crossing cord.

change it up

As shown in the purple/bronze rope, use 11º and 15º seed beads in multiple colors for a thinner, textured look. String the cords as follows: Cords 1, 3, and 7: String 9 in. (23 cm) of color A 15º seed beads. Cord 2: String 12 in. (30 cm) of 11º seed beads. Cords 4, 5, 6, and 8: String 9 in. (23 cm) of color B 15º seed beads.

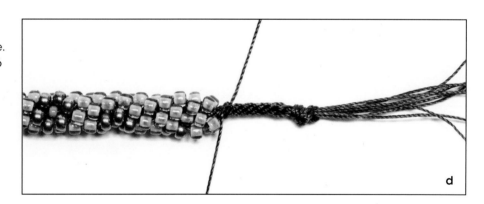

d

If they do, carefully unbraid the cords to the loose bead (being sure to maintain the correct cord order), tuck the loose bead under the crossing cord, and resume braiding.

4 When you have braided all of the beads, or when the cord is the desired length, work ½ in. (1.3 cm) of unbeaded rope.

5 Unwind the cords from the bobbins, remove the cords from the disk, and gather them together. Tie an overhand knot close to the braid. Trim the loose cords close to the knot, and dab with E6000 if desired.

Clasp

1 Cut a 6-in. (15 cm) piece of C-Lon cord, and tie it tightly with a square knot around the unbeaded braid at the starting end of the rope **(photo d)**. Apply a small drop of E6000 to the square knot, and trim the tails of this cord. Repeat this step at the other end of the rope. Allow the glue to dry.

2 Cut through the braid between the overhand knot and the square knot you made in the previous step. Repeat on the other end of the rope.

3 Using E6000 or two-part epoxy, glue one end cap to each end of the rope.

4 Open a jump ring, and attach half of the clasp to an end cap on the rope. Repeat at the other end of the rope. ◉

Keep tension

When using a disk, braiding is most successful when the cords are stretched taut across the hole. If the point of the rope begins to drop down below the face of the disk, gently pull the opposing sets of cords tight so the point of the braid rises up to the desired spot.

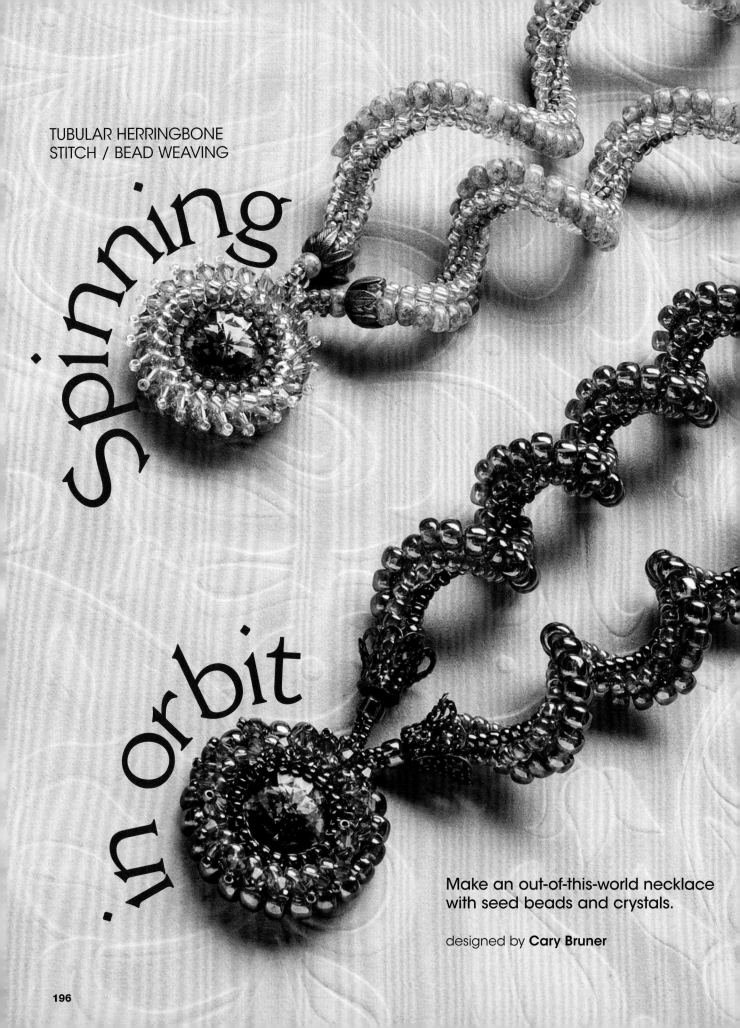

TUBULAR HERRINGBONE
STITCH / BEAD WEAVING

Spinning in orbit

Make an out-of-this-world necklace
with seed beads and crystals.

designed by **Cary Bruner**

a

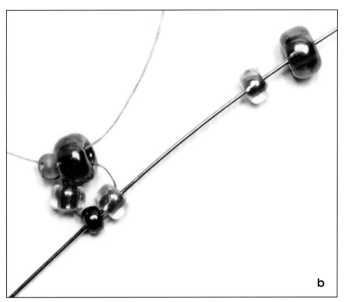

b

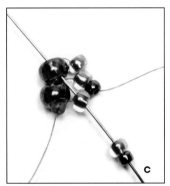

c

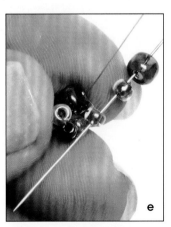

e

g

d

f

Pendant

1 On a comfortable length of thread, string a stop bead, leaving an 8-in. (20 cm) tail. Pick up a 6º seed bead, an 8º seed bead, an 11º seed bead, and an 8º, and sew through the 6º again. Pull the thread tight to form the beads into a ring **(photo a)**.

2 Pick up a 6º and an 8º, and sew through the following 8º and 11º **(photo b)**.

3 Pick up an 11º and an 8º, and sew through the next 8º. Skip the following 6º, and sew through the next 6º added in step 2 **(photo c)**. Keeping the tension tight, shape the beads with your fingers into a tube with four columns with the same bead type in each column **(photo d)**.

4 Pick up a 6º and an 8º, and sew down through the next 8º in the previous round **(photo e)**, and continue up through the following 11º **(photo f)**.

5 Pick up an 11º and an 8º, and sew down through the next 8º in the previous round, and continue up through the 6º added in the new round **(photo g)**.

Materials

lavender necklace 16 in. (41 cm) with 1⅛-in. (2.9 cm) pendant

- **1** 14 mm rivoli (Swarovski, tanzanite)
- **23** 3 mm bicone crystals (Swarovski, light Colorado topaz)
- **20 g** 6º seed beads (Toho Y103, hybrid stone pink)
- **15 g** 8º seed beads (Miyuki 250, crystal AB)
- **3 g** 11º seed beads (Miyuki F356, purple oil)
- **1 g** 15º seed beads (Miyuki 250, crystal AB)
- **4** 10 x 8 mm bead caps
- **1** toggle clasp
- Fireline, 6 lb. test
- beading needles, #12

pink/amber necklace colors

- 14 mm rivoli (Swarovski, vitral medium)
- 3 mm bicone crystals (Swarovski, topaz)
- 6º seed beads (Miyuki 257, transparent topaz AB)
- 8º seed beads (Miyuki 264, raspberry-lined crystal AB)
- 11º seed beads (Miyuki 457, metallic dark bronze)
- 15º seed beads (Toho 221, bronze)

green pendant colors

- 14 mm rivoli (Swarovski, crystal verde)
- 3 mm bicone crystals (Swarovski, bronze shade)
- 6º seed beads (Toho Y182, opaque olive luster green)
- 8º seed beads (Toho 1704, gilded marble lavender)
- 11º seed beads (Miyuki 318i, green tourmaline amber)
- 15º seed beads (Miyuki F460i, green bronze matte)

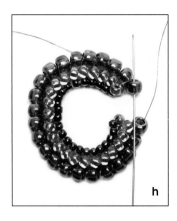
h

i

j

k

l

6 Work as in steps 4–5 20 more times for a total of 23 rounds. End and add thread as needed.

7 Join the tube into a ring as follows:

• With the working thread, make sure the beadwork isn't twisted, and sew through the 6º on the opposite end **(photo h)**.

• Sew back through the 8º in an adjacent column on the same end of the tube, and continue through the corresponding 8º on the opposite end of the tube **(photo i)**.

• Sew up through the 11º in the adjacent column on this end of the tube, and continue through the

corresponding 11º on the opposite end of the tube **(photo j)**.

• Sew down through the 8º in the remaining column, and continue through the corresponding 8º on the opposite end of the tube **(photo k)**. Pull the thread tight.

8 Sew through the beadwork to exit an 11º, and sew through the round of 11ºs to cinch up the beads. Sew through the beadwork to exit an 8º in an adjacent round.

9 Pick up three 15º seed beads, sew through the 8º your thread exited at the beginning of this step to form a picot, and continue through the following 8º

(figure 1, a–b).

10 Pick up two 15ºs, sew down through the first 15º added in the previous picot and the 8º your thread exited at the beginning of this step, and continue through the following 8º to form a new picot **(b–c)**. Repeat this step around the ring of 8ºs, ending when there is one 8º left for a total of 22 picots.

11 Sew up through the end 15º in the first picot. Pick up a 15º, and sew down through the end 15º in the last picot **(figure 2, a–b)**. Continue through the 8º your thread exited at the beginning of this step, the next 15º, and the 15º just added **(b–c)**.

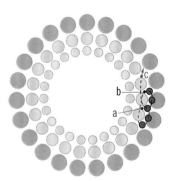

FIGURE 1

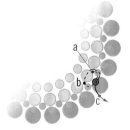

FIGURE 2

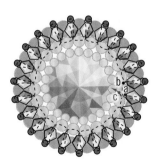

FIGURE 3

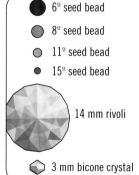

● 6º seed bead

● 8º seed bead

○ 11º seed bead

● 15º seed bead

14 mm rivoli

⬡ 3 mm bicone crystal

for a simpler look

Instead of making neck straps, string the pendant on satin cord, or add additional 15ºs when making the bail, and slide the pendant on a chain.

cream/topaz pendant colors

- 14 mm rivoli (Swarovski, golden shadow)
- 3 mm bicone crystals (Swarovski, golden shadow)
- 6º seed beads (Miyuki 577, dyed butter cream silver-lined alabaster)
- 8º seed beads (Miyuki 457L, metallic light bronze)
- 11º seed beads (Miyuki F460S, purple frosted iris matte)
- 15º seed beads (Toho 465A, crystal-lined bright gold)

12 Place the rivoli face down inside the bezel, and sew through the center 15ºs of the picots **(photo l)**. Pull the thread tight to cinch the beads, and retrace the thread path of the ring of 15ºs twice to secure the rivoli.
13 Sew through the beadwork to exit an 8º on the front of the bezel. Pick up a 3 mm bicone crystal and a 15º. Sew back through the 3 mm, and continue through the following 8º **(figure 3, a–b)**. Repeat this step around the ring of 8ºs for a total of 23 crystal embellishments **(b–c)**.
14 To make a bail: Sew through the beadwork to exit a 6º, pick up six 15ºs, and sew through the same

6º again to form a loop. Retrace the thread path to reinforce the connection. End the working thread, remove the stop bead, and end the tail.

Neck straps

1 Work as in steps 1–5 of "Pendant" for your desired length. Gentle spirals will naturally form as the tube is stitched. The length will shorten when the columns are cinched after steps 2 and 3, so for a 16-in. (41 cm) necklace, make each neck strap approximately 11 in. (28 cm) long when laid out flat without stretching the spirals. Depending on the thread tension, this will result

in a 7-in. (18 cm) neck strap when cinched. End and add thread as needed.
2 With the working thread exiting the end 6º, sew through the beadwork to exit the second-to-last 11º with the needle pointing toward the tail. Sew through the entire column of 11ºs, and exit the end 11º. Gently pull the thread tight to cinch the beads, which will form distinct spirals. Make a few half-hitch knots to secure the spiral shape.
3 Sew through the beadwork to exit an end 6º with the needle facing the other end. If your working thread is shorter than 18 in. (46 cm), end the thread and add a

new one. Sew through the entire column of 6ºs with your thread exiting the end 6º to cinch up the beads.
4 With the working thread, pick up a bead cap, a 6º, three 11ºs or 15ºs, half the toggle clasp, and three 11ºs or 15ºs. Sew back through the 6º, the bead cap, and the 6º your thread exited at the start of this step. Retrace the thread path to reinforce the connection.
5 Remove the stop bead, and attach a needle to the tail. Work as in step 4, but sew through the bail on the pendant instead of the toggle loop. End the tail.
6 Work as in steps 1–5 to make a second neck strap. ●

RIGHT-ANGLE WEAVE / BEAD WEAVING

TWICE AS NICE
bracelet

Work in right-angle weave around a suede cord to make this stunning double-wrap bracelet embellished with sparking crystals.

designed by **Cary Bruner**

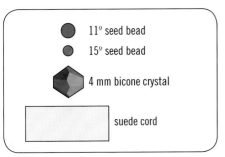

- ● 11º seed bead
- ● 15º seed bead
- ◆ 4 mm bicone crystal
- ▭ suede cord

FIGURE 1

Materials

mauve bracelet 12 in. (30 cm) (double wrap)
- **3** 7 mm round metal beads with 3 mm hole (brass)
- **120** 4 mm bicone crystals (Swarovski, lilac shadow)
- **10 g** 11º seed beads (Toho 1704, mauve 24K gilded marble opaque)
- **4 g** 15º seed beads (Miyuki 460, metallic dark raspberry)
- **14 in. (36 cm)** ⅛ in. (3 mm) faux suede cord
- jump rings
  - **1** 8 mm (brass)
  - **1** 6 mm (brass)
- **2** 5 x 3 mm fold-over cord ends
- **1** lobster claw clasp
- Fireline, 6 lb. or 8 lb. test
- beading needles, #11
- **2** pairs of chainnose, flatnose, and/or bentnose pliers

blue bracelet colors 6½ in. (16.5 cm) (single wrap)
- **1** 5 x 9 mm metal bead with 5 mm hole (silver)
- **60** 4 mm bicone crystals (Swarovski, light turquoise AB2X)
- **5 g** 11º seed beads (Miyuki 2008, matte metallic patina iris)
- **2 g** 15º seed beads (Miyuki 1816, black-lined chartreuse)
- **7 in. (18 cm)** ⅛ in. (3 mm) faux suede cord (turquoise)

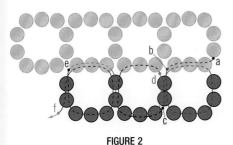

FIGURE 2

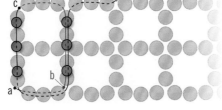

FIGURE 3

Beaded segments

1 On a comfortable length of thread, pick up 10 11º seed beads, and sew through the beads again (not shown in the figure for clarity) to form a ring, leaving a 6-in. (15 cm) tail. Tie a square knot, and sew through the first five beads again **(figure 1, a–b)**.

2 Pick up eight 11ºs, and sew through the last two beads your thread exited in the previous stitch, and continue through the first five beads added in this stitch **(b–c)**.

3 Work as in step 2 for a total of 15 right-angle weave (RAW) stitches to form row 1, ending and adding thread as needed. After the final stitch, sew through the next three 11ºs on the bottom of the last stitch **(figure 2, a–b)**.

4 To start row 2, pick up seven 11ºs, and sew through the three 11ºs on the bottom edge of the last stitch in row 1 to form a ring, and continue through the first two 11ºs picked up in this stitch **(b–c)**.

5 Pick up five 11ºs, and sew through

the adjacent three 11ºs on the bottom edge in the previous row **(c–d)**. Continue through the next two side 11ºs in the previous stitch, the five 11ºs picked up in this stitch, and the following three 11ºs of the next stitch in the previous row **(d–e)**.

6 Pick up five 11ºs, and sew through the two side 11ºs in the previous stitch in this row, and continue through the three 11ºs your thread exited at the start of this step and the next two 11ºs added in this stitch **(e–f)**.

7 Work as in steps 5–6 to complete the row, and sew through the bottom edge of 11ºs in the last stitch **(figure 3, a–b)**. End and add thread as needed.

8 Fold the beadwork in half lengthwise to create a V-shape (with the open side facing upward). Pick up three 15º seed beads, and sew through the edge three 11ºs in the corresponding stitch of the opposite row **(b–c)**. Pick up three 15ºs, and sew through the three 11ºs your thread exited at the start of this step. Continue through the three 15ºs

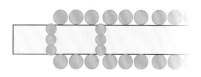

FIGURE 4

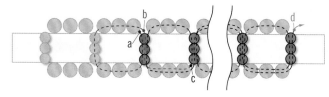

FIGURE 5

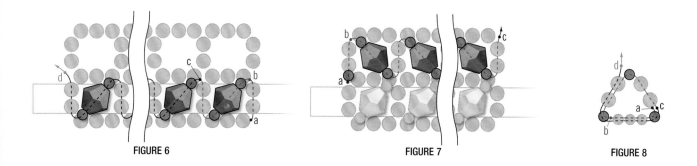

FIGURE 6

FIGURE 7

FIGURE 8

just added and the next three 11ºs on the other edge **(c–d)** to form a three-sided tube shape.

9 Slide the suede cord through the tube so the cord lies flat against the 15ºs. Pull the cord through the tube until 5/16 in. (8 mm) extends out the tube end **(figure 4)**. If needed, cinch up the 15ºs by pulling the thread tight.

10 Keeping the cord flat in the beadwork, pick up three 15ºs, sew through the corresponding three 11ºs on the opposite edge, the three 15ºs added in the previous stitch, and the three 11ºs your thread exited at the start of this step **(figure 5, a–b)**. Continue through the three 15ºs just added and the next three 11ºs on the other edge **(b–c)**.

11 Repeat step 10 for the remainder of the row. On the last stitch, stop after sewing through the last three 15ºs just added **(c–d).** The side with 15ºs will be the bottom edge of the bracelet.

Embellishment

1 Rotate the tube toward you, and sew through the next two 11ºs of the end RAW stitch of the base **(figure 6, a–b)**.

2 Pick up a 15º, a 4 mm bicone crystal, and a 15º, cross the RAW stitch diagonally, and sew through the corresponding two 11ºs going in the same direction **(b–c)**. Repeat this stitch to complete the row **(c–d)**, adding a total of 15 crystals. End and add thread as needed.

3 Pick up a 15º, and sew through the next two end 11ºs **(figure 7, a–b)**. Work as in step 2 to complete the row **(b–c)**.

4 To fill in the gaps between the RAW stitches on the end of the tube (only the end view of the beadwork is shown in the figure for clarity): Pick up a 15º, and sew through the next three end 15ºs **(figure 8, a–b)**. Pick up a 15º, and sew through the following two end 11ºs. Repeat this stitch once **(b–c)**, and continue through the next seven end beads **(c–d)** to position the thread exiting between the two rows of crystals.

5 To fill in the gaps in the spine of 11ºs between the two rows of crystals (only the top view of beadwork is shown in the figure for clarity): Sew through the next three 11ºs **(figure 9, a–b)**. Pick up an 11º, and sew through the following three 11ºs **(b–c)**. Repeat this stitch to complete the row **(c–d)**, and sew down through the end 15º **(d–e)**.

6 Work as in step 4 to fill the gaps at this end with 15ºs, but add only two 15ºs (the third 15º was added in step 3). End the tail, but not the working thread.

7 Slide a 7 mm metal bead onto the suede cord next to the beaded segment.

Keep on going

Continuing on the same suede cord, work as in "Beaded segment" and "Embellishment" to make a total of four beaded segments, placing a metal bead between each pair of segments.

make it a single

If desired, make a single wrap bracelet by making two instead of four beaded segments with a metal bead in the center. Each segment measures approximately 3 in. (7.6 cm) long.

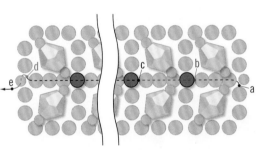

FIGURE 9

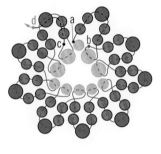

FIGURE 10

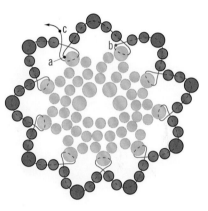

FIGURE 11

Clasp

1 Trim the suede cord, leaving ⁵⁄₁₆ in. (8 mm) exposed on each end (or enough space for a fold-over cord end).
2 Align a fold-over cord end finding at one end of the cord, and use chain-nose pliers to gently push each side of the finding flat to secure the cord.
3 Open a 6 mm jump ring, attach the loop of the fold-over finding and the loop of a lobster clasp, and close the jump ring.
4 Repeat step 2 on the other end of the bracelet, and attach an 8 mm jump ring to the loop of the fold-over finding.

Clasp embellishment

If desired, cover both fold-over cord ends with loops of seed beads:
1 With the working thread of the first beaded segment, pick up two 15ºs, an 11º, and two 15ºs, and sew through the previous end 11º, with the needle exiting toward the 15º your thread exited at the start of this step to form a loop (only the end view of the beadwork is shown

in figures 10–11 for clarity) **(figure 10, a–b)**. Repeat this stitch eight times to complete the round **(b–c)**.
2 Sew through the last two 15ºs added and the 11º in the last loop with the needle exiting to the left **(c–d)**.
3 Pick up two 15ºs, an 11º, and two 15ºs, and sew through the 11º in the next loop with the needle exiting to the left **(figure 11, a–b)**. Repeat this stitch eight times to compete the round **(b–c)**. End the working thread.
4 Add loops on the other end of the clasp: With the working thread, sew through the row of 11ºs between the rows of crystals to reach the clasp end, and then sew up through the end 15º. Repeat steps 1–3. End the working thread on all the beaded segments. ◗

did you know?

When using a lobster clasp, it's easy to make the length of jewelry adjustable. Just add five or more jump rings or a piece of chain to the first jump ring. Then attach the lobster clasp to any one of these jump rings or links.

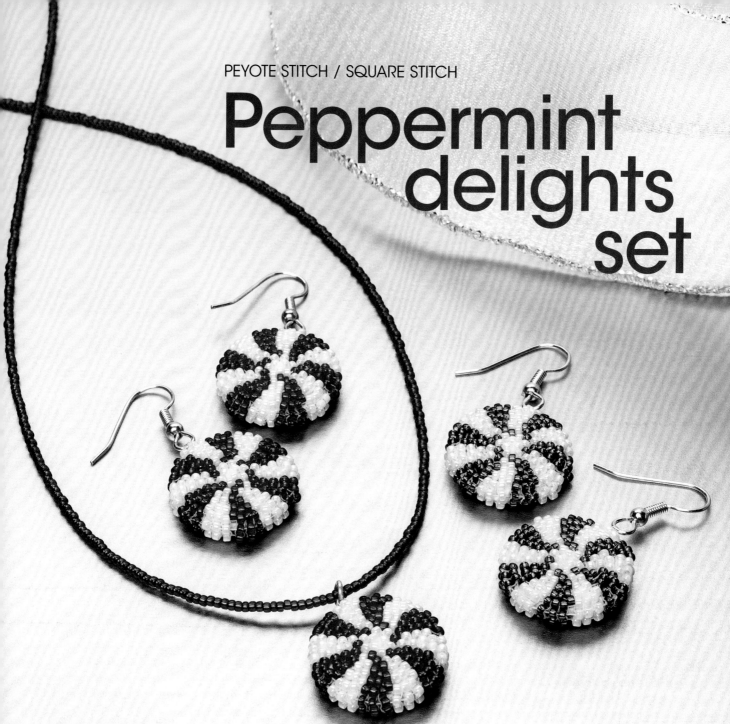

Peppermint delights set

Cook up fresh and minty swirled beaded beads into a cute jewelry set that gives the impression you're wearing real peppermint candy!

designed by
Lane Landry

Peppermint piece

1 On a comfortable length of thread, pick up three color A 15º seed beads, and sew through the beads again, leaving a 6-in. (15 cm) tail. Continue through the first bead added. Pull the thread tight, and position the beads into a triangle-shaped ring.

to help keep track

Before each round, count out the number of beads needed. When all the beads are used, the round should be completed, and it's time to step up to start the next round.

2 Work rounds of increasing circular peyote as follows, ending and adding thread as needed:

Round 1: Pick up two As, and sew through the following A in the ring. Repeat this stitch twice, and step up through the first A added in the round **(figure 1, a–b)**.

Round 2: Pick up a color B 15º seed bead, and sew through the next A in the pair

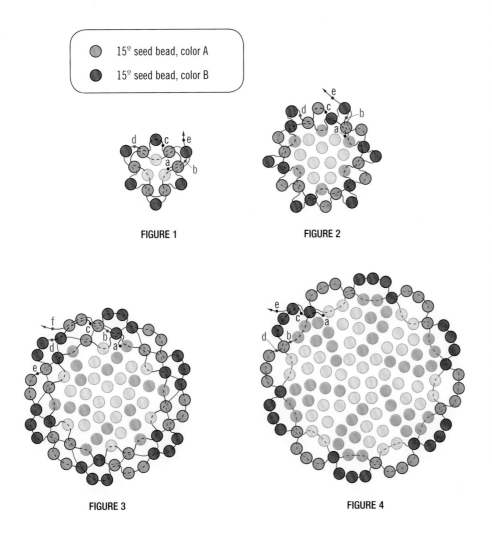

15º seed bead, color A
15º seed bead, color B

FIGURE 1

FIGURE 2

FIGURE 3

FIGURE 4

Difficulty rating

    ⬡

Materials

earrings ⅞ in. (2.2 cm)

• 15º seed beads
  - **3 g** color A (Toho 121, opaque white luster)
  - **3 g** color B (Toho 25C, silver-lined dark ruby or Toho 36, silver-lined emerald green)
• **1** pair of earring findings
• **2** dimes
• white tissue paper
• Fireline, 6 lb. test
• beading needles, #12

make it a necklace

Use a 5 mm closed jump ring in place of an ear wire to make a cute pendant, and string matching seed beads onto beading wire to make a coordinating neck strap.

(b–c). Pick up a B, and sew through the next A in the previous round **(c–d)**. Repeat these stitches twice to complete the round, and step up through the first A added in the round **(d–e)**.

Round 3: Work six stitches using both an A and a B in each stitch, and step up through the first A added in the round **(figure 2, a–b)**.

Round 4: Pick up a B, and sew through the next B **(b–c)**. Pick up an A, and sew through the following A **(c–d)**. Repeat these two stitches five times to complete the round, and step up through the first B added in the round **(d–e)**.

Round 5: Work 12 stitches

(using one bead per stitch) in an alternating pattern of a B and an A, and step up through the first B added in the round **(figure 3, a–b)**.

Round 6: Work 12 stitches (using one bead per stitch) in an alternating pattern of an A and a B, and step up through the first A added in the round **(b–c)**.

Round 7: Pick up two As, and sew through the following B **(c–d)**. Pick up two Bs, and sew through the following A **(d–e)**. Repeat these two stitches five times to complete the round, and step up through the first two As added in the round **(e–f)**.

Round 8: Pick up a B, and sew through the following

two beads in the previous round **(figure 4, a–b)**. Repeat this stitch 11 times in an alternating pattern of an A and a B to complete the round, and step up through the first B added in the round **(b–c)**.

Round 9: Pick up three Bs, and sew through the next bead in the previous round **(c–d)**. Repeat this stitch 11 times in an alternating pattern of three As and then three Bs to complete the round, and step up through the first B added in the round **(d–e)**.

Round 10: Working in square stitch, pick up a B, sew through the B your thread is exiting (going in the same direction), and

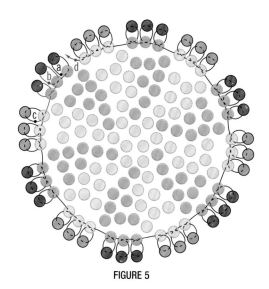

FIGURE 5

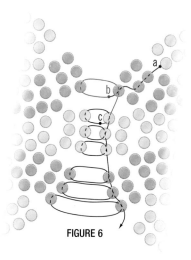

FIGURE 6

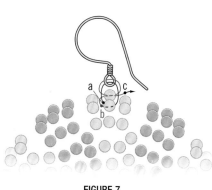

FIGURE 7

continue through the next B in the round **(figure 5, a–b)**. Repeat this stitch twice, but on the second stitch, skip the next "down" bead, and sew through the following "up" bead **(b–c)**. Repeat these stitches to complete the round, alternating between adding a set of three As and a set of three Bs so that each new bead is the same color as the bead you're attaching it to **(c–d)**. Sew through the beadwork as shown to exit an edge bead **(figure 6, a–b)**. End the tail, but not the working thread.
3 Repeat steps 1–2 to make a second peppermint piece, but end the working thread and tail.

Assembly
1 Stack the two peppermint pieces so that they are a mirror image of each other.
2 With the working thread, work a square stitch thread path (without picking up any new beads) to join the peppermint pieces (illustration is shown with the two pieces flat for clarity, but this works best when the pieces are stacked): Sew through the corresponding B on the edge of the second peppermint piece, and continue through the B your thread exited at the start of this step and the next A on the same edge **(b–c)**. Repeat this stitch until approximately

half of the circumference is joined.
3 To add firmness and stability to the beadwork, wrap a dime inside a 2½-in. (6.4 cm) square of white tissue paper. The paper should lie flat with no large lumps. Place the wrapped dime inside the beadwork. Adjust the paper if needed for a better fit by using scissors to round the corners, or remove a layer of the paper.
4 Continue working as in step 2 to complete the round. Sew through the next three beads to exit a center A bead **(figure 7, point a)**.
5 Sew through the loop of an ear wire, and the bead

your thread just exited, going in the same direction **(a–b)**. Sew through the adjacent A on the other peppermint piece, and continue through the ear wire loop and the bead your thread exited at the start of this step, going in the same direction **(b–c)**. The ear wire will sit on top of the two As. Retrace the thread path to reinforce the join, and end the thread.
6 Make a second earring. ●

Crystal crossings bracelet

Embellish a peyote-stitched base with crystals and pearls to create an exquisite bracelet.

designed by **Jackie Schwietz**

Base

1 On a comfortable length of thread, attach a stop bead, leaving a 12-in. (30 cm) tail. Pick up 11 8º hex beads, and work in flat odd-count peyote stitch for the desired bracelet length less ¾ in. (1.9 cm) for the clasp. End and add thread as needed, end on an odd numbered row with six up-beads, and end the working thread.

2 Place the base horizontally on your bead mat, and attach a needle to each end of a comfortable length of thread. With the right needle, sew through the third top edge hex from the right end of the base, with the needle pointing away from the base **(figure 1, point a)**. With the left needle, sew through the adjacent fourth hex on the top edge **(point aa)**.

note *If desired, leave five or six rows unembellished on each end of the base, as shown in the blue bracelet, p. 207.*

Top embellishment

1 With each needle, pick up a color A 15º seed bead, a 3 mm pearl, and an A. With one needle, pick up a pearl, and cross the other needle through it **(a–b and aa–bb)**. Repeat this stitch twice **(b–c and bb–cc)**. With each needle, pick up an A, a pearl, and an A, and sew through the corresponding hexes on the bottom edge of the base with the needles pointing toward the middle of the base **(c–d and cc–dd)**.

not all the same

Size 8º hex beads can vary in length. Depending on the hex, your base might be wider, and you may need to repeat the embellishment stitch three times instead of twice. Add or remove beads in the embellishment row to comfortably fit on top of the base.

2 Get into position to start the next row of embellishment: With each needle, zigzag through the next three edge

beads. The needles should be exiting the sixth and seventh edge beads **(figure 2, point a and aa)**.

3 Work as in step 1, but use 4 mm bicone crystals in place of the pearls **(figure 2)**. Repeat step 2.

4 Continue working as in steps 1–3, alternating pearls and crystals for the length of the base. End both working threads.

Clasp

1 Remove the stop bead, thread a needle on the tail, and sew back through the hex your thread is exiting. Place half of the clasp along the end of the base.

2 Pick up two color B 15º seed beads, the end loop of half the clasp, and two Bs, and sew back through the end hex **(figure 3, a–b)**. Sew through the beadwork as shown to exit the next up-bead on the edge **(b–c)**.

3 Work as in step 2 for the remaining loops on the clasp, sewing back through the hex your thread exited

---

■ 8º hexagon bead

● 15º seed bead, color A

○ 3 mm pearl

⬡ 4 mm bicone crystal

● 15º seed bead, color B

○ 8º seed bead

---

edge embellishment option

As shown in the blue bracelet, p. 207, instead of picking up an 8º and a 15º in step 2 of "Edge embellishment," pick up two 8ºs, and sew through the next hex. Skip a row as in step 4, and continue adding sets of 8ºs in this manner on both edges of the base.

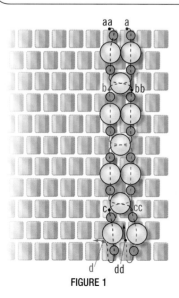

FIGURE 1

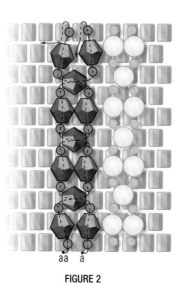

FIGURE 2

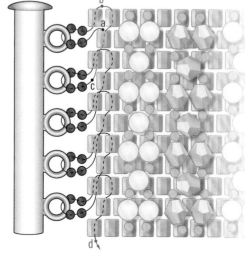

FIGURE 3

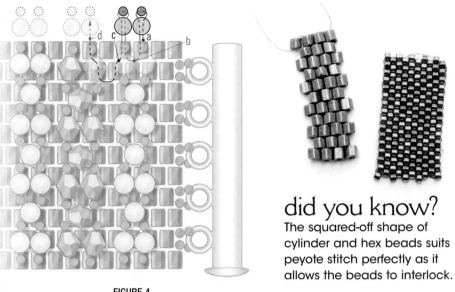

FIGURE 4

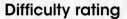

did you know?

The squared-off shape of cylinder and hex beads suits peyote stitch perfectly as it allows the beads to interlock.

Materials

amethyst bracelet 7½ in. (19.1 cm)

- **110** 4 mm bicone crystals (Swarovski, amethyst)
- **110** 3 mm pearls (Swarovski, vintage gold)
- **34 g** 8º hexagon beads (Toho F460A, matte raspberry bronze iris)
- **2 g** 8º seed beads (Toho PF557, permanent galvanized starlight)
- **15º** seed beads
  - **2 g** color A (Toho P471, permanent galvanized gold)
  - **1 g** color B (Toho 460A, metallic raspberry bronze iris)
- **1** 5-strand slide-tube clasp
- Fireline, 6 lb. or 8 lb. test
- beading needles, #11

blue bracelet colors

- 4 mm bicone crystals (Swarovski, Pacific opal)
- 3 mm glass pearls (Swarovski, bright gold)
- 8º hexagon beads (Toho F650, matte olivine)
- 8º seed beads (Toho 457, metallic bronze)
- 15º seed beads
  - color A (Toho 457, metallic bronze)
  - color B (Toho 952, rainbow topaz seafoam-lined)

at the start of each stitch **(c–d)**, and end the tail.

4 Add a comfortable length of thread to the opposite end of the base, exiting an end edge bead with the needle heading toward the beadwork. Work as in steps 2–3 to add the other half of the clasp. Do not end the working thread.

Edge embellishment

1 With the working thread, sew through the base to exit the third top edge hex from the right end of the base, with the needle pointing away from the base **(figure 4, point a)**. For clarity, part of the embellishment in **figure 4** has been faded to show the thread path.

2 Pick up an 8º seed bead and an A, and sew back through the 8º and the

hex your thread exited at the start of this step **(a–b)**.

3 Sew through the adjacent hex, and repeat step 2 to complete the first set of edge embellishments **(b–c)**.

4 Sew through the beadwork as shown to skip a row, and get into position to add the next set of edge embellishments **(c–d)**.

5 Work as in steps 2–4 for the length of the base. End and add thread as needed.

6 Sew through the beadwork to exit the corresponding hex on the other edge, and repeat steps 2–5. If any end hex beads are left unembellished, embellish them if you desire. ●

PEYOTE STITCH / HERRINGBONE STITCH /
CROSSWEAVE TECHNIQUE

FESTIVE BY DESIGN
NECKLACE

Combine popular stitches
to create a party-perfect
necklace glimmering with
pearls and rose montées.

designed by **Janice Chatham**

Rose montée components

1 On 1 yd. (.9 m) of thread, pick up
a 4 mm rose montée and seven 15°
seed beads. Sew through the rose
montée again in the same direction,
leaving a 6-in. (15 cm) tail **(figure 1,
a–b)**. This forms a loop of 15°s around
one side of the montée. Pick up seven
15°s, and sew through the montée
again to form a loop on the other
side **(b–c)**. Sew through the seven
15°s just added. Pick up a 15°, and
sew through the next seven 15°s. Pick

up a 15°, and sew through the following
four 15°s to form a tight ring around the
montée **(figure 2, a–b)**.
2 Sew through the open hole of the
montée and the opposite 15°. Sew
back through the same hole of the
montée, and continue through the
15° your thread exited at the start
of this step **(b–c)**.
3 Pick up an 11° seed bead, a 15°,
and an 11°, and sew through the
15° your thread exited at the start
of this step and the next 15° in the

ring **(figure 3, a–b)**. Pick up an 11° and
a 15°, and sew through the adjacent
11° in the previous set, the 15° in the
ring, and the next 15° **(b–c)**. Repeat
this stitch 13 times **(c–d)**. For the last
stitch in the round, sew through the
adjacent 11° in the first stitch, pick up
a 15°, and sew down through the 11°
added in the last stitch and the 15°
in the ring again **(d–e)**. End the tail
but not the working thread.
4 Make a total of five rose montée
components.

5 Add embellishment to one rose montée component: With the working thread, sew through the beadwork to exit an outer round 15º. Pick up three 15ºs, a crystal teardrop bead, and three 15ºs, and sew through the 15º your thread exited at the start of this step, going in the same direction **(figure 4)**. Don't end the working thread.

Pearl components

1 On 1 yd. (.9 m) of thread, pick up 24 15ºs, tie them into a ring with a square knot, leaving an 8-in. (20 cm) tail, and sew through the next 15º. These beads will shift to form rounds 1 and 2 as the next round is added.

Round 3: Working in circular peyote stitch, pick up a 15º, skip the next bead in the ring, and sew through the following 15º **(figure 5, a–b)**. Repeat this stitch 11 times, and step up through the first 15º added to complete the round **(b–c)**.

note If desired, substitute 5 mm round glass or crystal pearls in place of freshwater pearls.

2 Thread a needle on the tail, and sew through an adjacent bead in round 1. Pick up a 5 mm pearl, and center it in the middle of the ring. Sew through the opposite 15º, and sew back through the pearl and the 15º your thread exited at the start of this step **(figure 6, a–b)**. End the tail.

3 Round 4: With the working thread, pick up an 11º cylinder bead, and sew through the next 15º in round 3 **(c–d)**. Repeat this stitch to add a total of 12 cylinders **(d–e)**.

4 Sew through the following 15º in round 2, pick up a 15º, and sew through the next 15º in round 2 **(figure 7, a–b)**. Repeat this stitch 11 times to complete the round. Step up through the first 15º added **(b–c)**. The 15ºs in this round will sit on top of the 15ºs in rounds 1 and 3.

Difficulty rating

Materials
necklace 16½ in. (41.9 cm)

- 1 15 x 7.5 mm teardrop bead (Swarovski, Siam)
- pearls
  - 3 4.5–5 mm round or semi-round pearls (freshwater, white)
  - 22 4 mm rice pearls (freshwater, white)
  - 38 2 mm pearls (freshwater, white)
- **5** 4 mm rose montées (SS16, Siam)
- **2 g** 11º seed beads (Miyuki 4222, Duracoat galvanized pewter)
- **2 g** 11º cylinder beads (Miyuki DB251, galvanized gray)
- **3 g** 15º seed beads (Toho F464B, metallic matte silver)
- Fireline, 6 lb. test
- beading needles, #12 or #13

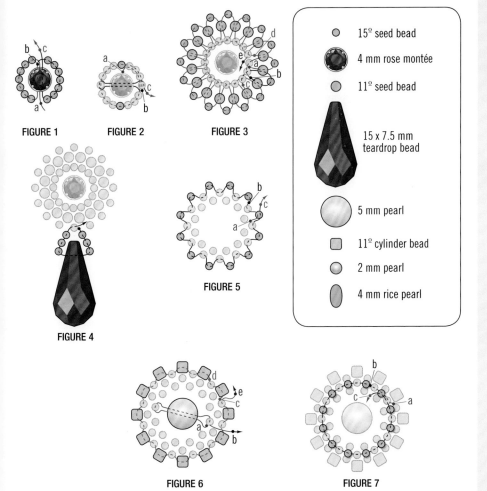

FIGURE 1

FIGURE 2

FIGURE 3

FIGURE 4

FIGURE 5

- 15º seed bead
- 4 mm rose montée
- 11º seed bead
- 15 x 7.5 mm teardrop bead
- 5 mm pearl
- 11º cylinder bead
- 2 mm pearl
- 4 mm rice pearl

FIGURE 6

FIGURE 7

5 Pick up an 11º, and sew through the next 15º added in step 4 **(figure 8, a–b)**. Repeat this stitch 11 times to complete the round **(b–c)**, and sew through the following cylinder in round 4 to step up **(c–d)**.

6 Work in modified herringbone stitch: Pick up two cylinders, and sew through the next cylinder in round 4 **(d–e)**. The cylinders will naturally sit at an angle. Repeat this stitch 11 times, and step up by sewing through the first cylinder added **(e–f)**.

7 Pick up two cylinders, sew down through the following cylinder in the stack and the next cylinder in round 4, and continue through the first cylinder in the next stack **(figure 9, a–b)**. Repeat this stitch 11 times to complete the round, and step up through the first cylinder added **(b–c)**.

8 Pick up two cylinders, and sew down through the next two cylinders in the stack, the following cylinder in round 4, and the next two cylinders in the following stack **(figure 10, a–b)**. Repeat this stitch 11 times to complete the round, but after the last stitch, sew through only the cylinder in round 4 **(b–c)**.

9 Pick up a 2 mm pearl, and sew through the following cylinder in round 4 **(figure 11, a–b)**. Repeat this stitch 11 times to complete the round **(b–c)**, and end the working thread.

10 Repeat steps 1–9 to make a total of three pearl components.

Assembly
Side segments
1 With the working thread of a rose montée component (one without a teardrop), sew through the beadwork to exit an edge 15º with the topside of the component facing up **(figure 12, point a)**.

2 Sew down through two cylinders on a pearl component **(a–b)**.

3 Pick up a 15º, and sew up through two corresponding cylinders in the following stack **(b–c)**. Pick up a 15º, and sew down through the next two cylinders **(c–d)**. Repeat these two stitches four times **(d–e)**.

4 Pick up a 15º, and sew up through two cylinders in the next stack **(e–f)**. Sew through an outer 15º of a new rose montée component, and then

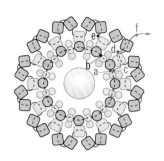

FIGURE 8

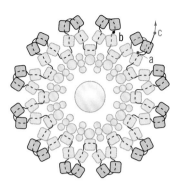

FIGURE 9

FIGURE 10

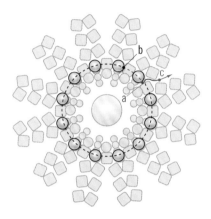

FIGURE 11

sew down through the next two cylinders in the following stack on the pearl component **(f–g)**.

5 Repeat step 3 **(g–h)**. To complete the round, pick up a 15º, sew up through the two end cylinders in the next stack, continue through the next three beads **(h–i)**, and end the thread.

6 Repeat steps 1–5 to make a second side segment.

Center focal
1 With the working thread of the rose montée component with the teardrop, sew through the beadwork to exit the 15º opposite the teardrop.

2 Attach this rose montée component to the remaining pearl component as in steps 2–3 of "Side segments," but in step 3, repeat the two stitches twice instead of four times.

3 Connect a side segment: Work as in step 4 of "Side segments," sewing through the edge 15º of a rose montée component in a side segment opposite the 15º attached to the pearl component.

4 Work as in step 3 of "Side segments"

for a total of three stitches, and then attach the remaining side segment.

5 Finish embellishing the center pearl component as in step 3 of "Side segments," and end the threads.

Neck straps
1 Attach a needle to each end of a comfortable length of thread. In a side segment, center the thread in the seventh 15º away from the connection to the pearl component **(figure 13, point a and aa)**.

2 With the needle facing the eighth 15º from the connection, pick up a 15º, and sew through the eighth 15º. Pick up a 15º, and sew through the next 15º **(a–b)**.

3 With each needle, pick up five 15ºs **(b–c and aa–bb)**. With one needle, pick up an 11º, a 4 mm rice pearl, and an 11º, and sew through these three beads with the other needle **(c–d and bb–cc)**.

4 On each needle, pick up two 15ºs. With one needle, pick up two 15ºs, and sew through these two beads with the other needle **(d–e and cc–dd)**. On each needle, pick up two 15ºs. With one needle, pick up an 11º, a rice

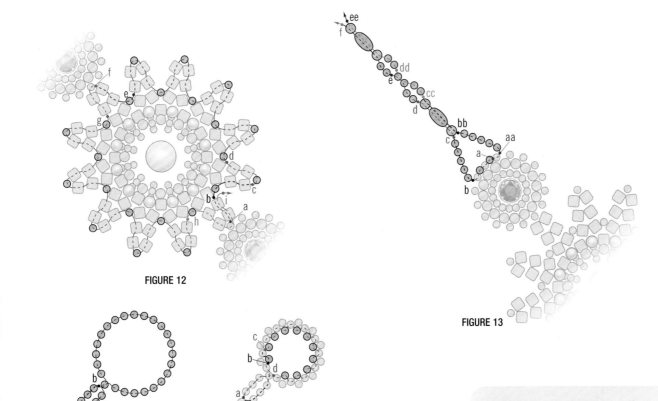

FIGURE 12

FIGURE 13

FIGURE 14

FIGURE 15

FIGURE 16

glass pearls 101

Glass pearls are a great alternative to freshwater pearls. They consistently have a perfect smooth shape, a uniform size, and the hole diameter is typically larger than those of freshwater pearls, allowing for several thread paths through the hole.

pearl, and an 11º, and sew through these three beads with the other needle **(e-f and dd-ee)**.
5 Repeat step 4 nine times. End and add thread as needed. Do not end the working threads.
6 Repeat steps 1–5 to make a second neck strap on the opposite side.

Toggle clasp
Toggle ring
1 At the end of a neck strap, with one needle, pick up 27 15ºs, and sew back through the fourth 15º to form a ring **(figure 14, a–b)**. Pick up three 15ºs, and sew back through the following 11º, rice pearl, and 11º in the neck strap **(b–c)**.
2 With the other needle, sew through the last three 15ºs added in step 1, and continue through the next two 15ºs on the left-side of the ring **(figure 15, a–b)**. Working in circular peyote stitch, pick up a 15º, skip a 15º, and sew through the next 15º in the ring **(b–c)**. Repeat this stitch 10 times **(c–d)**. Sew back through the first four 15ºs added in step 1 and the following 11º, rice pearl,

and 11º in the neck strap **(d–e)**. Tie the two working threads into a square knot, and end the threads.

Toggle bar
1 On 24 in. (61 cm) of thread, attach a stop bead, leaving a 6-in. (15 cm) tail. Pick up 10 15ºs, and work in flat even-count peyote stitch for a total of 10 rows. Zip up the ends to form a tube, and sew through the center of the tube to exit the other side.
2 Pick up a 2 mm pearl and a 15º, and sew back through the pearl and the center of the tube. Repeat this step once to add a pearl to the other side of the tube. End the working thread, remove the stop bead, and end the tail.

3 With a working thread from the

second neck strap, pick up six 15ºs, and sew through two adjacent 15ºs in the center of the toggle bar. Pick up two 15ºs, and sew back through the fourth 15º added in this step **(figure 16, a–b)**. Pick up three 15ºs, and sew back through the end 11º, rice pearl, and 11º in the neck strap **(b–c)**. With the other working thread, retrace the thread path to reinforce the join, and end the threads. ●

213

KUMIHIMO ■ BEAD WEAVING

Springtime garden

necklace

Braid seed beads and two-hole beads within a kumihimo rope to lay the foundation for embellishments that resemble nature.

designed by **Julia Hecht**

Setup

1 Cut six 5-ft. (1.5 m) pieces of regular-weight cord (Tex 210) and two 5 ft. (1.5 m) pieces of fine (Tex 135) or micro (Tex 70) weight cord. Gather the ends of the cords, and tie them together with an overhand knot 1½ in. (3.8 cm) from one end. Feed the knot through the center of the kumihimo disk from front to back.

note Avoid using a heavy-weight cord to secure the knot when working the braid, as it can cause the pattern to form an undesirable twist. Consider skipping that weight altogether for this project.

2 Using a Big-Eye needle, string 100 beads on each cord according to the bead stringing order (below). This will make a rope of approximately 15 in. (38 cm) without the clasp.

bead stringing order

Each cord should have 100 beads.
Cords 1, 2, 3, 5, 6, and 7: String 100 color A 8ºs on regular-weight cord.
Cord 4: String a repeating pattern of a lentil, an A, a SuperDuo, and an A 25 times on fine- or micro-weight cord.
Cord 8: String a repeating pattern of a SuperDuo, an A, a lentil, and an A 25 times on fine- or micro-weight cord.

After you load a cord, push the beads up to within 3 in. (7.6 cm) of the disk, and wrap the beaded cord around a bobbin, leaving about 4 in. (10 cm) of cord hanging from the edge of the disk. Label the bobbin with the appropriate cord number, and slip the cord into the appropriate slit in the disk.

make it longer

To make an 18-in. (46 cm) rope, string an additional 15 As on each end of all eight cords. This will evenly add 3 in. (7.6 cm) of unembellished length to the rope. Add an additional 12 in. (30 cm) to each cord if making a rope longer than 18 in. (46 cm).

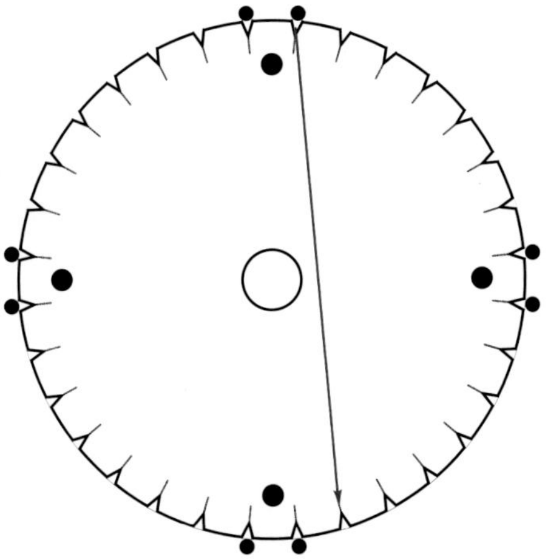

Difficulty rating

Materials

necklace 16 in. (41 cm)

- **12** 12 x 7 mm leaf beads (Czech, auburn gold inlay)
- **39** 5 x 7 mm Pip beads (jet Vega)
- **50** 3 x 6 mm two-hole lentil beads (CzechMates, opaque olive)
- **11 g** 2.5 x 5 mm SuperDuos (pastel emerald)
- **24** 4 mm fire-polished beads (matte metallic lava)
- 8º seed beads
  - **20 g** color A (Miyuki 457N, raspberry bronze)
  - **2 g** color B (Miyuki D4208, Duracoat copper rose)
- **1 g** 11º seed beads (Miyuki 14, silver-lined chartreuse)
- **2** 6 mm bullet end caps
- **1** hook-and-eye clasp
- **2–4** 6–7 mm jump rings
- C-Lon or S-Lon cord in regular weight (Tex 210) and fine (Tex 135) or micro weight (Tex 70) (brown)
- Fireline, 6 lb. test
- kumihimo disk with **8** bobbins
- beading needles, #11 or #12
- Big-Eye beading needle
- E6000 or 2-part epoxy adhesive
- **2** pairs of chainnose, bentnose, and/or flatnose pliers

FIGURE 1

cord 1   cord 2

cord 8

cord 3

cord 7

cord 4

cord 6   cord 5

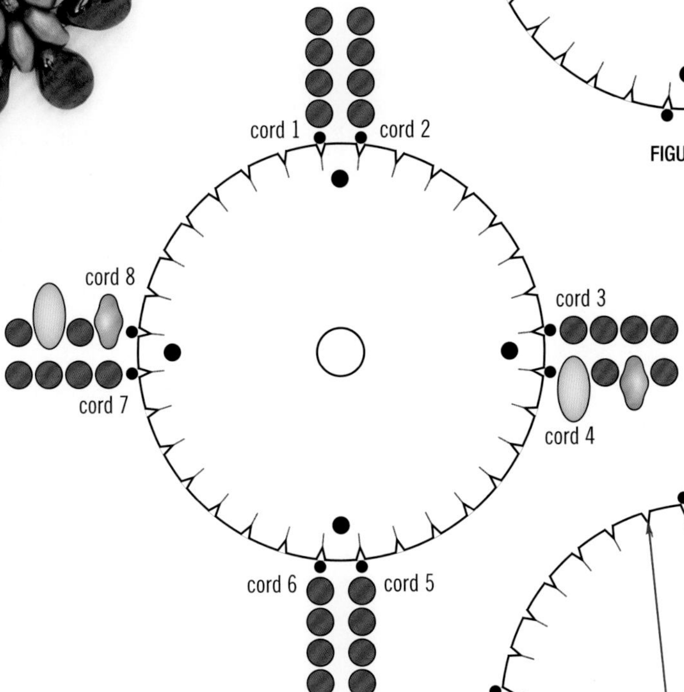

PATTERN

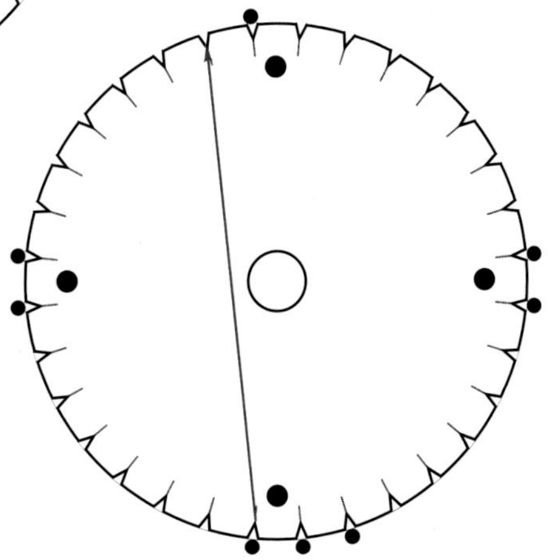

FIGURE 2

Braid

1 Position the kumihimo disk as shown in the **pattern** with cords 1–2 at the top.
2 Work a section of rope without the beads: Pick up the top-right cord, and slide it into the slit to the right of the bottom two cords **(figure 1)**. Pick up the bottom left cord, and slide it into the slit to the left of the top cord **(figure 2)**.

215

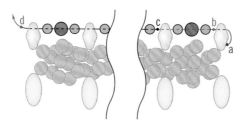

FIGURE 3

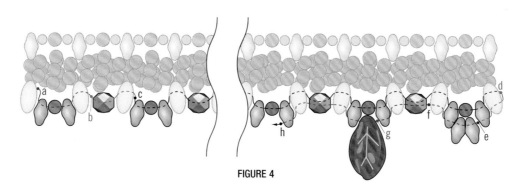

FIGURE 4

Rotate the disk clockwise one-quarter turn. Repeat this step until you have about ½ in. (1.3 cm) of unbeaded rope. Make sure you end with cords 1 and 2 at the top of the disk and all the cords in numerical order.

3 Continue braiding with the same motions as in step 2, but add beads: Pick up a cord, slide the next bead up to the point of the rope, and tuck the bead under the cord that crosses over it. Complete the move by sliding the cord into the appropriate slit. As you work, make sure the beads don't pop out from under the crossed cord. If they do, carefully unbraid the cords to the loose bead (being sure to maintain the correct cord order), tuck the loose bead under the crossing cord, and resume braiding.

note Braiding is most successful when the cords are stretched taut across the hole in the disk. If the point of the rope begins to drop down below the face of the disk, gently pull the opposing sets of cords tight so the point of the braid rises up to the desired spot.

4 When you have braided all of the beads, or when the cord is the desired length, work ½ in. (1.3 cm) of unbeaded rope.
5 Unwind the cords from the bobbins, remove the cords from the disc, and gather them together. Tie an overhand knot close to the braid. Trim the loose cords close to the knot, and dab with E6000 if desired.

Embellishment

1 Add a comfortable length of Fireline to one end of the rope, exiting the inner hole of the end SuperDuo, with the needle facing away from the beadwork (**figure 3, point a**). Sew through the open hole of the same SuperDuo (**a–b**).
2 Pick up an 11º seed bead, a color B 8º seed bead, and an 11º, and sew through the open hole of the next SuperDuo (**b–c**). Repeat this stitch for the length of the rope (**c–d**). End and add thread as needed.
3 Sew through the beadwork to exit the inner hole of the end lentil, with the needle pointing toward the beadwork (**figure 4, point a**).
4 Pick up a SuperDuo, a B, and a SuperDuo, and sew through the inner hole of the next lentil (**a–b**). Pick up a 4 mm fire-polished bead, and sew

FIGURE 5

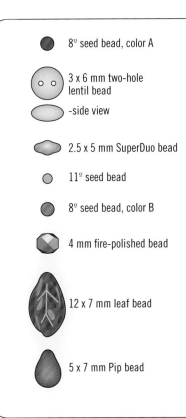

- 8º seed bead, color A
- 3 x 6 mm two-hole lentil bead
- -side view
- 2.5 x 5 mm SuperDuo bead
- 11º seed bead
- 8º seed bead, color B
- 4 mm fire-polished bead
- 12 x 7 mm leaf bead
- 5 x 7 mm Pip bead

a

b

c

through the inner hole of the next lentil **(b–c)**. Repeat these stitches for the length of the rope **(c–d)**.

5 Sew through the open hole of the same lentil, and continue through the open hole of the next SuperDuo **(d–e)**.

6 Pick up two SuperDuos, and sew through the open hole of the next SuperDuo and lentil **(e–f)**. Continue through the next fire-polished bead and the open hole of the following lentil and SuperDuo **(f–g)**.

7 Pick up a leaf bead, and sew through the open hole of the following SuperDuo, lentil, fire-polished bead, lentil, and SuperDuo **(g–h)**.

8 Repeat steps 6–7 for the length of the rope, ending with step 6. On the final repeat of step 6, you will sew through only the end SuperDuo and lentil **(figure 5, point a)**. Sew through the other hole of the same lentil **(a–b)**. Sew around the closest thread bridge,

and sew back through the hole your thread just exited and the other hole of the same lentil to position the needle facing toward the beadwork **(b–c)**.

9 Continue through the nearest hole of the next three SuperDuos **(c–d)**. Pick up a Pip bead, and sew back through the open hole of the same SuperDuo **(d–e)**. Pick up a Pip bead, and sew through the open hole of the next SuperDuo **(e–f)**. Pick up a Pip bead, sew through the other hole of the same SuperDuo, and continue through the following SuperDuo **(f–g)**. Sew through the nearest hole of the next 10 beads as shown **(g–h)**.

10 Work as in step 9 for the length of the rope, ending after sewing through the end lentil. End the Fireline.

Clasp

1 Cut a 6-in. (15 cm) piece of regular-weight C-Lon or S-Lon cord, and tie it tightly with a square knot around the unbeaded braid at the starting end of the rope **(photo a)**. Apply a small drop of E6000 to the knot, and trim the tails of this cord. Repeat this step at the other end of the rope. Allow the glue to dry.

2 Cut through the braid between the overhand knot and the square knot you made in the previous step **(photo b)**. Repeat on the other end of the rope.

3 Using E6000 or 2-part epoxy, glue one end cap to each end of the rope **(photo c)**.

4 Open a jump ring, and attach half of the clasp to an end cap on the rope. Repeat at the other end of the rope. If additional length is desired, attach more than one jump ring to each end cap before adding the clasp. **◐**

Checkered path
bracelet

Chessboard rhinestone assembly

Apply a thin coat of E6000 to the back of one of the chessboard rhinestones. Center another chessboard rhinestone on top of the glued area, and allow the glue to dry.

Bracelet straps

1 On a comfortable length of thread, work in ladder stitch in an alternating pattern of a color A triangle bead and a color B triangle bead to make a 10-bead ladder, leaving a 12-in. (30 cm) tail **(figure 1)**.

note Position the triangles so that all of the As have their flat side resting on one side of the ladder and all the Bs have their flat side resting on the opposite side of the ladder, thus making the pointed

edge of the opposite color triangle nestle between the flat sides of each alternate color triangle **(photo)**. The triangles should naturally position themselves in this manner after the first two triangles are added. Make sure the ladder stays straight and doesn't curve.

2 To even the tension, zigzag back through the triangles in the opposite direction **(figure 2)**.
3 Pick up an A and a B, sew down through the next B in the previous row, and continue up through the following A **(figure 3, a–b)**. Pull the thread tight. Make sure the sides of the A and B mirror the positions of their counterparts in the ladder. Repeat this stitch four times to complete the row, ending after sewing down through the last B in the previous row **(b–c)**.

4 Turn to start the next row by picking up two color C 11º seed beads and sewing up through the last B added **(c–d)**. Pull the thread tight.
5 Continue working in herringbone stitch: Pick up a B and an A, sew down through the next A in the previous row, and continue up through the following B **(figure 4, a–b)**. Make sure the triangles are positioned in the same manner as before. Repeat this stitch four times to complete the row, ending after sewing down through the last B in the previous row **(b–c)**.
6 Turn to start the next row by picking up two color D 11º seed beads and

Use complementary bead colors to create
a cleverly designed reversible bracelet that
features a chessboard rhinestone bezel setting.

designed by **Cary Bruner**

Materials

**gray/silver bracelet 7½ x 1 in.
(19.1 cm x 2.5 cm)**

- 20 mm chessboard circle flat-
  back rhinestones (Swarovski 2035)
    - **1** silver shade
    - **1** golden shadow
- **22** 3 mm fire-polished beads (opaque
  green luster)
- 3 mm bicone crystals (Swarovski)
    - **22** color E (crystal metallic light gold 2X)
    - **22** color F (crystal golden shadow)
- 11º sharp triangle beads (Miyuki)
    - **3 g** color A (F451D, gray mist matte metallic)
    - **3 g** color B (F470, galvanized silver matte)
- 11º seed beads (Miyuki)
    - **1 g** color C (F451D, gray mist matte metallic)
    - **1 g** color D (PF470, galvanized matte silver)
- 15º seed beads (Miyuki)
    - **1 g** color G (PF470, galvanized matte silver)
    - **1 g** color H (F451D, gray mist matte metallic)
- **1** 3-strand tube clasp
- Fireline, 6 lb. test
- beading needles, #11 or #12
- E6000 adhesive

pink/bronze bracelet colors

- 20 mm chessboard circle flat-
  back rhinestones (Swarovski 2035)
    - crystal
    - golden shadow
- 3 mm fire-polished beads (gold)
- 3 mm bicone crystals (Swarovski)
    - color E (rose AB)
    - color F (light Colorado topaz AB)
- 11º sharp triangle beads
    - color A (Toho 223, metallic
      antique bronze)
    - color B (Toho 553F, galvanized matte
      vintage rose)
- 11º seed beads
    - color C (Toho 221, bronze)
    - color D (Miyuki 1061L, galvanized rose)
- 15º seed beads
    - color G (Miyuki 395, color-lined dusty rose)
    - color H (Toho 221, bronze)

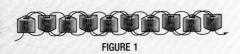

FIGURE 1

FIGURE 2

FIGURE 3

FIGURE 4

 11º triangle bead, color A

 -flat side

 11º triangle bead, color B

 -flat side

 11º seed bead, color C

11º seed bead, color D

 3 mm fire-polished bead

 3 mm bicone crystal, color E

 3 mm bicone crystal, color F

 15º seed bead, color G

 15º seed bead, color H

sewing up through the last A added **(c–d)**. Pull the thread tight.

7 Work as in steps 3–6 to complete one bracelet strap to the desired length, ending and adding thread as needed. Do not end the working thread or tail. For a 7½-in. (19.1 cm) bracelet, the strap should be 2¾ in. (7 cm) long. Three rows is approximately ¼ in. (6 mm) in length.

note If using a tight tension, the triangles will naturally start to angle properly after the first few rows are added.

8 Repeat steps 1–7 to make a second strap of identical length.

Bezel

1 On a comfortable length of thread, pick up a 3 mm fire-polished bead, a color E 3 mm bicone crystal, a C, and an E, and sew through the fire-polished bead again to form a ring **(figure 5, a–b)**.

2 Pick up a color F 3 mm bicone crystal, a D, and an F, and sew through the fire-polished bead again to form a ring to the left of the previous ring **(b–c)**.

3 Pick up a fire-polished bead, an E, and a C, and sew through the adjacent E. Continue through the fire-polished bead just added, going in the same direction, to form a ring on the right side of the fire-polished beads **(c–d)**.

4 Pick up an F and a D, sew through the adjacent F, and continue through the fire-polished bead again to form a ring on the left side of the fire-polished bead **(d–e)**.

5 Repeat steps 3–4 19 times for a total of 21 fire-polished beads in the strip.

6 Join the strip into a ring: Pick up a fire-polished bead, and sew through the end E in the first stitch of the strip **(figure 6, a–b)**. Pick up a C, sew through the end E in the last stitch of the strip, and continue through the fire-polished bead just added **(b–c)**. Sew through the end F in the first stitch of the strip, pick up a D, and sew through the end F in the last stitch of the strip. Continue through the fire-polished bead added at the beginning of this step and the next fire-polished bead **(c–d)**. If needed, pull the tail thread to cinch up any

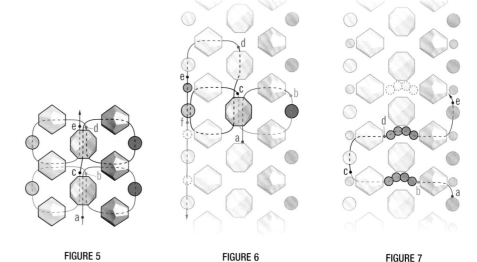

FIGURE 5   FIGURE 6   FIGURE 7

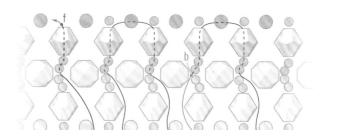

FIGURE 8

loose beads.

7 Sew through the beadwork to exit an edge D **(d–e)**. Pick up a color G 15º seed bead, and sew through the next edge D **(e–f)**. Repeat this stitch 21 times to complete the round. Insert the assembled chessboard rhinestones into the center of the bezel setting, and retrace the thread path of the last round to cinch up the beads.

8 Sew through the beadwork to exit a C on the opposite edge. Work as in step 7 to add color H 15º seed beads to this side of the bezel setting.

9 Sew through the adjacent E **(figure 7, a–b)**. Pick up two Hs and two Gs, position the 15ºs between the fire-polished beads, and sew through the adjacent F on the other side **(b–c)**. Sew through the next D and the adjacent F **(c–d)**. Pick up two Gs and two Hs, and sew through the adjacent E and the follow-

ing C **(d–e)**. Repeat these stitches 10 times to add a total of 22 arched bead sets. End the working thread and tail.

Assembly

1 Position a bracelet strap with the side of flat As facing up next to the bezel with the rhinestone surrounded by the Cs and Hs facing up. Align the strap tail thread along the edge of the bezel.

2 Using the tail, pick up a fire-polished bead, sew through the two corresponding Hs on the bezel, and continue through the next E, edge C, E, and the following two Hs **(figure 8, a–b)**. Pick up a C, and sew through the next A on the end of the strap **(b–c)**. Working toward the opposite edge of the strap, skip the next B, and sew through the following A **(c–d)**.

3 Repeat step 2 except pick up a C in place of a fire-polished bead **(d–e)**.

Pick up a fire-polished bead, sew through the next two corresponding Hs on the bezel, and continue through the next E **(e-f)**.

4 Sew through the beadwork of the bezel and the strap to exit an edge end B on the opposite surface of the strap, with the needle facing toward the bezel. Work as in steps 2–3, but sew through the fire-polished beads added in the previous step and add three Ds (in place of Cs) on this surface of the strap. Sew through corresponding pairs of Gs instead of Hs, and Fs instead of Es.

5 Repeat steps 1–4 to attach the other strap to the bezel, making sure to have

six unattached 15º arched bead sets on each open side of the bezel. End the tail.

Clasp

1 Check the bracelet fit, and use the working thread to add or remove herringbone rows evenly on each strap if necessary, allowing ⁹⁄₁₆ in. (1.4 cm) for the clasp.

2 To secure the loose stacks of herringbone, zigzag through the end row of a strap in the opposite direction.

3 Sew through the adjacent triangle in the same row with the needle pointing away from the strap **(figure 9, a-b)**.

4 Pick up a fire-polished bead, sew through the end loop of the clasp, and continue back through the fire-polished bead just added and the next triangle in the end row **(b-c)**. Skip the next triangle in the end row, and sew through the following triangle **(c-d)**. Repeat these stitches with the remaining two clasp loops **(d-e)**. Retrace the thread path to reinforce the clasp connections, and end the thread.

5 Work as in steps 2–4 to add the other half of the clasp to the other strap. ●

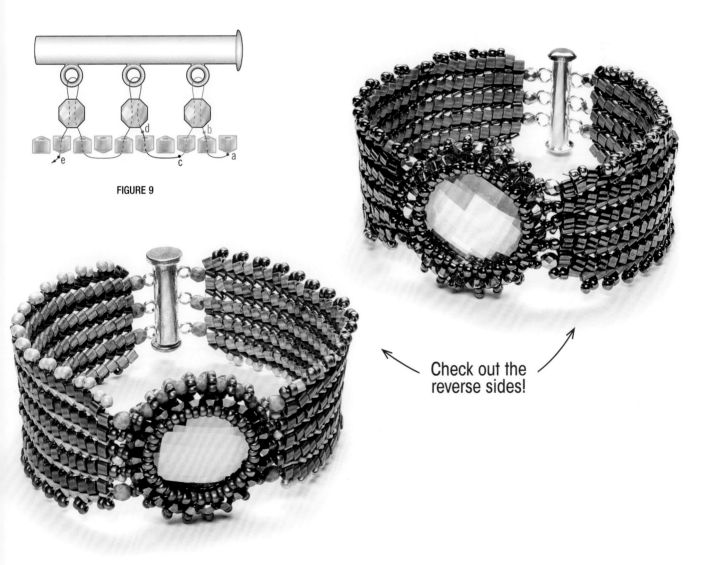

FIGURE 9

Check out the reverse sides!

TUBULAR AND CIRCULAR PEYOTE / BEAD WEAVING

Magnificent
mandala
pendant

Work several rounds of beadwork off a bezeled center
for a stunning and intricate mandala-style pendant.

designed by **Zsuzsanna Veres**

Difficulty rating

   ◇ ◇

Materials

pendant 2 in. (5 cm)

- **1** 14 mm rivoli (Swarovski, purple haze)
- **9** 4 mm fire-polished beads (polychrome olive mauve)
- **45** 2.5 x 5 mm SuperDuo beads (pearl coat purple velvet)
- **27** 8º cylinder beads (Miyuki DBL0023, metallic smoky gold iris)
- **11**º cylinder beads (Miyuki)
  - **2 g** color A (DB1055, matte metallic gray dusk gold iris
  - **2 g** color B (DB0611, dyed silver-lined wine)
- **1 g** 15º seed beads (Toho 221, bronze)
- **1** 12 x 5 mm bail (TierraCast "Legend," antique copper)
- **1** 6 mm jump ring (antique copper)
- Fireline, 6 lb. test
- beading needles, #11 or #12
- **2** pairs of chainnose, flatnose, and/or bentnose pliers
- thread bobbin or piece of cardboard

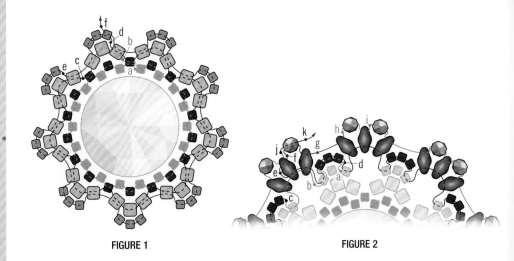

FIGURE 1   FIGURE 2

Bezel

1 On 3 yd. (2.7 m) of thread, pick up 36 color B 11º cylinder beads, and sew through the first three beads again to form a ring, leaving an 8-ft. (2.4 m) tail. These beads will shift to form rounds 1 and 2 as the next round is added. Wrap the tail on a thread bobbin or piece of cardboard.

2 Work rounds of tubular peyote stitch for the front of the bezel as follows, and step up at the end of each round:

Round 3: Work a round using color A 11º cylinder beads.

Rounds 4-5: Work both rounds using 15º seed beads. End this thread.

3 Unwind the tail from the thread bobbin, and attach a needle. Flip the beadwork over, and place the rivoli face down into the beadwork. Stitching off the B cylinders in round 1, work two rounds using 15ºs for the back of the bezel, using a tight tension.

4 Sew through the beadwork to exit a B cylinder in round 1 of the bezel. This is the round of cylinders nearest the 15ºs on the back of the bezel.

Edge embellishment

1 Work rounds of circular peyote stitch as follows:

Round 1: Working off round 1 of the bezel, stitch a round using As **(photo)**, and step up at the end of the round.

Round 2: Flip the beadwork to the front. Working off the As just added, stitch another round using As, and step up at the end of the round **(figure 1, a-b)**. For clarity, only round 1 of "Edge embellishment" is shown in the figure.

2 Pick up three 8º cylinder beads, skip

the next A in the previous round, and sew through the following A to form a picot **(b-c)**. Repeat this stitch eight times to complete the round, and sew through the first 8º added **(c-d)**.

3 Pick up three Bs, skip the center 8º, and sew through the next 8º in this picot and the first 8º in the next picot **(d-e)**, positioning the beads in front of the center 8º. Repeat this stitch eight times to complete the round, and step up through the first B added **(e-f)**.

4 Pick up three As, skip the center B, and sew through the next B **(figure 2, a-b)**. Pick up three SuperDuo beads, and sew through the first B in the next picot **(b-c)**. Repeat these stitches eight times to complete the round **(c-d)**. Sew through the next six beads as shown to exit the inner hole of the center SuperDuo **(d-e)**, and continue through the open hole of the same SuperDuo **(e-f)**.

5 Pick up a 3 mm fire-polished bead, and sew through the open hole of the next SuperDuo **(f-g)**. Skip the next picot, and continue through the open hole of the following SuperDuo **(g-h)**. Pull the thread tight to bring together the last

223

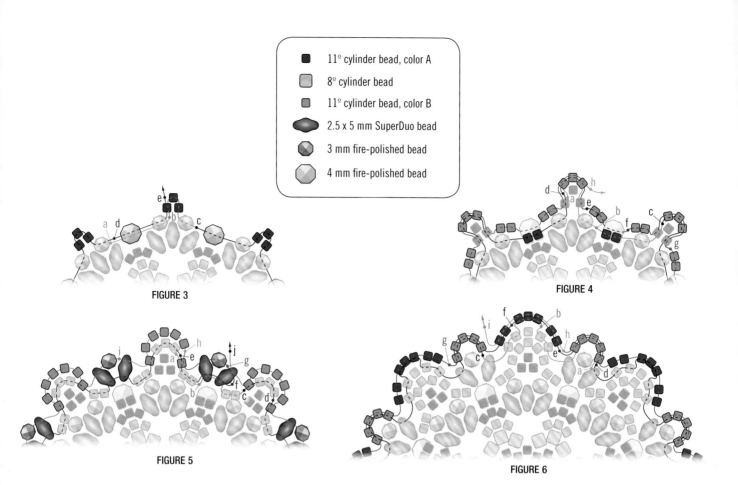

FIGURE 3

FIGURE 4

FIGURE 5

FIGURE 6

Legend:
- 11° cylinder bead, color A
- 8° cylinder bead
- 11° cylinder bead, color B
- 2.5 x 5 mm SuperDuo bead
- 3 mm fire-polished bead
- 4 mm fire-polished bead

two SuperDuos, positioning the picot in front of the SuperDuos. Pick up a 3 mm, and sew through the open hole of the next SuperDuo **(h–i)**. Repeat these stitches eight times to complete the round **(i–j)**, and sew through the first 3 mm added at the beginning of this step **(j–k)**.

6 Pick up 4 mm fire-polished bead, and sew through the next 3 mm **(figure 3, a–b)**. Pick up three As, and sew through the following 3 mm **(b–c)**. Repeat these stitches eight times to complete the round **(c–d)**, and sew through the next 4 mm, the 3 mm, and the first A in the following picot **(d–e)**.

7 Pick up three Bs, skip the center A, and sew down through the next A and 3 mm **(figure 4, a–b)**. Pick up two As, cross in front of the next 4 mm, and sew through the following 3 mm and A **(b–c)**. Repeat these stitches eight times to complete the round **(c–d)**, and sew through the first three Bs added and the next A **(d–e)**.

8 Pick up two Bs, and sew through the next 4 mm **(e–f)**. Pick up two Bs, and sew through the following A, three Bs, and A **(f–g)**. Repeat these stitches eight

times to complete the round, but only sew through the A and three Bs for the last stitch **(g–h)**.

9 Pick up a B, and sew through the next two Bs **(figure 5, a–b)**. Pick up two SuperDuos, skip the next 4 mm, and sew through the following two Bs **(b–c)**. Pick up a B, and sew through the next three Bs **(c–d)**. Repeat these stitches eight times to complete the round **(d–e)**. Sew through the first B added in this round, the next two Bs, and the first two SuperDuos **(e–f)**. Continue through the open hole of the same SuperDuo **(f–g)**.

10 Pick up a 3 mm, sew through the open hole of the next SuperDuo, skip the next two Bs, and continue through the B added in the previous step **(g–h)**. Pick up five Bs, skip the next three Bs, and sew through the following B added in the previous step and the open hole of the next SuperDuo **(h–i)**. Repeat these stitches eight times to complete the round **(i–j)**, pulling tight as you go so the outer edge of the beadwork curves slightly toward the back. If it is not curving, gently push the 4 mm fire-polished beads from the back of the

beadwork toward the front, and pull tight again.

11 Pick up five Bs, skip the next 3 mm, sew through the outer hole of the next SuperDuo, and continue through the first two Bs in the picot added in the previous round **(figure 6, a–b)**. Pick up three As, skip the center B, and sew through the next two Bs in the same picot and the outer hole of the following SuperDuo **(b–c)**. Repeat these stitches eight times to complete the round **(c–d)**, and sew through the first five Bs added in this round **(d–e)**.

12 Pick up two As, and sew through the next set of three As added in the previous round **(e–f)**. Pick up two As, and sew through the next set of five Bs added in the previous round **(f–g)**. Repeat these stitches eight times to complete the round **(g–h)**.

13 Sew through the next seven Bs from the last two rounds to reinforce the next three-bead picot **(h–i)**. Open a 6 mm jump ring, slide it under the three-bead picot just reinforced and through the loop in the bail. Close the jump ring and end the thread. ●

RIGHT-ANGLE WEAVE / PEYOTE STITCH / NETTING

Ring around the barrel bead

Create a cleverly constructed beaded bead using a wood barrel, seed beads, and fire-polished beads.

designed by **Fatima Mensen-Potter**

change it up
Alter the look by interchanging pearls, crystals, and fire-polished beads of the same size within the design.

Difficulty rating

Materials

blue/silver bead 1⁷⁄₁₆ in. x 1³⁄₈ in. (3.7 x 3.5 cm)

- 1 32 x 22 mm wood barrel bead with a 9 mm hole (www.thebeadedbead.etsy.com)
- **39** 4 mm pearls (Swarovski or Preciosa, white)
- **13** 4 mm bicone crystals (Swarovski, crystal AB)
- **26** 4 mm fire-polished beads (jet)
- 3 mm fire-polished beads
  - **52** color A (silver half coat)
  - **26** color B (jet AB)
- **1 g** 8º seed beads (Preciosa, jet hematite)
- **1 g** 11º seed beads (Toho 21F, frosted silver-lined crystal)
- **1 g** 15º seed beads (Miyuki 451, metallic hematite)
- Fireline, 6 lb. test
- beading needles, #11 or #12

multi-colored bead colors

- **36** 4 mm pearls (Preciosa, bronze)
- **12** 4 mm bicone crystals (Swarovski, fuchsia AB2X)
- **24** 4 mm fire-polished beads (azurite halo fire)
- 3 mm fire-polished beads
  - **48** color A (tanzanite AB)
  - **24** color B (olivine AB)
- 8º seed beads (Toho 945, jonquil mint julep-lined)
- 11º seed beads (Toho 377, teal-lined aqua)
- 15º seed beads (Toho PF562, galvanized saffron)

get a grip
For extra stability, slide the barrel onto a pen or marker, and use your fingers to grasp the beadwork, keeping it centered on the barrel while working.

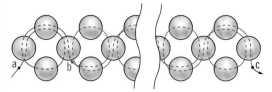

FIGURE 1

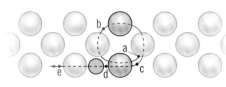

FIGURE 2

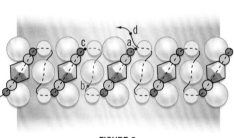

FIGURE 3

variable size
To accommodate slight variances in the diameter of the wood barrel beads and pearls, the number of RAW stitches might need to be adjusted up or down to fit properly around the center of the barrel. The blue/silver bead started with a flat strip of 12 RAW stitches before being joined into a ring, and the other two beads started with 11 RAW stitches.

RAW center ring

1 On a comfortable length of thread, pick up four 4 mm pearls, leaving a 6-in. (15 cm) tail. Sew through the first three pearls again to form a ring **(figure 1, a–b)**. Picking up three pearls per stitch, work a total of 11 or 12 right-angle weave (RAW) stitches **(b–c)**.

2 Form the strip into a ring: Wrap the strip around the center of the wood barrel bead, pick up a pearl, and sew through the end bead of the first stitch **(figure 2, a–b)**. Pick up a pearl, and sew through the end pearl of the last stitch **(b–c)**. Test the fit, and make adjustments if necessary. It's okay if the ring fits slightly loosely around the center of the barrel as the beadwork will cinch up when future rounds of peyote stitch are added. Retrace the thread path to reinforce the join (not shown in the figure for clarity), and continue through the adjacent edge bead of the same stitch **(c–d)**.

3 Pick up an 8º seed bead, and sew through the next edge pearl **(d–e)**. Repeat this stitch to complete the round.

4 Sew through the beadwork to exit a pearl on the opposite edge. Work as in step 3 to add 8ºs on this edge of the ring **(photo above)**, and then sew through the first 8º added at the start of this step.

5 Add an embellishment on top of each RAW stitch: Pick up a 15º seed bead, an 11º seed bead, a 4 mm bicone crystal, an 11º, and a 15º. Cross the RAW stitch diagonally, and sew through the corresponding 8º on the other edge, going in the same direction **(figure 3, a–b)**. Sew through

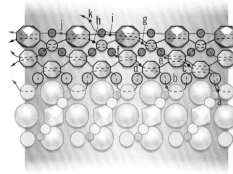

FIGURE 4

the adjacent center pearl, and continue through the next 8º on the original edge with the needle facing away from the beads just added **(b-c)**.

6 Work as in step 5 to add embellishment sets on top of each RAW stitch **(c-d)**. End and add thread as needed. End the tail, but not the working thread.

Sides

To keep the beadwork tension evenly distributed around the barrel, you will be using two working threads to work mirror image rounds of tubular netting/peyote on each side of the RAW center ring.

1 Add a comfortable length of thread to the beadwork, exiting the edge 8º opposite the existing working thread.

2 Work in rounds using one thread to complete the round on one side of the RAW center and then using the other working thread to repeat the round on the opposite side of the ring.

Round 1: With either working thread, pick up an 11º, a color A 3 mm fire-polished bead, and an 11º, skip the next pearl, and sew through the following 8º **(figure 4, a-b)**. Repeat this stitch to compete the round, and step up through the first 11º and A added in this round **(b-c)**.

Round 2: With either working thread, pick up an A, and sew through the next A in the previous round **(c-d)**. Pull the thread tight. Repeat this stitch to complete the round, and step up through the first A added in this round **(d-e)**. The beadwork will start to cinch after

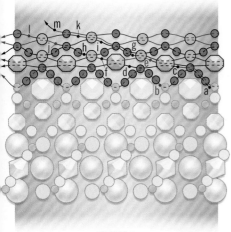

FIGURE 5

this and future rounds are completed.

Round 3: With either working thread, pick up a 15º, an 11º, and a 15º, and sew through the next A in the previous round **(e-f)**. Repeat this stitch to complete the round, and step up through the first 15º and 11º added **(f-g)**.

Round 4: With either working thread, pick up a 4 mm fire-polished bead, and sew through the next 11º in the previous round **(g-h)**. Repeat this stitch to complete the round, and step up through the first 4 mm fire-polished bead added **(h-i)**.

Round 5: With either working thread, pick up a 15º, and sew through the next 4 mm fire-polished bead in the previous round **(i-j)**. Repeat this stitch to complete the round, and step up through the first 15º added **(j-k)**.

Round 6: Pick up five 15ºs, and sew through the next 15º in the previous round **(figure 5, a-b)**. Repeat this stitch to complete the round, and step up through the first three 15ºs added **(b-c)**.

Round 7: Pick up a color B 3 mm fire-polished bead, and sew through the next center 15º in the previous round **(c-d)**. Repeat this stitch to complete the round, and step up through the first B added **(d-e)**.

Round 8: Pick up an 11º, and sew through the next B in the previous round **(e-f)**. Repeat this stitch to complete the round, and step up through the first 11º added **(f-g)**.

Round 9: Pick up three 15ºs, and sew through the next 11º in the previous round **(g-h)**. Repeat this stitch to complete the round, and step up through the first two 15ºs added **(h-i)**.

Round 10: Pick up an 11º, and sew through the next center 15º in the previous round **(i-j)**. Repeat this stitch to complete the round, and step up through the first 11º added **(j-k)**.

Round 11: Pick up a 15º, and sew through the next 11º in the previous round **(k-l)**. Repeat this stitch to complete the round, and step up through the first 15º added **(l-m)**. Pull the thread tight, and retrace the thread path to cinch the beads. End the working threads. ●

pink/gold bead colors
- **36** 4 mm pearls (Swarovski, powder rose)
- 4 mm bicone crystals (Swarovski)
  - **12** light rose
  - **24** rosaline (in place of 4 mm fire-polished beads)
- 3 mm beads
  - **48** bicone crystals, color A (Preciosa, golden flare 2X)
  - **24** fire-polished beads, color B (gold)
- 8º seed beads (Toho 221, bronze)
- 11º seed beads (Toho 221, bronze)
- 15º seed beads (Toho 221, bronze)

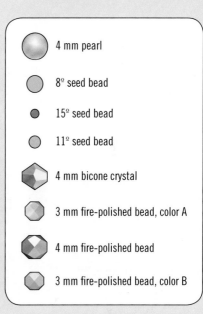

4 mm pearl

8º seed bead

15º seed bead

11º seed bead

4 mm bicone crystal

3 mm fire-polished bead, color A

4 mm fire-polished bead

3 mm fire-polished bead, color B

Holiday garland
bracelet

Relive days gone by with
a bracelet reminiscent of
an old-fashioned popcorn-
and-cranberry garland.

designed by **Jeanette Dailey Bobby**

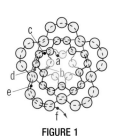

FIGURE 1

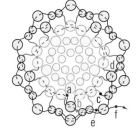

FIGURE 2

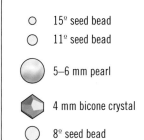

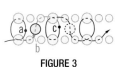

FIGURE 3

helping hand

Pearl holes are small, so throughout this project, if you encounter tight spots, use a pair of chainnose pliers or a needle gripper to gently pull the needle through the beads.

Difficulty rating

Materials

bracelet 7 in. (18 cm)
- **148** 5–6 mm freshwater pearls (mix of peach, cream, and wine)
- **64** 4 mm bicone crystals (olivine)
- seed beads (Miyuki 4201, silver)
  - **1 g** 8º seed beads
  - **1 g** 11º seed beads
  - **6 g** 15º seed beads
- **2** ⁷⁄₁₆-in. (11 mm) 2-hole buttons (clear)
- beading needles, #13
- Fireline, 4 lb. test
- chainnose pliers or needle gripper (optional)

Beaded buttons

1 On 30 in. (76 cm) of thread, pick up five 15º seed beads. Leaving a 6-in. (15 cm) tail, tie the beads into a ring with a square knot, and sew through the next 15º.

2 Work rounds of peyote stitch:

Round 2: Pick up a 15º, and sew through the next 15º in the ring **(figure 1, a–b)**. Repeat this stitch four times, and step up through the first 15º added in the round **(b–c)**.

Round 3: Work a round picking up two 15ºs per stitch, and step up through the first two 15ºs added in this round **(c–d)**.

Round 4: Work a round picking up one 11º seed bead per stitch, and sewing through the pairs of 15ºs in the previous round. Step up through the first 11º added in this round **(d–e)**.

Round 5: Work a round with three 11ºs per stitch, and step up through the first three 11ºs added in this round **(e–f)**.

Round 6: Work a round picking up one 11º per stitch, and sewing through the trios of 11ºs in the previous round. Step up through the first 11º added in this round **(figure 2, a–b)**.

Round 7: Pick up two 15ºs, and sew through the middle 11º in the next trio of 11ºs **(b–c)**. Pick up two 15ºs, and sew through the next 11º in round 6 **(c–d)**. Repeat these two stitches four times to complete the round, and step up through the first two 15ºs added in this round **(d–e)**.

Round 8: Pick up an 11º, and sew through the next two 15ºs in the previous round. Repeat this stitch nine times to complete the round, and step up **(e–f)**. Sew through all the beads in rounds 7 and 8 again, and pull the thread snug. End the working thread and tail.

3 With 42 in. (1.1 m) of thread, repeat steps 1–2 but leave a 12-in. (30 cm) tail.

4 Align the two sections so the outer edge 11ºs are stacked on top of each other. With the thread exiting an edge 11º on one layer, sew through the corresponding 11º on the other layer, and then sew through the 11º in the first layer again and the following 15º **(figure 3, a–b)**. Pick up an 11º, and sew through the next 15º and the following 11º in the other layer **(b–c)**. Repeat these stitches until you have attached seven 11ºs. Slide a ⁷⁄₁₆-in. (11 mm) button between the layers, and continue stitching the layers together. End the working thread.

5 With the tail, sew through a button hole, and exit the other layer. Pick up an 11º, a size 8º seed bead, and an 11º, and sew through the other button hole and the other layer of beadwork. Pick up four 15ºs, and sew through the first button hole again. Retrace the thread path at least once more, and end the thread.

6 Repeat steps 1–5 to make another beaded button.

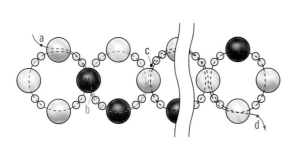

FIGURE 4

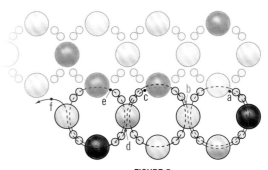

FIGURE 5

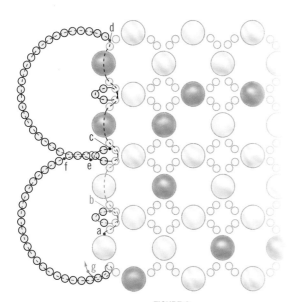

FIGURE 6

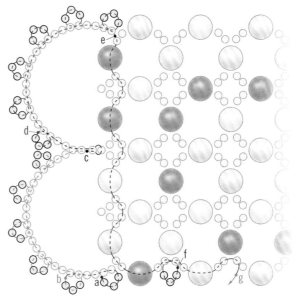

FIGURE 7

Bracelet base

1 On a comfortable length of thread, pick up a repeating pattern of a 5–6 mm pearl and two 15ºs four times. Leaving a 6-in. (15 cm) tail, tie the beads into a ring, and sew through the first pearl, two 15ºs, and the next pearl **(figure 4, a–b)**.

mix it up

Throughout the bracelet base, pick up the pearl colors in a random order.

2 Working in right-angle weave (RAW), pick up a repeating pattern of two 15ºs and a pearl three times, and then pick up two 15ºs. Sew through the pearl your thread exited at the start of this step, and continue through the next two 15ºs, pearl, two 15ºs, and pearl **(b–c)**.

3 Repeat step 2 until you have a total of 16 right-angle weave stitches, but after the last stitch, sew through only two 15ºs and one pearl, exiting a side pearl **(c–d)**. This completes the first 16-stitch row.

4 To begin the next row, work as in step 2 but after adding the beads, sew through two 15ºs, a pearl, two 15ºs, a pearl, two 15ºs, and a pearl **(figure 5, a–b)**.

5 Pick up two 15ºs, and sew through the adjacent pearl in the previous row **(b–c)**. Pick up two 15ºs, a pearl, two 15ºs, a pearl, and two 15ºs, and sew through the adjacent pearl in the previous stitch and the following two 15ºs, pearl, two 15ºs, and pearl **(c–d)**.

6 Pick up two 15ºs, a pearl, two 15ºs, a pearl, and two 15ºs, and sew through the adjacent pearl in the previous row **(d–e)**. Pick up

two 15ºs, and sew through the adjacent pearl in the previous stitch and the following six beads **(e–f)**.

7 Repeat steps 5–6 until you reach the end of the row. After adding the beads in the last stitch, sew through only three beads instead of six to exit a side pearl.

8 Repeat steps 4–7 twice for a base that is four stitches wide by 16 stitches long. End and add thread as needed. When the base is complete, end the working thread and the tail.

Embellishment
Edges

1 Add a comfortable length of thread at one end of the base, and exit the end pearl in the bottom row, with the needle facing toward the opposite edge **(figure 6, point a)**. Sew through the next three 15ºs **(a–b)**. Create a picot: Pick up three 15ºs, and sew

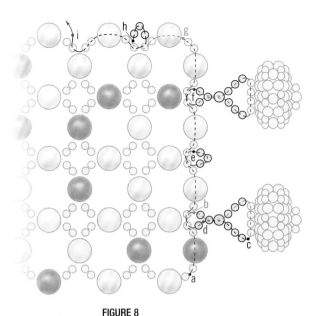

FIGURE 8

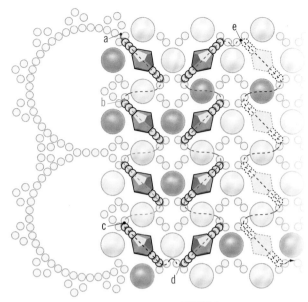

FIGURE 9

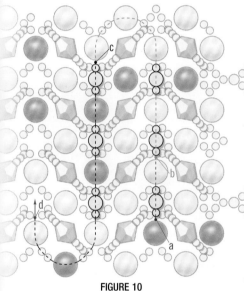

FIGURE 10

through the last two 15ºs your thread exited and the following 15º, pearl, and three 15ºs (b-c). Repeat this stitch twice, but end the second picot by sewing through one 15º instead of three (c-d).
2 Pick up 27 15ºs, sew through the middle 15º in the second picot made on this end (d-e), and sew back through the last three 15ºs added (e-f). Pick up 24 15ºs, sew through the corner 15º, and sew back through the last two 15ºs added (f-g).
3 Pick up three 15ºs, and sew through the two 15ºs your thread just exited, and continue through the following four 15ºs (figure 7, a-b). Repeat this stitch five times to complete six picots around this

loop (b-c). Sew through the beadwork as shown to exit the fourth 15º on the adjacent loop (c-d), and then work six picots around this loop (d-e). Sew through the end of the band to exit the third 15º on the opposite edge (e-f).
4 Work as in step 1 (f-g) to add picots along this edge.
5 To add the clasp buttons, sew through the beadwork to exit the adjacent bottom end pearl and the following three 15ºs (figure 8, a-b). Pick up two 15ºs, an 11º, and three 15ºs, and sew through the four 15ºs on the bottom of a beaded button (b-c). Pick up three 15ºs, and sew back through the 11º just added and the following 15º (c-d). Pick up a 15º, sew through the two 15ºs your thread exited at the start of this step, and continue through the next five beads on the base (d-e).
6 Work a picot, and sew through the next five beads (e-f). Attach the other clasp button as in step 5 (f-g), and then sew through the next four beads (g-h).
7 Add a picot, and sew through the next four beads (h-i). Repeat to add picots on this edge. End the thread.

Surface embellishment
1 Add a comfortable length of thread at one end of the base, exiting between the pair of 15ºs at the corner (figure 9, point a). Position the band horizontally on your work surface.
2 Pick up three 15ºs, a 4 mm bicone crystal, and three 15ºs. Cross diagonally over the adjacent RAW stitch, and sew through the opposite 15º, pearl, and 15º (a-b). Repeat this stitch twice (b-c). Work another stitch, but sew through two 15ºs instead of a 15º, pearl, and 15º (c-d). This puts you in position to embellish the next row.
3 Repeat step 2 (d-e) to embellish the remaining rows. The embellishment on each row will angle opposite that of the previous row. End and add thread as needed.
4 Flip the bracelet over to work on the underside. Sew through the beadwork to exit a pearl with a vertical hole (figure 10, point a). Pick up a 15º, an 8º, and a 15º, and sew through the next vertical pearl (a-b). Repeat this stitch twice, and then sew through the next two 15ºs, pearl, two 15ºs, and pearl in the RAW stitch (b-c). Repeat these stitches (c-d) to embellish the remaining rows, and end the thread. ●

Modern
ANTIQUES

Use bright colors of English-cut antique-style beads — also known as rough-cut beads — to make a quick and stylish bracelet.

designed by **Kerrie Slade**

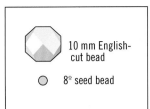

	10 mm English-cut bead
○	8º seed bead

FIGURE 1

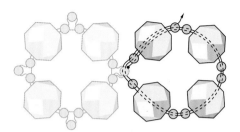

FIGURE 2

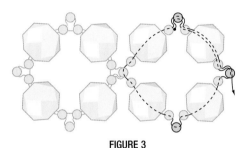

FIGURE 3

Materials

teal blue bracelet 8 in. (20 cm)
- **32** 10 mm English-cut antique-style beads (teal blue)
- **4 g** 8º seed beads (Toho PF558, galvanized aluminum)
- clasp
- **2** 8 mm jump rings
- Fireline 14 lb. test
- beading needles, #10
- **2** pairs of chainnose, flatnose, and/or bentnose pliers

red bracelet colors:
- 10 mm English-cut antique-style beads (tomato red)
- 8º seed beads (Toho PF557, galvanized starlight and Toho PF558, galvanized aluminum)

fuchsia bracelet colors:
- 10 mm English-cut antique-style beads (fuchsa)
- 8º seed beads (Toho 37F, silver-lined frosted olive)

1 On 7 ft. (2.1 m) of thread, pick up a repeating pattern of two 8º seed beads and a 10 mm English-cut bead four times. Sew through the beads again to form a ring, pulling tight and leaving an 8-in. (20 cm) tail. Continue through the first 8º added.

2 Pick up an 8º, and sew through the next 8º, 10 mm, and 8º, keeping a tight tension. Repeat this stitch to complete the round, and step up through the first 8º added in this round **(figure 1)**.

3 Pick up an 8º, a 10 mm, two 8ºs, a 10 mm, two 8ºs, a 10 mm, two 8ºs, a 10 mm, and an 8º, and sew through the 8º your thread exited at the start of this step. Sew through all the beads again, keeping a tight tension, and continue through the first three beads added in this step **(figure 2)**.

4 Pick up an 8º, and sew through the next 8º, 10 mm, and 8º, keeping a tight tension. Repeat this stitch twice, and then continue through the beads as shown to exit the second 8º added in this step **(figure 3)**.

5 Repeat steps 3 and 4 for the desired length bracelet, leaving approximately 1¼ in. (3.2 cm) for the clasp. End the working thread and tail (Basics).

6 Open an 8 mm jump ring (Basics), attach half of the clasp, and slide the jump ring around the three 8ºs at one end of the bracelet. Close the jump ring. Repeat for the other end of the bracelet. ●

Other Techniques

Tribal moon necklace

Make an easy mixed-metal necklace with ready-made chain and components.

designed by **Marcy Kentz**

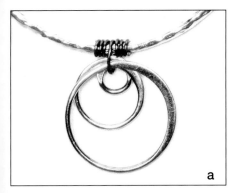

a

b

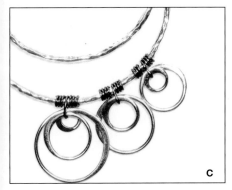

c

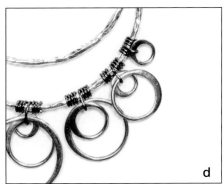

d

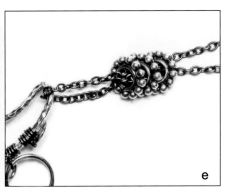

e

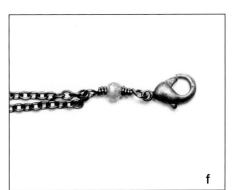

f

Difficulty rating

Materials

necklace 18 in. (46 cm)

- **1** 42 mm crescent moon pendant (item #S2779)*
- brass circle links*
  1 15 mm (item #VNS2405)
  2 12 mm (item #VNS2366)
  4 10 mm (from item #VNS2687)
  2 8 mm (from item #VNS2687)
  5 5 mm (from item #VNS2687)
- **2** 3 mm beads
- **6** 8 mm flat spacers (item #S385)*
- 27 in. (69 cm) 24-gauge wire, bronze finish (item #UVW419)*
- **2** 16-in. (41 cm) brass cable chains with attached lobster claw clasp (item #UVCH100)*
- chainnose pliers
- roundnose pliers
- wire cutters

Available at www.ninadesigns.com

1 The three smallest ring sizes come connected together. In order to use them, you'll need to cut the links apart. Cut the center link from five components, leaving the 5 mm and 10 mm links loose. Cut the end links from two additional components to leave the 8 mm links loose.

2 Cut a 3-in. (7.6 cm) piece of 24-gauge wire, and bend it in half. Pass one end of the wire through a 15 mm link, a 10 mm link, and a 5 mm link. Align the cluster of links with the center outer curve of the crescent pendant, and wrap each end of the wire around the crescent three times, working in opposite directions **(photo a)**. Trim the wire ends.

3 On each side of the crescent pendant, work as in step 2 to add:

- a 12 mm and an 8 mm cluster **(photo b)**
- a 10 mm and a 5 mm cluster **(photo c)**
- a single 5 mm link **(photo d)**

4 Cut the clasp off of a 16-in. (41 cm) chain. Center the chain through one end of the crescent pendant, and string three spacers over both chain ends **(photo e)**.

5 Cut a 3-in. (7.6 cm) piece of wire, and make the first half of a wrapped loop (Basics). String each end of the chain into the loop, and complete the wraps. String a 3 mm bead, and make the first half of a wrapped loop. String a lobster claw clasp into the loop, and complete the wraps **(photo f)**.

6 Repeat steps 4 and 5 for the other side of the necklace, but substitute a 10 mm link for the clasp. ●

WEAVING

Metal&leather
bracelet

Combine two classic materials in a
trendy woven bracelet. Add a customized
button clasp for extra flair!

designed by **Marla Salezze**

a

b

c

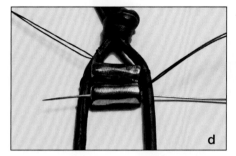

d

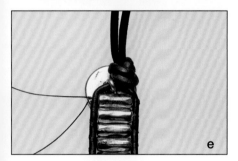

e

Materials

bracelet 7¾ in. (19.7 cm)

- **48** 8 x 3 mm metal tube beads (**16** each in gold, silver, and copper)
- **1** 13.5 mm button shank blank (silver)
- image transfer collage sheet (Nature)
- epoxy clay (Crystal Clay, white)
- 24 in. (61 cm) 1.5 mm leather cord (brown)
- nylon beading thread, size D (brown)
- beading needle, #10
- paper towel
- **1** or **2** binder clips
- clipboard or rigid beading board
- G-S Hypo Cement

Button

1 Following the manufacturer's instructions, pinch off a pea-sized amount of both part A and part B epoxy clay, and mix until blended.

2 Press the clay into the button blank so the clay is flush with the top of the blank.

3 Cut the desired image from the image transfer sheet, making sure the image will fit within the edges of the button. If you want the image to be oriented a certain way when it is on the bracelet, make sure to figure that out now. Place the image face down on the epoxy clay, and burnish it onto the clay with your fingernail. Leave the image on the clay for about five minutes.

4 Apply a wet paper towel to the paper backing on the image. Dab the paper backing until it is thoroughly damp, and then gently slide the backing off of the clay **(photo a)**. The image should remain on the clay. Following the manufacturer's instructions, allow the clay to dry completely.

Bracelet

1 Fold the leather cord in half, and tie an overhand knot (Basics) about ½ in. (1.3 cm) away from the fold **(photo b)**. Make sure the button can fit through the knot before pulling it tight.

2 Attach a binder clip to each end of your beading board. If you are using a clipboard instead, attach one binder clip to the edge opposite the existing one. Insert the knotted end of the leather into one clip and the loose ends into the other, pulling the leather taut.

3 Center a needle on 3 yd. (2.7 m) of thread. Working with doubled thread, tie the end of the thread to the left-hand leather strand with a square knot (Basics), positioning it ¼ in. (6 mm) from the knot in the leather.

4 Pick up an 8 x 3 mm tube bead (any color), and position the bead between the two strands of leather. Pass your needle around the right-hand strand, back through the bead **(photo c)**, and then around the left-hand strand.

5 Repeat step 4 **(photo d)**, picking up the three bead colors in a repeating pattern, until you have added all the beads or you have reached the desired length. Each set of three beads adds about ⅜ in. (1 cm) to the length of the bracelet.

6 Cut the needle off the thread, and tie the thread to one of the leather strands with a couple of square knots.

7 String the button onto one of the leather strands, and tie the leather strands with an overhand knot so that the button is snug against the last bead **(photo e)**.

8 Apply a dab of glue to the knots in the thread and the leather, and allow the glue to dry. Trim the thread and leather close to the knots. ●

Cascading floral *bracelet*

Embark on a creative journey using a commemorative bead to create a multifaceted, flowing design.

designed by **Cassie Donlen**

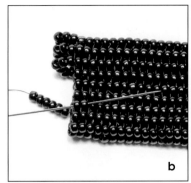

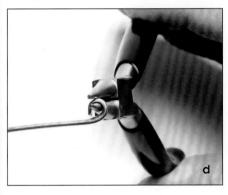

Materials

bracelet 8¼ in. (21 cm)

- **1** commemorative bead (this bead is by Andrea Guarino-Slemmons, www.BeadAndButton.com/showbead)
- **18 g** 11º seed beads (Miyuki 9458-TB, metallic iris brown)
- **14** 2 mm round beads, sterling silver
- **6 x 1 in.** (15 x 2.5 cm) 20-gauge silver sheet metal, dead soft
- silver wire, round, dead soft
  - **7 in.** (18 cm) 14-gauge
  - **5 in.** (13 cm) 16-gauge
- **16** 2½-in. (6.4 cm) 22-gauge ball-end head pins, fine silver
- **6** 18-gauge 4.5 mm silver jump rings
- **1** 12 x 12 mm 2-strand toggle clasp
- Fireline 6 lb. test
- beading needles, #11 or #12
- fine-tip permanent marker
- **2** pairs of chainnose, flatnose, and/or bentnose pliers
- 1.25 mm metal hole-punch pliers
- roundnose pliers
- wire cutters
- **2** hammers (chasing and light utility)
- center punch
- dapping set with block
- disc cutter set
- steel bench block or anvil

Base

1 The base is formed from two identical sections of tubular herringbone that have been flattened to form a double layer. On a comfortable length of thread, pick up four 11º seed beads, leaving a 20-in. (51 cm) tail. Sew through all the beads again, and form them into two stacks of two beads each. Working in two-bead ladder stitch, pick up two 11ºs, sew through the previous stack of beads, and continue through the two 11ºs just picked up to form a new stack. Continue working in two-bead ladder stitch until you have 18 stacks of two beads each. Form the ladder into a ring.

2 Working off the ladder and using 11ºs, work in tubular herringbone stitch for 41 rounds. End and add thread as needed. If the working thread is less than 20 in. (51 cm) after the final round, end the thread and start a new thread that is 2 ft. (61 cm) long.

3 Flatten the tube to create two layers. There should be nine columns on each side with the working thread and tail located in the same column (either layer) of an outer edge.

4 Pick up six 11ºs, and sew through the top two 11ºs in the corresponding column on the opposite side **(photo a)**.

Continue through the adjacent top two 11ºs in the next column. Repeat these stitches for the next two columns to create three loops. Retrace the thread path of the loops several times.

5 Sew through the top edge 11ºs in the next three columns (same side as your working thread), and repeat step 4 on the remaining three columns **(photo b)**. End the working thread and tail.

6 Repeat steps 4–5 using the tail for the other end of the base.

7 Repeat steps 1–6 to make another base section.

Wire components

1 Cut four 1¾-in. (4.4 cm) pieces of 14-gauge round wire. On a bench block, use a chasing hammer to flatten approximately ¼ in. (6 mm) at one end of each piece of wire **(photo c)**.

2 With the tips of a roundnose pliers, grasp the flattened end of a piece of wire, and rotate to form a small loop **(photo d)**. Repeat for the other three wire pieces, and set aside.

3 Use a disk cutter and utility hammer to punch 12 ¹⁵⁄₆₄-in. (6 mm) disks (small), 12 ⁵⁄₁₆-in. (8 mm) disks (medium), and two ⅜-in. (1 cm) disks (large) from 20-gauge silver sheet **(photo e)**.

f

g

h

i

j

k

no disk cutter?

Order the disks precut in 22-gauge (6.4 mm, 8.0 mm, and 9.5 mm).

4 Use a marker to identify the center on each disk, and use hole-punching pliers to make a hole **(photo f)**.

5 Place each disk on a bench block, and use a center punch and utility hammer to texture one side of each disk **(photo g)**.

6 Place each disk, textured side up, in the corresponding depression of a dapping block, and use dapping punches to create a concave dome **(photo h)**.

no doming block?

No worries — just opt to keep the disks flat.

7 On a head pin, string a large disk, and make a wrapped loop. Repeat to create dangles with the second large disk, six of the medium disks, and eight of the small disks **(photo i)**.

Clasp

1 Open two 4.5 mm jump rings, slide one through each loop on the toggle ring, and close the rings.

2 Slide a 14-gauge wire component (from steps 1–2 of "Wire components") through three of the seed bead loops on one end of a bracelet base and the two jump rings attached to the toggle ring. Continue through the remaining three seed bead loops **(photo j)**.

3 If needed, trim the wire so that only 7/16 in. (1.1 cm) is exposed from the edge of the last beaded loop. Work as in steps 1–2 of "Wire components" to flatten this end and form a loop **(photo k)**. This loop should face the same direction as the first one.

4 Repeat step 1 with the toggle bar, but add a second pair of 4.5 mm jump rings to each loop on the toggle bar. Con-tinue with steps 2–3 to attach the toggle bar to one end of the other base.

Assembly

1 Cut a 5-in. (13 cm) piece of 16-gauge round wire, and make a wrapped loop on one end. Slide the commemorative bead onto the wire, and make another wrapped loop **(photo l)**.

2 Lay the base flat on a hard surface, and slide a 14-gauge wire component through the outer seed bead loop on the remaining end of a herringbone base. String a medium and a small disk dangle onto the wire, and slide the wire through the second loop. String a small disk dangle onto the wire, and slide the wire through the third loop.

3 String a small disk dangle, a loop from the lampwork bead, and a large disk dangle onto the wire **(photo m)** before sliding the wire through the next loop. String a small disk dangle onto the wire, and slide the wire through the second-to-last loop. String a small and a medium disk dangle, and slide the wire through the last loop **(photo n)**.

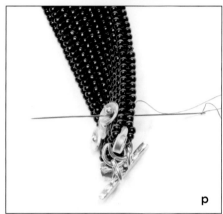

4 If needed, trim the wire so that only ⁷/₁₆ in. (1.1 cm) is exposed from the edge, and work as in steps 1–2 of "Wire components" to flatten the wire **(photo o)** and form a loop.
5 Repeat steps 2–4 on the second base.

Embellishments

1 On 1 yd. (.9 m) of thread and leaving a 6-in. (15 cm) tail, sew up through a her-ringbone base about ³/₁₆ in. (5 mm) from the end where the clasp is attached. Exit the center column. Pick up a med-ium disk and a 2 mm round silver bead, and sew back through the disk and the base. Retrace the thread path.
2 Sew through the beadwork to exit two columns over from where you attached the medium disk. Pick up a small disk and a 2 mm bead, and sew back through the disk and the base **(photo p)**. Retrace the thread path.

3 Work as in step 2 to add a small disk on the other side of the medium disk **(photo q)**. End the working thread and tail.
4 Repeat steps 1–3 on the second base.
5 Work as in steps 1–4 to add two medium disks and two small disks for embellishment next to the disk dangles on each base. Position the disks as desired to make them look as if they are cascading or flowing away from the focal bead **(photo r)**. ●

STRINGING

GEMS & PEARLS
MULTISTRAND NECKLACE

String an artfully composed piece with your favorite materials.

designed by **Deb Lonergan**

Difficulty rating

Materials
adjustable necklace
15–20 in. (38–51 cm)
• 1 16-in. (41 cm) strand of 8 mm pearls
  in each of **2** colors
  - color A (light lavender)
  - color B (white)
• **65–75** 5–6 mm pearls, color C
  (mix of purples)
• **20–30** 3–5 mm pearls, color B (white)
• **36 in. (.9 m)** total of assorted 3–6 mm
  gemstone chips, rondelles, rounds, and
  drops (amethyst, peridot, citrine, pink
  quartz, iolite, and aquamarine)
• **1 g** 11º seed or cylinder beads
• **2** 16 mm cones (with 13–15 mm opening)
• **3** 4 mm spacer beads
• **5 in. (13 cm)** chain
• **1** lobster claw clasp
• **1** 2-in. (5 cm) head pin
• **4** 4 mm jump rings
• **12** crimp beads
• **12** wire guards
• **6 in. (15 cm)** wire, 22-gauge
• flexible beading wire, .014
• **12** Bead Stoppers or tape
• chainnose pliers
• crimping pliers
• roundnose pliers
• wire cutters

1 On a spool of beading wire, string 13¼ in. (33.7 cm) of color A 8 mm pearls. Trim from the spool, leaving about 2 in. (5 cm) of bare wire on each end, and secure them temporarily with a Bead Stopper or a piece of tape.
  String five more strands, making each about ⅛–¼ in. (3–6 mm) shorter than the last strand you strung (make them all different lengths):
• One strand of color B 8 mm pearls
• One stand of color C 5–6 mm pearls
• Three strands of mixed gemstone chips, rondelles, rounds, and drops, randomly interspersed with color D 3–5 mm pearls along the strand (there is no specific stringing order).

2 Remove the tape or Bead Stopper from one end of one strand. String a crimp bead and a wire guard, and then go back through the crimp bead. Being sure to leave enough working wire to finish the other end, crimp the crimp bead, and trim the excess wire. Repeat on the other end of the strand.
  Repeat this step with the other strands. On the strands with the larger beads, string two or three 11º seed or cylinder beads on each end to make it easier to fit all the strands into the cone later.

3 SECRETS OF THE PERFECT MULTISTRAND
1. Vary the length of your strands by ⅛–¼ in. (3–6 mm).
2. Use a wire guard at the end of each strand for strength and a professional touch.
3. String the strands in the order you want them to fall when the necklace is untwisted.

4 Use 4 mm jump rings to attach a 1-in. (2.5 cm) piece of chain to a lobster claw clasp and the wrapped loop at one end of the necklace.

5 Use a 4 mm jump ring to attach a 4-in. (10 cm) piece of chain to the other wrapped loop. On a head pin, string a 4 mm spacer bead and two gemstones, and make a wrapped loop. Use a 4 mm jump ring to attach this wrapped loop to the end of the 4-in. (10 cm) chain. ◉

3 Cut 3 in. (7.6 cm) of 22-gauge wire, and make the first half of a large wrapped loop on one end. String one end of each strand onto the loop, and complete the wraps. Over the remaining wire end, string a cone and a 4 mm spacer bead and make a wrapped loop. Repeat on the other end of the strands.

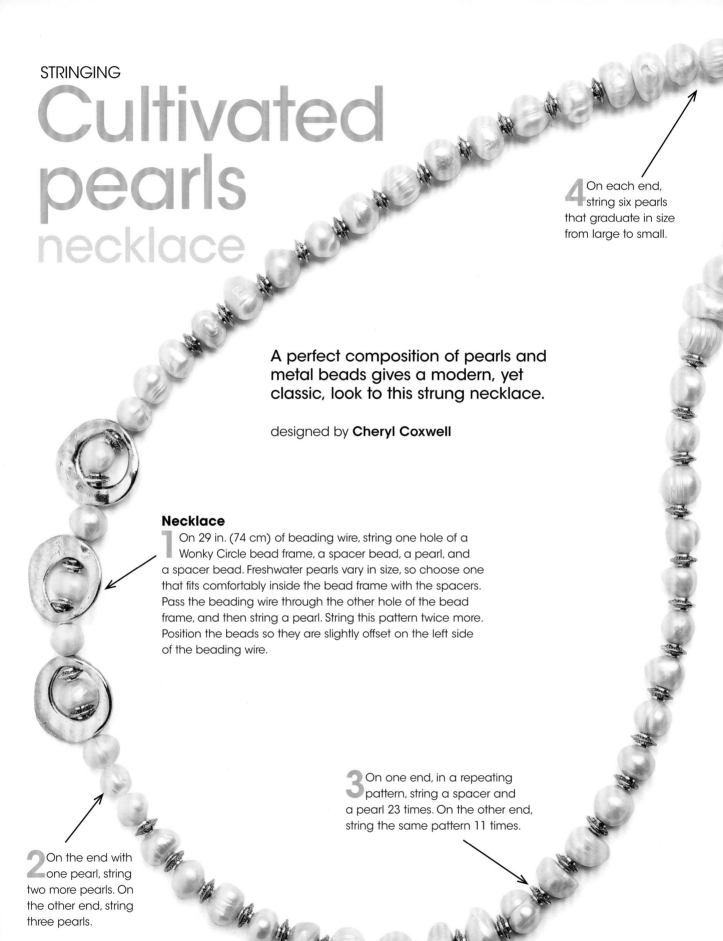

Cultivated pearls
necklace

4 On each end, string six pearls that graduate in size from large to small.

A perfect composition of pearls and metal beads gives a modern, yet classic, look to this strung necklace.

designed by **Cheryl Coxwell**

Necklace

1 On 29 in. (74 cm) of beading wire, string one hole of a Wonky Circle bead frame, a spacer bead, a pearl, and a spacer bead. Freshwater pearls vary in size, so choose one that fits comfortably inside the bead frame with the spacers. Pass the beading wire through the other hole of the bead frame, and then string a pearl. String this pattern twice more. Position the beads so they are slightly offset on the left side of the beading wire.

3 On one end, in a repeating pattern, string a spacer and a pearl 23 times. On the other end, string the same pattern 11 times.

2 On the end with one pearl, string two more pearls. On the other end, string three pearls.

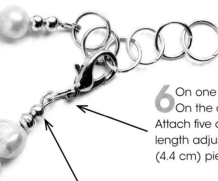

6 On one end, use a jump ring to attach the lobster clasp. On the other end, attach a jump ring to the Wire Guardian. Attach five additional linked jump rings to make the necklace length adjustable. As an alternative, you can also use a 1¾ in. (4.4 cm) piece of chain in place of the linked jump rings. ●

5 On each end, string two crimp beads and a Wire Guardian. String the wire back through both crimp beads, and pull the wire tight. Crimp both crimp beads on each end, and attach a crimp cover over each crimp bead.

Make matching earrings

On a 3-in. (7.6 cm) head pin, string one hole of a Wonky Circle bead frame, a spacer bead, a pearl, and a spacer bead. Pass the head pin through the open hole of the bead frame, and make a wrapped loop. Open the loop of an ear wire, and attach it to the wrapped loop. Close the loop.

Difficulty rating

Materials
necklace 26 in. (66 cm)
- **3** 20 mm Wonky Circle bead frames (gold, Impossible Things Bead Emporium; 305-294-3500)
- **57** 8-9 mm pearls (freshwater, white)
- **40** 3 x 6 mm spacer beads (gold)
- **1** lobster clasp
- **7** 10 mm jump rings
- **4** crimp beads (gold)
- **4** 5 mm crimp covers
- **2** Wire Guardians
- **29 in. (74 cm)** flexible beading wire, .014
- **2** pairs of chainnose, flatnose, and/or bentnose pliers
- crimping pliers

Prefer beads to a metal frame?

Use 15º and 11º seed beads to make your own bead frame for this project.

Beaded frame

1 On 1 yd. (.9 m) of thread, pick up 36 15º seed beads. Tie the beads into a ring with a square knot, leaving a 6-in. (15 cm) tail. These beads will shift to form the first two rounds as the third round is added.

2 Working in tubular peyote stitch, work a round using 15ºs, and step up through the first 15º added in this round. Work three rounds using 11ºs, stepping up at the end of each round.

3 Sew through the beadwork to exit a 15º "up" bead on the opposite edge, and work two rounds using 11ºs.

4 Zip up the two edge rounds to form a ring, and end the threads.

5 Repeat steps 1–4 to make a total of three beaded frames for use in place of the metal bead frames. To help ease the beading wire through the beaded frame, use a Speeder Beader Needle, or gently push a thick head pin through the middle section of the ring to help form a path for the beading wire. Remove the head pin, and thread the wire through the created space, taking special care to not break the thread.

A GEM OF A FIND
JEWELRY SET

Create stunning jewelry using dainty
aquamarine gemstones that hang from
gold chain to create a delicate set.

designed by **Jennifer Robinson**

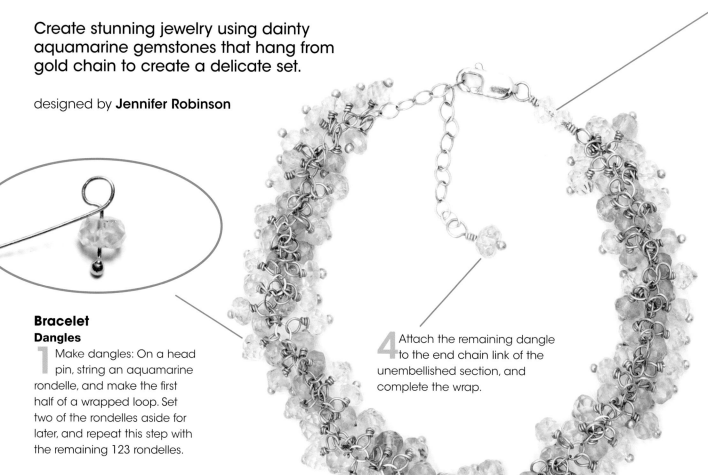

Bracelet
Dangles

1 Make dangles: On a head
pin, string an aquamarine
rondelle, and make the first
half of a wrapped loop. Set
two of the rondelles aside for
later, and repeat this step with
the remaining 123 rondelles.

4 Attach the remaining dangle
to the end chain link of the
unembellished section, and
complete the wrap.

Assembly

2 For an adjustable bracelet length of 6–7½ in. (15–19.1 cm),
cut a 6¾-in. (17.1 cm) piece of flat oval cable chain. Working
from one end of the chain, attach two dangles to each chain link,
completing each wrap as you go. If desired, alternate varying
shades of dangles on each link. Stop when you have one dangle
left unattached. This remaining dangle will be used in step 4. There
should be approximately 1¼ in. (3.2 cm) of unembellished chain
that will serve as the catch for the clasp.

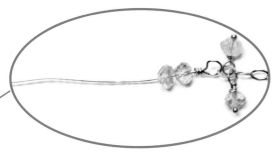

3 On one end of a 4-in. (10 cm) piece of 26-gauge wire, make the first half of a wrapped loop. Attach the loop to the end of the chain with the dangles, and complete the wrap. String two rondelles onto the wire. Make the first half of a wrapped loop on this end of the wire, attach the loop to the lobster clasp, and complete the wrap.

note
If a longer bracelet length is desired, cut the chain to your desired length minus the length of the clasp. Approximately 22 rondelles and head pins are required for each additional 1-in. (2.5 cm) in length.

Materials
adjustable bracelet
6–7½ in. (15–19.1 cm)
- **125** 3.5 mm aquamarine rondelles (multiple shades on one strand)
- **1** lobster clasp (gold)
- **4 in. (10 cm)** 26-gauge wire (gold-filled)
- **6 ¾ in. (17.1 cm)** flat oval cable chain, 2.3 mm width (gold-filled)
- **123** 1³⁄₁₆ in. (30 mm) 27-gauge head pins with single ball tip (gold vermeil)
- chainnose pliers
- roundnose pliers
- wire cutters

earrings 1⅛ in. (2.9 cm)
- **36** 3.5 mm aquamarine rondelles
- **1** pair of earring findings
- **1½ in. (3.8 cm)** flat oval cable chain, 2.3 mm width (gold-filled)
- **36** 1³⁄₁₆-in. (30 mm) 27-gauge head pins with single ball tip (gold vermeil)

Earrings
1 On a head pin, string a rondelle, and make the first half of a wrapped loop. Repeat this step to make a total of 18 dangles. Complete the wraps on two of the dangles, and set them aside.
2 Cut a ¾-in. (1.9 cm) piece of flat oval cable chain. Working from one end of the chain, attach two dangles to each chain link, completing each wrap as you go. If desired, add the dangles in gradating colors.
3 Open the loop of an ear wire, and attach a wrapped dangle, the end link of the chain with dangles, and a wrapped dangle. Close the loop.
4 Repeat steps 1–3 to make a second earring. ●

Tempting treasures
wire frame earrings

Shape simple wire frames, and fill them with pearls and gemstone beads to make earrings that overflow with rich abundance.

designed by **Bonnie Riconda**

Frames

1 Flush cut 6 in. (15 cm) of 18-gauge wire. With a marker, make marks ¾ in. (1.9 cm), 2¾ in. (7 cm), 3¼ in (8.3 cm), and 5¼ in. (13.3 cm) from one end **(photo a)**.

2 Using roundnose pliers, make a loop on each end, making sure they face the same way **(photo b)**.

3 Using chainnose or flatnose pliers, make a right-angle bend at each mark to form a rectangular shape, making sure the loops are on the outside. If the loops don't overlap, trim and re-shape them as needed **(photo c)**.

4 Place the frame on the bench block, and hammer it to slightly flatten and texture the wire **(photo d)**. Don't hammer the loops when they are overlapped. Instead, sep-arate them, hammer them individually, and squeeze them back together.

5 Repeat steps 1–4 to make another frame.

Embellishment

1 Cut 3 ft. (.9 m) of 26-gauge wire, and wrap it several times around the top-left edge of a frame **(photo e)**.

2 String enough gemstone rondelles to reach the other side of the frame, and make several wraps **(photo f)**. Repeat this step with the desired beads, altering the number of wraps as needed to match the height of each row of beads.

3 At the bottom, if you wish to add a couple of vertical beads (as in the sample earrings), first make a spot for them: Stop adding rows when the space remaining is the same height as the beads you want to add. Attach a 3 mm pearl to the side of the frame by stringing a pearl on the wire, and wrapping it once or twice around the frame. Repeat to add another pearl in the corner, but wrap the wire around the bottom edge of the frame several times. Next, string the bead that you want to position vertically, and wrap the wire between two adjacent beads in the previous row **(photo g)**. String another vertical bead, being sure to position it correctly in the remaining space (bend the 26-gauge wire horizontally to position the bead properly), and then wrap the wire around the bottom of the frame.

4 Trim and tuck the wire tail, pressing it in close to the frame.

5 Repeat steps 1–4 to embel-lish the other frame, making it a mirror image of the first.

Ear wires and assembly

1 Cut 2 in. (5 cm) of 22-gauge wire, and make a tiny loop at one end. Use roundnose pliers to bend the wire to match the **template**. Place the ear wire on the bench block, and use a hammer to slightly flatten and texture the wire. Use a file or cup bur to smooth the end of the wire. Repeat to make a second ear wire.

2 Open the loop of an earwire, pass it through the two loops at the top of an earring frame, and close the loop.

3 Repeat steps 1–2 to complete the other earring. ●

TEMPLATE

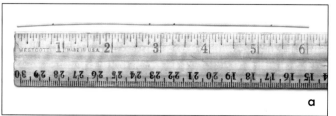

a

b

go wild!

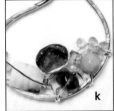

h

i

j

k

Materials

pair of earrings 2½ x ½ in. (6.4 x 1.3 cm)

- **12 in. (30 cm)** 18-gauge wire
- **4 in. (10 cm)** 22-gauge wire
- **6 ft. (1.8 m)** 26-gauge wire
- assorted beads, such as:
  - 2 x 3 mm gemstone rondelles
  - 3 mm pearls
  - 4 x 6 mm pillows/rectangles
- chainnose pliers
- roundnose pliers
- wire cutters
- steel bench block or anvil
- hammer
- file or cup bur
- marker

You don't have to restrict yourself to rectangles and straight lines. Flex your creativity to make freeform earrings, keeping these guidelines in mind:

- Draw a shape with one continuous line to represent your wire, and then bend your wire to match the shape **(photo h)**.
- Fill your shapes completely or partially. Begin filling by wrapping 26-gauge wire along one side or the bottom of the shape. String one or more beads, slide the bead(s) up to the previous wraps, and make two wraps around the frame **(photo i)**. Repeat along the inner edge of the frame, picking up one or more beads each time.

- Once the first "row" is established, work the next row in the same manner but wrap the 26-gauge wire around a wire in the previous row **(photo j)**.
- To add a drop bead or other top-drilled bead where desired, string the bead, slide it up to the previous wraps, and make a wrap around the frame or other internal wire. Now make several wraps around the bottom of the bead **(photo k)**, ending with one or two additional wraps around the frame or internal wire. It's okay if these wraps look somewhat "organic" compared to the more regular wraps made around the frame.

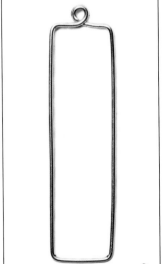

c

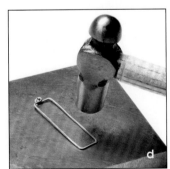

d

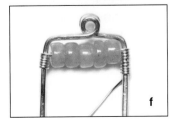

f

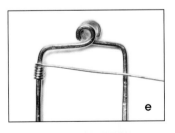

e

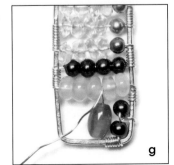

g

Contributors

Marcia Balonis started making jewelry as a teenager and her passion has continued in many forms. Often inspired by nature, she focuses on wearable art suitable for the casual lifestyle in rural Fl. Contact her at marcia@baublesbybalonis.net, and see her work at www.baublesbybalonis.etsy.com or www.baublesbybalonis.net.

Eileen Barker was taught how to bead by her grandmother in the 1950s. In 1986 she opened her own store called Bead Street, providing a venue for teaching a variety of classes. Contact her at beadstreetonline@gmail.com or visit www.beadstreetonline.com.

Jimmie Boatright is a retired public school educator who teaches her original designs at Beadjoux Bead Shop in Braselton, Georgia. Contact her at dboatri931@aol.com or visit www. beadjoux.com.

Jeanette Daily Bobby got hooked on beading in 2002. She completed the NYIAD (New York Institute of Art & Design) Jewelry Design Program in 2014, through which she learned her favorite stitch, RAW. She lives in Milwaukee, Wisc., with her husband and pets and also enjoys gardening, listening to jazz, and reading. Contact Jeanette at jlbobby@ameritech.net, www.distinctleedifferent.etsy.com, or www.beadartbyjeanette.com.

Cary Bruner works and teaches at Bead Haven in Las Vegas. She finds that patience comes naturally when she remembers her own humble start. Email her at creationsbycary@aol.com or visit www.creationsbycary.etsy.com.

Alicia Campos is from Spain and started beading about five years ago. She enjoys designing and creating unique jewelry. Contact her at malizzia23@hotmail.com or visit www.complementosalicia.etsy.com.

Contact **Janice Chatham** at bighjh2@aol.com.

Svetlana Chernitsky has been beading for more than eight years and loves working with two-hole beads. Email her at lirigal@gmail.com, or visit www.lirigal.com and www.etsy.com/shop/lirigal.

Cheryl Coxwell has loved beads from a very young age. Growing up, she was inspired by her great-aunt's fashion sense, and spent many hours creating designs using beads from old jewelry. Cheryl finds designing jewelry to be relaxing and enjoys placing colors together to create unique pieces. Contact Cheryl at citron95@att.net or visit her Etsy store at www.summerztreasures.etsy.com.

Cassie Donlen is a former Associate Editor at *Bead&Button* and has recently relocated to Florida. See more of her work at www.cassiedonlen.etsy.com..

Josie Fabre, author of *Fast Peyote Stitch Jewelry* (available from Kalmbach Books), is a designer and avid bead weaver from Slidell, LA. Email jpfabre@fabres.net or visit www.josie.etsy.com.

Margherita Fusco lives in Cremona, Italy, and started beading about ten years ago just for fun. She has found her true passion in bead weaving. Contact her at fusco_margherita@yahoo.it, or visit www.75marghe75.etsy.com or 75marghe75.blogspot.it.

Adrienne Gaskell is passionate about teaching and encouraging innovations in the ancient art form of kumihmo braiding. She can be contacted at agaskell@me.com or via her website www.KumihimoResource.com.

Julia Gerlach is the editor of *Bead&Button* magazine. Contact her at jgerlach@beadandbutton.com.

Stephanie Goff owns and operates Beadjoux Bead store in Braselton, Georgia with her mom, Monica. She has been published in national beading magazines, is a 2015-2016 Starman TrendSetter, and teaches at the Bead&Button Show. Contact her at beadjoux@att.net or visit www.beadjoux.com.

Graehound is a mixed-media studio artist, and a recent BFA graduate working full time as a comic illustrator (and bead addict). Contact her at autobot@graehound.com, or visit her website, www.graehound.com.

Julia Hecht had a busy life as a pediatrician. While on a leave of absence from work, she discovered the joy of beading. Several years later she left her medical practice to pursue beading full-time. She owns and teaches classes at Poppyfield Bead Company in Albuquerque, New Mexico. She feels that teaching beadwork is another form of practicing edicine. Email her at poppyfieldbeadco@gmail.com or visit poppybeads.com.

Debora Hodoyer has been involved in various artistic disciplines and since she discovered the beads's world, she never came back. Contact her at crownofstones@outlook.it or visit www.crownofstones.etsy.com.

Marcy Kentz is a full time product designer at Nina Designs and a part time jewelry designer. You can find her creations at www.marcykentz.etsy.com.

Alice Kharon has been beading for more than a dozen years. She specializes in designing contemporary wearable jewelry. She lives in the Chicago suburbs with her husband and their cat. You can reach her at alice.kharon@yahoo.com.

Renee Kovnesky is a full-time beadweaving jewelry designer who creates and teaches her own designs in Appleton, WI. She is working on her first book, due to be published in 2018. She can be contacted at elegancebyrenee@yahoo.com or via her web site, etsy.com/shop/ElegancebyRenee.

Cara Landry works with her mom, Lane, creating beautiful beading tutorials that feature detailed instructions and full color close-up photos of each and every step, which they offer at SimpleBeadPatterns.com.

Lane Landy works with her daughter, Cara, creating beautiful beading tutorials that feature detailed instructions and full color close-up photos of each and every step, which they offer at SimpleBeadPatterns.com.

Contact **Deb Lonergan** in care of Kalmbach Books.

Alla Maslennikova of Moscow, Russia, likes to incorporate unusual elements in her beadwork. Alla's works have won several awards, including 1st place and Best of Show Runner Up in the Finished Jewelry category in BeadDreams 2015. Contact Alla at beadlady.ru@gmail.com, or visit her website, www.beadlady.ru.

Andrea Mazzenga is a registered nurse and lampwork artist. In 2007 she decided to leave medicine, and opened her bead shop, Buttercup Beads, in Audubon, Pennsylvania. Contact her at buttercupbeads@aol.com or visit www.buttercupbeads.com.

Fatima Mensen-Potter is an inspiring artist, always looking at the bright side of the world. "I see beauty everywhere" is her motto and purpose. She can be contacted at fatima@shewalksin crystal.com or via her website, www.SheWalksinCrystal.Etsy.com, www.shewalksincrystal.etsy.com, or www.shewalksincrystal.com.

Angie Mézes is a a full-time jewelry designer in Budapest, Hungary. Her favorite technique is bead embroidery.

Contact her at redtulipinfo@gmail.com, www.etsy.com/shop/RedTulipDesign, or www.facebook.com/redtulipdesign.by.angie.mezes.

Marina Montagut is a jewelry artist in Sarasota, Fla. Contact Marina at marinabeads@hotmail.com, or visit marinabeads.com.

Maria Teresa Moran used to be a floral designer and owned a flower shop. Now semi-retired, she is still inspired by flowers as she designs beaded jewelry. Email her at mmoran@nbcguild.com.

Meg Mullen fell in love with bead embroidery more than 20 years ago because the design possibilities are endless. Meg owns Bead My Love. Check her website at www.beadmylove.com for beads and embroidery supplies. When she is not traveling, she hosts Beautiful Bead Embroidery Retreats in Rehoboth Beach, Del. Contact Meg at beadmylove@aol.com.

Marie New is an award-winning British beadwork designer and a member of the Starman Trendsetters Team. She loves playing with color, texture, and form, and when not playing with seed beads, she is teaching textile design at a high school. Contact her at mail@maztexdesigns.co.uk or visit maztexdesigns.co.uk.

Szidonia Petki is a self-taught beader who lives in Gallipoli, Italy. She loves the rich colors and intricate patterns of vintage-inspired jewelry. Email her at spetki@gmail.com, or visit www.sidoniasbeads.com. or www.sidoniasbeads.etsy.com.

Lori Phillips is a custom interior seamstress and uses her beaded buttons in her décor. Contact her at makedrapes@gmail.com or or visit www.LoriGetsCarriedAway.com or www.etsy.com/shop/LoriGets CarriedAway.

Contact **Bonnie Riconda** in care of Kalmbach Books.

Jennifer Robinson is a full-time jewelry designer from Ontario. Her work is full of colour, detail and lots of sparkle. See her collection at www.livjewellery.etsy.com or contact her at livjewellery@gmail.com.

Hannah Rosner is an award-winning artist and has been a beading instructor for over 20 years. She has taught classes at the Bead&Button Show, bead societies, and bead stores throughout the U.S. Hannah is also a Starman TrendSetter. To see more of her tutorials, kits, and finished work, visit www.goodrivergallery.com. Email Hannah at goodrivergallery@aol.com.

Marla Salezze is a jewelry designer and teacher of bead weaving. She is on the Nunn Design Innovations Team and a member of the Bead Society of Eastern Pennsylvania. Contact her at marla@beadedbymarla.com and purchase kits for her projects at www.beadedbymarla.com.

Yasmin Sarfati is a self-taught designer from Israel. She stumbled across a bead store years ago when she got off at the wrong bus stop. After a few years, she decided to open a bead store in Israel and has been teaching the art of jewelry making ever since. Email Yasmin at service@beading-with-beads.com or visit her website at www.beadingwithbeads.com.

Jackie Schwietz was formerly a painter in oils and acrylics. She turned to beading after moving to Florida. She enjoys working with various sizes and shapes of beads. Jackie also teaches her designs at My Bead Gallery in Englewood, Florida. She served as President of the Gulf Coast Bead Society from 2013–2015. Contact Jackie at rjschwietz@comcast.net.

Candice Sexton is a full time bead crochet artist, author and national instructor from Chesterton, Indiana. Her finished work can be found at local galleries and her work, patterns, and kits can be found on her website at www.candicesexton.com or etsy site at www.etsy.com/shop/CandiceSexton.

Ora Shai lives in Jerusalem, Israel, and has been an avid beader for years. She loves to explore all beading techniques but has a fondess for right-angle weave.

Email her at orrrasha@gmail.com or visit www.beadtales.blogspot.co.il.

Kathy Simonds is a jewelry designer and Starman TrendSetter from Idaho Falls, Idaho. She can be reached at kbsimonds@gmail.com or through her KathySimondsDesigns Etsy store.

Kerrie Slade is a beadwork designer living in Mansfield, England. She has had her work published in numerous books and magazines around the world. Kerrie now teaches internationally and sells patterns through her website, www.kerrieslade.co.uk and blogs at kerrieslade.blogspot.co.uk.

Contact **Sue Sloan** in care of Kalmbach Books.

Donna Sutton was introduced to the world of beads in 2010 and found it to be the perfect medium for expressing her creativity and imagination. Kits for her project are available at www.dragonflydreamdesign.etsy.com or contact Donna at dragonflydream design@hotmail.com.

Justyna Szlezak was a talented bead artist from Poland. She passed away in 2015 after a battle with cancer. We first published her "Blooming flower pendant" in June, 2015, and her family is generously allowing us to publish this pattern. Find more patterns at www. inmemoryoferidhan.etsy.com.

Julie Moore Tanksley started beading about 10 years ago and started designing soon after. She is a member of the Dallas Bead society and teaches locally at bead stores and retreats. Julie and her husband own a small music store in Huntington, Texas. Julie enjoys being a grandmother and spending time with family and friends. Contact her at juellesdesigns@yahoo.com or visit www.juellesdesigns.etsy.com.

Liz Thompson lives in the metro Detroit (Michigan) area and works at a large urban hospital to support her beading and vacation habits. Contact Liz via email at ethomps1@gmail.com or visit www.thebadliz.blogspot.com.

Zsuzsanna Veres, also known as Vezsuzsi, is a full-time Hungarian designer who lives in Austria with her husband and two children. She has been designing and teaching since 2008, and has been published in several beading magazines. Contact her at vezsuzsi@gmail.com, see her blog at www.vezsuzsi.hu, or visit www.beadsbyvezsuzsi.etsy.com.

Nicole Vogt is a self-taught beader from Germany and lucky to have two sisters with the same hobby. They run a blog alll together at dreikleineperlen. blogspot.de and you can contact her at drei_kleine_perlen@gmx.de.

Agnieszka Watts finds beading relaxing and enjoys the endless possibilities it brings. Peyote stitch and netting are her favorite stitches, but she loves inventing new stitches also. Email her at me7asia@yahoo.pl, or visit www.agnesse.weebly.com.

Connie Whittaker is an associate editor at *Bead&Button* magazine. Contact her at cwhittaker@beadandbutton.com.

Gianna Zimmerman is from the Netherlands and has been beading for more than 10 years. She teaches via video on www.youtube.com/user/ beading4perfectionists. Contact her at beadingforperfectionists@yahoo.nl or visit www.youtube.com/user/B4Pbakup.

Index